Diane Mullen
Atlanta, Ga
July 1975

THE LETTERS OF
KING CHARLES I

UNIFORM WITH THIS VOLUME

King Charles I
By Van Dyck

THE
LETTERS
SPEECHES AND PROCLAMATIONS
OF
KING
CHARLES I

Edited by

SIR CHARLES PETRIE
Bart., C.B.E., M.A., F.R.Hist.S.

FUNK & WAGNALLS
NEW YORK

First published 1935
This edition © Sir Charles Petrie 1968
This edition first published 1968

All rights reserved.

Library of Congress Catalog Card Number: 68-25021
Published by Funk & Wagnalls, A Division of Reader's Digest Books, Inc.,
by arrangement with Cassell & Co. Ltd.
Printed in Great Britain.

INTRODUCTION TO THE FIRST EDITION

KING CHARLES I has undoubtedly hitherto suffered from the fact that he has rarely been allowed to speak for himself. He has been extravagantly praised by some writers, and as immoderately abused by others, but in the vast majority of cases the authors in question have been content to treat him as the personification of a principle, namely the Divine Right of Kings. In too many instances they have thus neglected to inquire what manner of man Charles really was, and how he arrived at the convictions for which in the end he laid down his life. The present volume is an attempt to remedy this defect, and to trace by means of the King's own words, from boyhood to the scaffold, not only his career, but the development of his ideas. It is, it may be remarked, in no sense a History of England during the period of his life, and events are given prominence solely from the standpoint of their effect upon Charles himself.

What these letters reveal, but what is too often forgotten, is that when he came to the throne he was not only a young man, but young for his age. As a rule the Stuarts matured early (Prince Charles Edward is a notable example of this), but Charles I was an exception. He was very greatly under the influence of Buckingham until the latter's death, and this dependence is in no way extraordinary : Buckingham had been his father's minister since Charles was little more than a boy, and, whatever his faults, he was just the type of man, full of worldly wisdom and only eight years older than the King, upon whom the somewhat diffident Charles would naturally come to rely. The letters which Charles and Buckingham wrote to James I from Madrid are evidence of their relationship while the former was still Prince of Wales, and his later ones, after he became King, tell the same story. The real ruler of England from 1623 until 1628 was Buckingham; and, incidentally, Charles is never again found writing to a subject in the same familiar strain that he did to ' Steenie '.

The death of James I ushers in the long struggle with the Parliament, and, apart from the religious issues involved, it is clear that neither Charles nor his opponents fully grasped what was the real cause of their difference. The value of money was steadily falling, and the price of wheat (a sure index) rose 250 per cent. between 1570 and 1648. It had become impossible for the King to live on his own resources. Parliament could not understand what was taking place, and it became increasingly suspicious of the Crown when it found that the money it voted was never enough to carry on the administration of the country. This, however, was not all, for the rich landowners and burghers who filled the House of Commons wanted glory without having to pay for it, and Hampden was soon to achieve immortality for his championship of this point of view. That the King had both precedent and common sense on his side can hardly be denied, and his justification for the dissolution of Parliament in 1629 is a masterpiece of close reasoning. Had Charles been the innovator some writers would have us believe, his methods would have been very different, and probably far more successful than was actually the case.

The third chapter of the present work covers that period during which the King governed without either a Parliament or what we should to-day term a Prime Minister, and it is impossible not to be struck with the immense variety of subjects which bear the imprint of his activity. The purchase of a collection of pictures, the matrimonial affairs of the great families, the training of the Militia, and the administration of the diocese of Wells, not to mention such important matters as the state of Ireland and Scotland, all come under review. It was the apogee of the reign, and we can see the character of Charles rapidly developing: behind and forgotten are the differences with the Queen, which had once caused him to write so sharply of her to Buckingham, while the Civil War and the scaffold at Whitehall are still far away in the distance. Benevolent despotism was the order of the day, and scant respect was paid, as the instructions in respect of the provision of saltpetre clearly show, to the vested interests of the rich. It was unfortunate both for King and nation that these latter were supreme in Parliament, with which impecuniosity and religious dissension rendered it impossible for Charles permanently to dispense.

It was the progress of events in Scotland and Ireland that brought Charles, like many a British administration in the centuries to come, down in the end. Half Englishman and half Scot, it was the irony of fate that made the King an Englishman at Holyrood, and a Scot at Westminster. What seemed to him to be but the orderliness of the Anglican Church was regarded as rank Popery in Edinburgh, while his English opponents never allowed for the dour stubbornness of the Scot in his nature, and so were the more irritated when they encountered it. In the letters to Strafford and Hamilton we see the gathering of the storm, and can already discern its ultimate consequences. The necessity of raising an army to suppress the Scots meant the summoning of the English Parliament to vote the money, and the House of Commons seized upon the King's attempt to bring troops over from Ireland as a pretext to get control out of the hands of the Crown into their own. Charles was beginning at last to realize the forces that were being marshalled against the monarchy and himself, but he did not yet know how to deal with them.

At this point we reach what was at once the greatest crime and the greatest blunder in the King's career, namely the treatment of Strafford. Whether out of a natural reluctance to take strong measures, or because he hoped by not doing so to conciliate his opponents, Charles hesitated too long to put Strafford at the head of the administration, and to allow him to strike at Pym and his friends for their treasonable negotiations with the Scottish rebels. This vacillation was fatal, for Pym struck first, and the King lost the only minister who might have saved the situation even at that late hour. Nor was this all, for the circumstances of Strafford's death remain an indelible blot upon the character of his master, even when every allowance has been made for the difficulties of the latter's position, for he had written 'upon the word of a King you shall not suffer in life, honour, or fortune'. That his minister's fate, and his own responsibility for it, were ever afterwards in his thoughts is clear, for years later Charles is found writing to the Queen that he had yielded to things that were against his conscience, 'for which I have been so deservedly punished'. Some of those who criticize him most severely would do well to ask themselves how they would have acted in his position.

As the Civil War drew on the King became an excellent exponent of his own case, and he begins ever more strongly to take the line that it is not he, but his opponents, who would overturn the Constitution. His actions did not belie his words, and the letter to the Governor of Dartmouth is an admirable illustration of his scrupulous regard for legality. When the clash came, too, Charles showed himself the most humane of men, and his letter to the Mayor of Newbury with regard to the rebel prisoners is the more commendable when one remembers the type of warfare that was being waged in contemporary Germany, and was so soon to be conducted by Cromwell in Ireland. At this stage there is also beginning to creep into the letters a note of resignation, which grows rapidly more pronounced, until, on the eve of his departure from Oxford in 1646, he is found writing to Digby, ' If I cannot live as a King, I shall die like a gentleman, without doing that which may make honest men blush for me.' Nevertheless, his patience was not inexhaustible, and he made no effort to conceal his anger when Rupert so unaccountably surrendered Bristol.

Was Charles dishonest? The record of his dealings with his opponents, and the circumstances in which they took place, must be considered before the question can be answered. From the moment that the King placed himself in the hands of the Scots until his death he was actually, if not always nominally, a prisoner. He had to negotiate with three separate factions, namely the Parliament, the Army, and the Scots; and while they all had force at their disposal, he had none. Furthermore, he had just been decisively beaten in a long civil war. Any man in his position who had not employed the one weapon left to him, dissimulation, would have been a fool, and Charles was assuredly not that. That he blundered badly from time to time, particularly when he sent Glamorgan to intrigue with the Irish, must be admitted, but that he was any more dishonest than his enemies, and therefore worthy of censure, it is impossible in face of the evidence to maintain. The Army, the Scots, and the Parliament merely sought to use Charles for their own ends, as he tried to play them off against one another for his. They were more successful; that is all.

So we come to the last scene, the trial, and to the letter which he wrote to his son, later Charles II. Here the mists are finally dispersed, and the naked soul of the King becomes clear. It is recorded that although all his life he had been handicapped by a stammer, there was no trace of it when he faced his judges in Westminster Hall, and the fact is significant. During those days he was the embodiment of a principle, the old English monarchy, and that was upon its trial in his person. With him, it was condemned, but Charles so behaved that its resurrection took place eleven years later, and that sense of continuity and tradition for which he stood has ever since been the keynote of the English character. His protest when Bradshaw had pronounced sentence upon him, ' I am not suffered for to speak : expect what justice other people will have,' has not been forgotten when minorities have on other occasions attempted to control our destinies for their own purposes.

For the King's behaviour on the scaffold itself, we may turn with greatest advantage to the well-known lines of Andrew Marvell, the Puritan poet :

> He nothing common did or mean
> Upon that memorable scene,
> But with his keener eye
> The axe's edge did try;
> Nor called the gods with vulgar spite
> To vindicate his helpless right,
> But bowed his comely head
> Down, as upon a bed.

In the pages that follow Charles may be studied both as a man and as a monarch. What difference of opinion there may be about him in the latter capacity, there can be none that a better man has never sat upon the throne of this country. A true Christian, he fought that religion might have its proper place in the national life, and there was a complete absence of rancour in his nature : in the very shadow of the scaffold he could write to the Prince of Wales that ' it is all I have now left me, a power to forgive those that have deprived me of all '. In success or in adversity, Charles always showed himself a very great gentleman.

In conclusion, it only remains to add that certain public documents have been included in the present work in order to make plainer the questions at issue between the King and his opponents. The spelling has throughout been modernized, but I have employed the old calendar with the modern notation of years.

CHARLES PETRIE.

LILLINGTON, DORSET.
November, 1934.

CONTENTS

CHRONOLOGICAL TABLE

1600, Nov. 19		Birth of Charles.
1605		Charles created Duke of York.
1612, Nov. 6		Death of Henry, Prince of Wales.
1619, Aug. 16		Frederick elected King of Bohemia.
1622		Frederick loses the Palatinate.
1623, Feb.-Sept.		Charles and Buckingham in Madrid.
1625, March 27		Accession of Charles.
	May	Marriage with Henrietta Maria.
	June-Aug.	First Parliament.
1626, Feb.-June		Second Parliament.
1627		War with France.
1627, June		Expedition to Rhé.
1628, March		Third Parliament meets.
	June	Petition of Right.
	Aug.	Murder of Buckingham.
1629, March		Third Parliament dissolved.
1630		Distraint of Knighthood.
1633, June		King visits Scotland.
	July	Wentworth sent to Ireland.
	Aug.	Laud, Archbishop of Canterbury.
1634, Oct.		First writ of Ship Money.
1638, Feb.		The Scottish National Covenant.
		The First Bishops' War.
1639, June		Treaty of Berwick.
1640, April-May		Short Parliament.
		The Second Bishops' War.
	Nov. 3	Long Parliament meets.
		Impeachment of Strafford.
1641, May 12		Execution of Strafford.
		The Ten Propositions.
	Aug.-Nov.	Charles in Scotland.
	Oct.	Irish rebellion begins.
	Nov.	The Grand Remonstrance.
1642, Jan.		The King leaves London.
	June	The Nineteen Propositions.
	Aug. 22	The King raises his standard at Nottingham.
	Oct. 23	Battle of Edgehill.
1643, Sept. 15		Armistice in Ireland.
	Sept. 20	First battle of Newbury.

1644,	Jan.	Scots enter England.
	July 2	Battle of Marston Moor.
	Aug. 31	The surrender at Lostwithiel.
	Oct. 27	Second battle of Newbury.
1645,	Jan.	Negotiations at Uxbridge.
	June 14	Battle of Naseby.
	Sept. 11	Rupert surrenders Bristol.
	Sept. 13	Montrose defeated at Philiphaugh.
1646,	May	The King goes to the Scots.
	Aug.	Propositions of Newcastle.
1647,	Feb.	The King delivered to the Parliament.
	June	Cornet Joyce at Holmby.
		The Heads of Proposals.
	Nov.	The King's flight from Hampton Court.
	Dec.	The King signs the engagement.
		The vote of no addresses.
1648,	Feb.-Aug.	Second Civil War.
	Aug.	Negotiations at Newport.
	Dec.	Pride's Purge.
1649,	Jan. 20-27	Trial of the King.
	Jan. 30	Execution of the King.

CHAPTER I

THE EARLY YEARS

1600-1625

The Prince, who was later to become King Charles I, was born at Dunfermline Palace on November 19th, 1600, about eleven o'clock at night. He was the youngest child of King James VI of Scotland and his wife Anne, daughter of Frederick II of Denmark and Norway. Two brothers and one sister had died in infancy, and, in addition to Charles, there only survived Henry, born in 1593, and Elizabeth, born in 1596. Owing to his own delicate health, Charles was christened within a few days of his birth, and on the same occasion he was created Duke of Albany. When his father succeeded to the English throne in 1603, the young Prince, again for reasons of health, was left behind in Scotland, and he did not go to England until the following year. In 1605 he was created Duke of York.

I. To James I

SWEET, SWEET FATHER,

I learn to decline substantives and adjectives. Give me your blessing.

I thank you for my best man.

Your loving son,
YORK.

To my father the King.

II. To the Queen

MOST WORTHY MISTRESS,

Seeing I cannot have the happiness to see Your Majesty, give me leave to declare by these lines the duty and love I owe to you, which makes me long to see you. I wish from my heart that I might help to find a remedy to your disease [i.e. gout]; the which I must bear the more patiently, because it is the sign of a long life. But I must for many causes be sorry; and specially because it is troublesome to you, and has deprived me of your most comfortable sight, and of many good dinners; the which I hope, by God's grace, shortly to enjoy. And when it shall please

3

you to give me leave to see you, it may be I shall give you some good recipe, which either shall heal you or make you laugh; the which wishing I may obtain by Your Majesty's most gracious favour, kissing in all humility your most sacred hands, and praying for your health and long prosperity, I end, most worthy mistress,

Your Majesty's most humble and obedient servant,

CHARLES.

In 1612, Henry, the elder brother of Charles, died, and the latter became heir to the throne, though he was not created Prince of Wales until four years later. George Villiers was chief minister at this time: he was made Viscount Villiers in 1616, Earl of Buckingham in 1617, and Marquess of Buckingham in 1618. At first relations between him and Charles were none too cordial, but they soon became very close, and remained such until Villiers was murdered in 1628. The following letter, which is undated in the original, was written at a time when the King had taken offence with Charles.

III. TO LORD VILLIERS

STEENIE,

There is none that know me so well as yourself, what dutiful respect and love I have ever, and shall ever carry to the King; and therefore you may judge what grief it is to me to have the ill fortune as that any of my actions should bear so ill an interpretation as I find by your letter, this message I sent by my Lord Montgomery has borne. I will no ways stand upon my justification, but desire that my good meaning may be taken instead of the ill message. That which made me think that this message would not displease the King, was the command you know he gave me a good while ago, that I should use all means to make the Queen make a will whereby she should make over to me her jewels; therefore, I sent to have the King's approbation of that which I thought he had desired, and therefore I thought he would rather be glad than any way displeased with the message. My meaning was never to claim anything as of right, but to submit myself as well in this as in all other things to the King's pleasure. It doth grieve me much that the King should be so much moved with it as you say he is, for the least show of his displeasure would make me leave to meddle or think of any such thing any more, without showing himself openly so angry with me. To conclude, I pray you to commend my most humble service to His Majesty, and tell him that I am very sorry that I have done anything to offend him, and that I will be content to have any penance inflicted upon me so he may forgive me, although I had never a thought nor never shall have to displease him; yet I deserve to be punished for my ill-fortune. So, hoping never to have occasion to write to you of so ill a subject again, but of many better, I rest,

Your true, constant, loving friend,
CHARLES P.

I had written to the King before I received yours, but I hope you will mend anything that is amiss in the other with this, for I did not think the King had been so angry before I received yours.

In 1613 Elizabeth, the sister of Charles, married the Elector Palatine, and six years later her husband was persuaded to accept the throne of Bohemia by those who were in rebellion against the Emperor. He was defeated at the battle of the White Mountain, and lost not only Bohemia, but also the Palatinate. The remainder of the reign of James I was spent in an effort by that monarch to secure the restoration of his son-in-law to his hereditary dominions. The threat to the Protestant cause aroused great feeling in the country, and in November, 1621, Parliament proceeded to discuss foreign policy. The King, relying upon precedent, which was on his side, objected to this, and there was a dispute between the Crown and Parliament concerning privileges. The views of Charles are sufficiently indicated in his two letters to Buckingham.

IV. TO THE MARQUESS OF BUCKINGHAM

STEENIE,

The Lower House this day has been a little unruly; but I hope it will turn to the best; for, before they rose, they began to

5

be ashamed of it. Yet I could wish that the King would send down a commission here, that (if need were) such seditious fellows might be made an example to others, by Monday next, and till then I would let them alone. It will be seen whether they mean to do good, or to persist in their follies; so that the King needs to be patient but a little while.

I have spoken with so many of the Council, as the King trusts most, and they are all of his mind, only the sending of authority to set seditious fellows fast is of my adding. I defy thee in being more mine than I am,

Thy constant, loving friend,
CHARLES P.

Friday, November 3, 1621.

v. TO THE MARQUESS OF BUCKINGHAM

STEENIE,

This day the Lower House has given the King a subsidy, and are likewise resolved to send a message, humbly to entreat him to end this session before Christmas. I confess that this they have done is not so great a matter that the King need to be indulgent over them for it; yet, on the other side (for his reputation abroad at this time), I would not wholly discontent them; therefore, my opinion is, that the King should grant them a session at this time, but withal I should have him command them not to speak any more of Spain, whether it be of that war, or my marriage.

This, in my opinion, does neither suffer them to encroach upon the King's authority, nor give them just cause of discontentment. I think you will find that all those of the Council that the King trusts most, are likewise of this mind. Sir Edward Cecil wrote me a letter from the Army, of much stuff, but it was of fashion; the most of the letter was of reasons why the King should enter into a war for the defence of the Palatinate, and trust no more treaties. Now, in earnest, I wish the gentleman well, but yet I would not have Sir Horace Vere (who has both endured so much misery, and so good service there) either to be discouraged or disgraced; therefore I think the King shall do

6

well to employ Cecil, but I would 'not have him come over other's head. So, praying you commend my humble service to the King, I rest

Yours more than can be expressed, and
as much as can be thought,
CHARLES P.

Parliament was adjourned shortly before Christmas, and dissolved in January.

The difference between James and the Parliament rendered impracticable any idea of restoring the Elector Palatine by force of arms, for the House of Commons would not vote the necessary funds. It was therefore necessary to resort to diplomacy, and this was set in motion with a view to securing the marriage of Charles to a Spanish Infanta, according to the terms of which the King of Spain, Philip IV, was to secure the restoration of the Elector. Accordingly, Lord Digby, who had represented King James in Madrid on a previous occasion, was created Earl of Bristol, and sent to the Spanish capital to conduct the negotiations for the marriage. These, however, proceeded too slowly for Charles and Buckingham who, on February 17th, 1623, set off for Madrid in disguise, and with few attendants. The following letters tell the story of their adventures.

VI. CHARLES AND BUCKINGHAM TO JAMES I

Paris, Saturday, February 22, 1623.

DEAR DAD AND GOSSIP,

We are sure before this, you have longed to have some news from your boys; but before this time we have not been able to send it you; and we do it with this confidence, that you will be as glad to read it as we to write, though it be now our best entertainment. And that we may give the perfecter account, we will begin this where my last ended.

First, about five or six o'clock on Wednesday morning, we wish to say, the first that fell sick was your son, and he that continued it longest was myself. In six hours we got over with as fair a passage as ever men had. We all got so perfectly well, when we but saw land, that we resolved to spend the rest of the day in riding post; and lay at Montreuil, three post off

7

Boulogne.   The next day we lay at Breteuil, eleven post farther; and the next to Paris, though no great need of it; yet I had four falls by the way, without any harm.   Your son's horses stumble as fast as any man's; but he is so much more stronger before than he was.   He holds them up by main strength of mastery, and cries still on! on!! on!!!   This day we went, he and I alone, to a perriwig-maker, where we disguised ourselves so artificially that we adventured to see the King.   The means how we did compass it was this : we addressed ourselves to the King's governor, Monsieur du Proes, and he courteously carried us where we saw him our fill.   Then we desired Monsieur Proes to make us acquainted with his son, because we would trouble the old man no longer, which he did; and then we saw the Queen-Mother at dinner.   This evening his son hath promised us to see the young Queen, with her sister and little Monsieur.   I am sure now you fear we shall be discovered; but do not fright yourself; for I warrant you the contrary.   And finding this might be done with safety, we had a great tickling to add it to the history of our adventures.

To-morrow, which will be Sunday, we will be (God willing) up so early, that we make no question but to reach Orleans; and so every day after we mean to be gaining something, till we reach Madrid.   I have nothing more to say, but to recommend my poor little wife and daughter to your care (and) that you will bestow your blessing upon

Your humble and obedient son and servant,

CHARLES.

Your humble slave and dog,

STEENIE.

Of the persons mentioned in this letter, the King of France was Louis XIII; Monsieur was his brother, Gaston, Duke of Orleans; the Queen-Mother was Marie de Medicis, widow of Henry IV; while the Queen of France was Anne, daughter of Philip III of Spain, and sister of the Infanta Maria whom Charles was on his way to Madrid to woo.   Charles also saw his future wife, Henrietta Maria, on this occasion.

8

VII.CHARLES AND BUCKINGHAM TO JAMES I

SIR,

Since the closing of our last, we have been at court again (and that we might not hold you in pain, we assure you we have not been known), where we saw the young Queen, little Monsieur, and Madame, at the practising of a mask that is intended by the Queen to be presented to the King; and in it there danced the Queen and Madame, with as many as made up nineteen fair dancing ladies, amongst which the Queen is the handsomest, which hath wrought in me a greater desire to see her sister. So, in haste, going to bed, we humbly take our leaves, and rest,

Your Majesty's most humble and
obedient son and servant,
CHARLES.
And your humble slave and dog,
STEENIE.

Paris, February 22, 1623.

VIII.CHARLES AND BUCKINGHAM TO JAMES I

DEAR DAD AND GOSSIP,

We are now got into Spain, free from harm of falls, in as perfect health as when we parted, and undiscovered by any Monsieur. We met Gresley a post beyond Bayonne. We saucily opened your letters, and found nothing either in that or any other which we could understand without a cipher, that hath made us repent our journey; but, by the contrary, we find nothing but particulars hastened, and your business so slowly advanced, that we think ourselves happy that we have begun it so soon; for yet the temporal articles are not concluded, nor will not be, till the dispensation comes, which may be, God knows when; and when that time shall come, they beg twenty days to conceal it, upon pretext of making preparations : this bearer's errand was answered by our journey thither, yet we have thought it fit he should go forward to bring you certain news of your boys, that crave your blessing, and rest.

Your Majesty's humble and obedient son and servant,

CHARLES.

And your humble slave and dog,

STEENIE.

The arrival of Charles and Buckingham in Madrid ushered in a series of negotiations for the marriage, in which the Spanish Government was never serious, but out of which it hoped to snatch some advantage. Charles had no intention of becoming a Catholic, and Philip IV was equally determined to do nothing to save the Elector Palatine from the wrath of his Habsburg cousin at Vienna. The Count-Duke of Olivares was the chief minister of Spain, while Gondomar had been the Spanish ambassador in London.

IX. CHARLES AND BUCKINGHAM TO JAMES I

DEAR DAD AND GOSSIP,　　　　　　　　　　*March* 10, 1623.

On Friday last we arrived here, at five o'clock at night, both in perfect health; the cause that we advertised you of it no sooner was, that we knew you would be glad to hear as well of the manner of our reception, as our arrival. First we resolved to discover the wooer, because, upon the speedy opening of the ports, we found posts making such haste after us, that we knew not it would be discovered within twelve hours after, and better we have the thanks of it than a postilion. The next morning we sent for Gondomar, who went presently to the Count of Olivares, and as speedily got me your dog Steenie a private audience of the King; when I was to return back to my lodgings, the Count of Olivares himself alone would accompany me back again to salute the Prince in the King's name. The next day we had a private visit of the King, the Queen, the Infanta, Don Carlos, and the Cardinal, in the sight of all the world, and I may call it a private obligation hidden from nobody; for there was the Pope's nuncio, the Emperor's ambassador, the French, and all the streets filled with guards and other people : before the King's coach went the best of the nobility, after followed all the ladies of the court : we sat in an invisible coach, because nobody was suffered to take notice of it, though seen by all the world.

In this form they passed three times by us; but, before we could get away, the Count of Olivares came into our coach and conveyed us home, where he told us the King longed and died for want of a nearer (sight) of our wooer. First, he took me in his coach to go to the King; we found him walking in the street, with his cloak thrown over his face, and a sword and buckler by his side; he leaped into the coach, and away he came to find the wooer in another place appointed, where there passed much kindness and compliment one to another. You may judge by this how sensible the King is of your son's journey; and if we can either judge by outward shows, or general speeches, we have reason to condemn your ambassadors for rather writing too sparingly than too much.

To conclude, we find the Count of Olivares so overvaluing of our journey, that he is so full of real courtesy, that we can do no less than beseech Your Majesty to write the kindest letter of thanks and acknowledgement you can unto him : he said, no later to us than this morning, that, if the Pope would give a dispensation for a wife, they would give the Infanta to thy son's baby as a wench; and hath this day written to the Cardinal Ludovisio, the Pope's nephew, that the King of England hath put such an obligation upon this King, in sending his son hither, that he entreats him to make haste with the dispensation, for he can deny him nothing that is in his kingdom. We must hold you thus much longer to tell you, the Pope's nuncio works as maliciously and as actively as he can against us, but he receives such rude answers, that we hope he will be soon weary on't : we make this collection of it, that the Pope will be very loath to grant a dispensation, which, if he will not do, then we would gladly have your direction how far we may engage you in the acknowledgement of the Pope's special power; for we almost find, if you will be contented to acknowledge the Pope chief head under Christ, that the match will be made without him. So, craving your blessing, we rest

Your Majesty's humble and obedient son and servant,
CHARLES.
Your humble slave and dog,
STEENIE.

11

It soon became apparent that the Spanish Government would not commit itself until the Pope (Gregory XV) had granted a dispensation for the marriage, and it was clear that this would be dependent upon conditions which it was extremely doubtful whether James would, or could, accept.

x.Charles and Buckingham to James I

DEAR DAD AND GOSSIP,

That Your Majesty may be the more particularly informed of all, we will observe our former order to begin still where we left, which was, we think, at the King's private visit in the night. The next day your baby desired to kiss his hands privately in the palace, which was granted, and thus performed. First, the King would not suffer him to come to his chamber, but met him at the stair-foot; then entered into the coach, and walked into his park. The greatest matter that passed between them, at that time, was compliments, and particular questions of our journey; then, by force, he would needs carry him half-way home, in which doing, they were both almost overthrown in brick-pits. Two days after, we met with His Majesty again in his park, with his two brothers; they spent their time in seeing his men kill partridges flying and conies running, with a gun. Yesterday, being Sunday, your baby went to a monastery called St. Jeronimo's, to dinner, which stands a little out of the town. After dinner came all the councillors in order, to welcome your baby; then came the King himself, with all his nobility, and made their entry, with as great triumph as could be, where he forced your baby to ride on his right hand, which he observes always. This entry was made just as when the Kings of Castille come first to the crown : all prisoners set at liberty, and no office or matters of grace falls, but is put in your baby's hands to dispose.

We trouble Your Majesty more particularly with these things of ceremony, that you may be better able to guide yourself towards this nobleman, who is sent of purpose to advertise you of your son's safe arrival here, for sooner than he was received in the palace, they took no notice of his coming. We had almost forgotten to tell you, that the first thing they did at their arrival into the palace was the visiting of the Queen, where grew a quarrel between your baby and lady, for want of a salutation; but your dog's opinion is, that this is an artificial forced quarrel, to beget hereafter the greater kindness.

For our main and chief business, we find them by outward shows as desirous of it as ourselves, yet are they hankering upon a conversion; for they say, there can be no friendship without union in religion, but put no question in bestowing their sister, and we put the other quite out of question, because neither our conscience nor time serves for it, and because we will not implicitly rely upon them. For fear of delays (which we account the worst denial), we intend to send, with all speed, Michael Andrew, to come to bring us certain word from Gage, how he finds our business prosper there, according to which we will guide ourselves. Yet ever resolving to guide ourselves by your directions, so craving your blessing we end

Your Majesty's humble son and servant,
CHARLES.

I beseech Your Majesty advise as little with your Council in these businesses as you can. I hope in writing jointly as we do, we please you best, for I assure Your Majesty, it is not for saving pains. This King did entreat me to send Your Majesty a great *recantho* in his name (which is a compliment), for which, in my poor opinion, it will not be amiss for Your Majesty to write him a letter of thanks for all the favours he has done me since I came hither, with that of the Count of Olivares.

CHARLES.
Your Majesty's humble slave and dog,
STEENIE.

Madrid, the 17th of March, 1623.

XI. CHARLES AND BUCKINGHAM TO JAMES I

DEAR DAD AND GOSSIP,

Since the writing of our other letter we have received news from Rome, which we send you here enclosed; you will find Gage hath a good hope of soon affecting the dispensation : we think our sending Michael Andrew thither will do no hurt. We are glad this paper gives us room to quarrel (with) you, for not sending to us all this while, for though we hear often from you by reports, yet nothing can satisfy except we have it under your own hand; therefore we beseech you to do it as oft as you can. So craving your blessing, we end

Your Majesty's humble and obedient son and servant,

CHARLES.

Your Majesty's humble slave and dog,

STEENIE.

Madrid, the 18*th of March,* 1623.

XII.CHARLES AND BUCKINGHAM TO JAMES I

DEAR DAD AND GOSSIP,

The post hath been delayed these three days, and should he be as many more, you should have every day a letter. This morning your dog Steenie hath been with the Count of Olivares, where was concluded that no time should be spared in setting forward the ships, which we desire may be well chosen, because we think the King, Queen, and all his court will see them. But once again we beseech you that there be no delays of our side, and by the next send us word how soon they will be ready. It's time now that you advertise my father, Rutland, that you intend him admiral of fleet. Thus craving your blessings, we rest

Your Majesty's humble and obedient son and servant,

CHARLES.

Your Majesty's humble slave and dog,

STEENIE.

Madrid, 25*th of March,* 1623.

XIII.CHARLES AND BUCKINGHAM TO JAMES I

March 27, 1623.

DEAR DAD AND GOSSIP,

According to our promise in our last, we write to you this day again, for our post is not yet parted; and that this may not altogether be empty, we think it not amiss to assure you, that neither in spiritual nor temporal things there is anything pressed upon us more than is already agreed upon.   Fain would they, in this time of expecting the dispensation, have treated upon the ends and effects of friendship; but we have avoided it with so many forcible arguments, that they now rest satisfied.   They were likewise in hope of a conversion of us both; but now excuses are more studied than reasons for it, though they say their love shall ever make them wish it.   To conclude, we never saw the business in a better way than now it is; therefore we humbly beseech you lose no time in hasting the ships, that we may make the more haste to beg that personally which now we do by letter—your blessing.

Your Majesty's humble and obedient son and servant,
CHARLES.
Your Majesty's humble slave and dog,
STEENIE.

Madrid.

During this time several communications passed between the Pope on the one hand, and James and Charles on the other.   The following letter gives a good idea of the latter's attitude, which was conciliatory, but firm.

XIV. TO THE POPE

April 20, 1623.

Your Holiness's letters I have received with no less gratitude and reverence than that feeling of uncommon good will and piety demanded, wherewith I know they have been indited. And that exhortation from Your Holiness has been to me especially welcome, that you have set before me the examples of my ancestors, which can never be sufficiently commended for my inspection and imitation.   They, although they encountered the difficulty of various fortunes, and the danger of life itself, that they might more widely propagate the Christian faith; yet never did they carry the standard of Christ's cross against his most violent enemies with a more cheerful spirit than I will use and endeavour, that the peace and unity of the Christian commonwealth, which hath been so long banished, may be brought

15

back, returning, as it were, from captivity or the grave; for, since the subtlety and malice of the father of discords hath sown the seeds of such unhappy differences among those who profess the Christian religion, this measure I deem most necessary, in order to promote more successfully the hallowed glory of God and our Saviour, his Christ; and I shall esteem it no less honour to myself to tread in the well-worn track of my ancestors, and to approve myself a zealous imitator of them in holy and religious undertakings, than to have derived my descent and origin from them. And to this same the inclination of my lord King and father very much fires me, and the ardent desire, wherewith he is animated to put forth a helping hand to so pious a work, as well as the grief which preys upon his royal breast, when he weighs and ponders what cruel slaughters, what deplorable calamities have arisen from the dissensions of Christian Princes.

Further—the judgement which Your Holiness hath formed of my desire of contracting affinity and marriage with the house of the Catholic prince, is a test both of your charity and wisdom; for never should I feel so earnest as I do to be joined to any one living in that close and indissoluble bond, whose religion I hated. Wherefore be Your Holiness persuaded that I am and ever shall be of such moderation as to keep aloof, as far as possible, from every undertaking, which may testify any hatred towards the Roman Catholic religion; nay, rather I will seize all opportunities, by a gentle and generous mode of conduct, to remove all sinister suspicions entirely; so that, as we all confess one undivided Trinity, and one Christ crucified, we may be banded together unanimously unto one faith. That I may accomplish this, I will reckon as trifling all my labours and vigilance, and even the hazards of kingdoms, and life itself.

It remaineth only that, in returning Your Holiness the greatest possible thanks for the letters which I hold in the light of an illustrious gift, I pray for your every prosperity and happiness everlasting.

Your Holiness's most devoted,
CHARLES P.

The Pope not unnaturally took advantage of his opportunity to exact better treatment for English Catholics in return for a dispensation.

XV. CHARLES AND BUCKINGHAM TO JAMES I

April 23, 1623. Madrid.

DEAR DAD AND GOSSIP,

We are sorry we are not able to continue the advertisement of the dispensation's arrival; it is certainly granted, and is as certainly upon the way hither; and although clogged with some new condition, yet such as we hope to remove with ease. They are these: two years more to the education of the children; no other oath to be ministered to the Roman Catholic subjects than that which is given to the Infanta's subjects, and that they may all have free access to her church. We hope in granting the first, yet making it hard, we shall not only facilitate the other two conditions, but, in a little time hereafter, bring more years back again with the two; to this we both recommend secrecy here, and to you there. If we receive your directions in time to this, we will punctually follow them. To the second our answer will be, the oath was made by Act of Parliament, and that you cannot abrogate it without the whole consent of your people. In the last, we hope to let them see, as it will bring but a pester and inconvenience to the Infanta herself, so it will less satisfy the Catholics, because it will make the act more public and less useful to their ends, than to have the exercises of their consciences freely in their own houses; for all meeting in one centre, the number will seem greater, and so make the State jealouser, and consequently make their security more uncertain, this being no less than in covered words to ask liberty of conscience, which you have neither mind nor power to grant; many other reasons we have, and so powerful, that we make neither question to speed the business end, nor to end it to your own liking, which sweet Jesus grant, and your blessing to Your Majesty's humble and obedient son and servant,

CHARLES.

Your Majesty's humble slave and dog,

STEENIE.

XVI. CHARLES AND BUCKINGHAM TO JAMES I

SIR,

I confess that you have sent more jewels than (at my departure) I thought to have had use of; but, since my coming, seeing many jewels worn here, and that my bravery (i.e. fashionable appearance) can consist of nothing else, besides that some of them which you have appointed me to give to the Infanta, in Steenie's opinion and mine, are not fit to be given to her; therefore I have taken this boldness to entreat Your Majesty to send more for my own wearing, and for giving to my mistress, in which I think Your Majesty shall not do amiss to take Carlisle's advice. So, humbly craving your blessing, I rest Your Majesty's humble and obedient son and servant,

CHARLES.

I, your dog, says you have many jewels, neither fit for your son's nor your daughter's wearing, but very fit to bestow on those who must necessarily have presents, and this way will be least chargeable to Your Majesty in my poor opinion.

Madrid, the 22nd of April, 1623.

XVII. CHARLES AND BUCKINGHAM TO JAMES I

Madrid, April 27, 1623.

DEAR DAD AND GOSSIP,

Michael Andrew is now come back from Rome, but the dispensation got hither before him; that you may the better judge of the conditions it is clogged with, we have sent you Gage's letters; this comfort yourself with, that we will not be long before we get forth of this labyrinth, wherein we have been entangled these many years; we beseech Your Majesty be secret in the conditions, and be assured we will yield to nothing but what you may perform both with your honour and conscience; if you should not keep them so, it will beget dispute, censures, and conclusions there to our prejudice. The chief end of sending this post, is to tell you that the Groyne [i.e. Corunna] is resolved on to be the fittest port for your ships, and us here; wherefore we pray Your Majesty to make no delay, but to send them with all speed thither. Sir, I, Steenie, am commanded by my wife to trouble you with a deed of honour and charity, to have a care of the widow, Mistress Murray, whom you promised in her husband's time to provide for, and her seven children. We have been both much comforted with the return of Dick Graeme, who hath made to me, your dog, in particular, such a relation of Your Majesty's constant care and love of me, in my absence, that now I shall follow your advice with a cheerful heart though not with a more trustful nor affectionate one; for he hath told me your carriage hath been such, that it hath calmed the mad malice of all my enemies, which was no small grief to me to hear they were of so great a number; and for that honour, [i.e. a dukedom] which Your Majesty tells me my Lord Treasurer hath been an importunate suitor for, though not a secret one, give me leave, out of the pride of my heart, to say, whensoever anything proceeds otherwise than immediately from your heart and affection, I shall kiss it, and lay it down at your feet again, for hitherto you have accustomed me to no other. Out of a certain report here that you had done it, I sent Edward Clarke purposely to entreat you to undo it, or to add one more for my sake; but now that it is undone, which I thank God heartily for, I beseech Your Majesty humbly, on my knees, to let it remain so, till I have the happiness to speak with yourself, which is infinitely desired by your two boys that crave your blessing.

P.S. by Prince Charles.

We send this post with such speed, that we have no time to write this better.

Your Majesty's humble and obedient son and servant,
CHARLES.

XVIII. To James I

Madrid, April 29, 1623.

SIR,

I do find that, if I have not somewhat under Your Majesty's hand to show, whereby that you engage yourself to do whatsomever I shall promise in your name, that it will retard the business a great while; wherefore I humbly beseech Your Majesty to send me a warrant to this effect:

'We do hereby promise, by the word of a King, that what-soever you, our son, shall promise in our name, we shall punctually perform.'

Sir, I confess that is an ample trust that I desire; and if it were not mere necessity, I should not be so bold, yet I hope Your Majesty will never repent you of any trust you put upon

Your Majesty's humble and obedient son and servant,

CHARLES.

XIX. CHARLES AND BUCKINGHAM TO JAMES I

June 6, 1623.

DEAR DAD AND GOSSIP,

The Pope having written a courteous letter to me your baby, I have been told to write him an answer, without Your Majesty's leave, the copy whereof is here enclosed; we make no doubt but to have the opinions of those busy divines reversed (for already the Count of Olivares hath put out ten of the worst), so Your Majesty will be pleased to begin to put in execution the favour towards your Roman Catholic subjects, that you will be bound to do by your oath, as soon as the Infanta comes over, which we hope you will do for the hastening of us home, with this protesta-tion to reverse all, if there be any delay of the marriage. We send you here the articles as they are to go, the oaths, private and public, that you and your baby are to take, with the Councils, wherein, if you scare at the least clause of your private oath (where you promise that the Parliament shall revoke all the penal laws against the Papists within three years) we sought good to tell Your Majesty our opinions, which is that if you think you may do it in that time (which we think you may) if you do your best, although it take not effect, you have not broken your word, for this promise is only as a security that you will do your best. The Spanish ambassador, for respect of the Pope, will present unto you the articles as they came from Rome, as likewise for to require that the delivery of the Infanta may be deferred till the spring, his commission is to press for this, but to be satisfied with what we have yielded to here. We both humbly beg of Your Majesty that you will confirm these articles soon, and press

earnestly for our speedy return.   So, craving your blessings, we
rest

> Your Majesty's humble and obedient son and servant,
>> CHARLES
> Your Majesty's most humble slave and dog,
>> STEENIE.

*By this time Buckingham was clearly beginning to realize
that he had placed Charles and himself in a false position; hence
the criticism of Olivares.   That James was right in his desire for
an understanding with Spain there can be no doubt, but the
question was as much a religious as a political one, and a settlement involved concessions to the English Roman Catholics which
no King of England dare have promised.*

xx.CHARLES AND BUCKINGHAM TO JAMES I

Madrid, June 26, 1623.

DEAR DAD AND GOSSIP,

Though late, yet at last we have gotten the articles drawn
up in form, which we sent you by the Lord Rochford, without
any new addition or alteration.   The foolery of the Count of
Olivares hath been the cause of this long delay, who would
wilfully against thee have pulled it out of the Junto's and
Council's hands, and put it into a wrangling lawyer's, a favourite
of his, who, like himself, had not only put it into an odious
form, but had slipped in a multitude of new, unreasonable,
undemanded, and ungranted conditions, which the Council
yielded unto, merely out of fear; for when we met the Junto,
they did not make one answer to any of our objections, but confessed, with blushing faces, that we had more than reason on
our sides, and concluded with us that the same should serve
which were between Queen Mary and King Philip, being put
to the end of every article which is to be sworn to.   By this you
may a little guess with what favour they proceed with us, first,
delaying us as long as possibly they can, then, when things are
concluded of, they throw in new particulars, in hope they will
pass, out of our desire to make haste; but when our business is
done, we shall joy in it the more we have overcome so many

difficulties; in the meantime we expect pity at your hands. But, for the love of God and our business, let nothing fall from you to discover anything of this, and comfort yourself that all things will end well, to your contentment and honour. Our return now will depend on your quick dispatch of these; for, thank God, we find the heats of such weight here, as we may very well travel both evenings and mornings.

The divines have not yet recalled their sentence, but the Count tells us he hath converted very many of them, yet keeps his old form in giving us no hope of anything till the business speaks itself. But we dare say they dare not break it upon this, nor (we think) upon any other, except the affairs of Christendom should smile strangely upon them, which will at all times and in all cases guide them. So craving your blessing, we end.

SIR,

In the midst of our serious business, little pretty Toby Mathews comes to entreat us to deliver to Your Majesty, which is, as he calls it, a picture of the Infanta, drawn in black and white. We pray you, let none laugh at it but yourself and honest Kate; he thinks he has hit the nail on the head, but you will find it the foolishest thing that you ever saw.

Your Majesty's humble and obedient son and servant,
CHARLES.
Your Majesty's most humble slave and dog,
STEENIE.

'Honest Kate' was the Marchioness of Buckingham, daughter of the 6th Earl of Rutland, whom Buckingham had married in 1620.

James now sent a command to Charles and Buckingham to return at once.

XXI.CHARLES AND BUCKINGHAM TO JAMES I

Madrid, June 27, 1623.

DEAR DAD AND GOSSIP,

Our other letter was written before William Crofts came; he hath brought with him letters to our hearts' desire; we have thus far made use of them already. This morning we sent for the Count of Olivares, and, with a sad countenance, told him of your peremptory command, entreating him, in the kindest manner we could, to give us his advice how we might comply with this, and not destroy the business. His answer was, that there were two good ways to do the business, and one ill one; the two good ways were either with your baby's conversion, or to do it with trust, putting all things freely, with the Infanta, into our hands; the ill one was to bargain, and stick upon conditions as long as they could. As for the first, we absolutely rejected it, and for the second, he confessed, if he were King, he would do it, and, as he is, it lay in his power to do it; but he cast many doubts lest he should hereafter suffer for it, if it should not succeed; the last he confessed impossible since your command was as peremptory. To conclude, he left us with a promise to consider of it, and when I, your dog, conveyed him to the door, he bade me cheer up my heart, and your baby's both.

Our opinion is, that the longest time we can stay here will be a month, and not that neither, without bringing the Infanta with us. If we find not ourselves assured of that, look for us sooner. Whether of these resolutions be taken, you shall hear from us shortly that you may in time accordingly give order for the fleet. We must once again entreat Your Majesty to make all the haste you can to return these papers confirmed, and in the meantime to give orders for the execution of all these things, and to let us here know so much.

So let the worst then come, we make no doubt but to be with you before you end your progress; therefore, we entreat you to take comfort, for in your health depends all our happiness. So craving your blessing, we end.

I, Your Majesty's dog, beseecheth you to tell Cottington that I love him, and I pray you to do the like, for he is an honest man, and deserves it, or else call me knave.

Your Majesty's humble and obedient son and servant,
CHARLES.
Your Majesty's most humble slave and dog,
STEENIE.

23

Buckingham by now wished to get away from Madrid at the earliest possible moment, not least because he feared the activities of his enemies in England. Charles, on the other hand, who was still only a boy, was extremely sensitive to the ridicule he might incur if he returned home without the Infanta, and consequently wished to remain in the hope of arriving at a settlement.

XXII.CHARLES AND BUCKINGHAM TO JAMES I

Madrid, June 29, 1624.

DEAR DAD AND GOSSIP,

By Killigrew's dispatch, you understood how we entreated the Count of Olivares to give us his advice how we might comply with your peremptory command, and not destroy that business our heart was so much set on; to give an answer to which he required some time. The next day, at night, we sent for him again, and pressed him for his opinion and counsel; to which he answered, on Monday the divines should meet and give in their opinions, and upon Tuesday or Wednesday at the farthest, His Majesty should send us his last and final answer; but perceiving that we all looked sadly, and were at a resolution to return speedily upon it, if it were not to Your Majesty's satisfaction and ours, which could not be, except they resolved presently to give her without any new or further conditions, he concluded that he would do his best, and bid us be of good comfort, for he was in no doubt himself but all would end well. This we have thought good to advertise Your Majesty of, to the end you may not grieve yourself, nor think the time long till our coming, nothing was done, or intended, you may be the better satisfied with this our stay. They shall no sooner declare themselves to us, but you shall have it; so we crave your blessing and end.

Your Majesty's most humble and obedient son and servant,

CHARLES.

Your Majesty's most humble slave and dog,

STEENIE.

A further complication arose at this point, for on July 8th the Pope died, and there was some delay before a successor was

*elected in the person of Urban VIII. The new Pontiff was no
less desirous than his predecessor to turn the proposed marriage
to the advantage of the English Catholics, and he brought all
the pressure he could to bear upon both James and Charles. He
wrote to the latter, ' You, who desire so greatly to wed a Catholic
maiden, should surely take to yourself that bride, by whose
beauty Solomon, that wisest of Kings, boasts that he was taken
captive,' and added, with unconscious irony, ' Consider how that
at the court of Spain you are now made a spectacle for God and
man.' Urban directed that articles should be inserted in the
contract providing that the children of the marriage should have
Catholic nurses, and that Catholic churches should be erected in
every county. Whether or not the Spanish Government was
whole-hearted in its desire for the marriage, there is no reason
to question the sincerity of the Pope, and the impossibility of
these conditions is evidence, not of Urban's bad faith, but of his
ignorance of Protestant feeling in the British Isles.*

XXIII. CHARLES AND BUCKINGHAM TO JAMES I

Madrid, July 15, 1623.

DEAR DAD AND GOSSIP,

You have understood by this time how we were forced to
resort to your last letter, sent to us by Crofts : they continue still
the same expressions of joy which we then advertised you of.
We have thought it fit again, at this time, to entreat you to put
all those things in present execution, in favour of your Roman
Catholic subjects, that you are bound hereafter to do by the
articles; for we are (in) good hope, if that be, to bring the Infanta
at Michaelmas with us. We have given them these reasons to
persuade them to it : the lengthening of Your Majesty's days;
the honour of your son; the satisfaction of your whole people in
general; and the easier and sooner performance of what is
promised, with the charge you have been this year already at, at
how much it will be increased more by her stay till the spring.
We have showed them three ways to do it; first by alleging the
Infanta's love to your son, which will serve to take off the blame
of the act from the Count of Olivares, if the people should dislike
it, which he seems much to fear, and for which, we find, he hath
little reason; but because he gives so ill and so unlikely a reason,

we philosophy upon the worst on his part, than to make another trial with the Junto of divines, where they may make use of the advertisement they received last, concerning execution, from their own ambassador's; but that, I hope, will be better strengthened by what they shall write hereafter; and lastly, while this is working, to send to Rome, to persuade the Pope to dispense with this King's oath, since Your Majesty, your son, and your Council, hath agreed to that, for which that oath was required.

Sir, we do not know whether this will take effect or not; if it do not, we will be the sooner with you : we know you will think a little more time will be well spent to bring her with us, when, by that means, we may upon equaller terms treat with them of other things.   Do your best there, and we will not fail of ours here.   You should do well to see the ambassador's letters, and send them in your own packets.   Of all this we must entreat you speak nothing; for (if you do, our labour will be harder here, and when it shall be hoped there, and not take effect, they will be the more discontented.   I, your baby, have, since this conclusion, been with my mistress, and she sits publicly with me at the plays, and within these two or three days shall take place of the Queen as Princess of England.   I, your dog, have also had a visit of her, to deliver your letter, and to give her the *par bien* of this conclusion.   As this prosper you shall hear from time to time.   So we crave your blessing, and end

Your Majesty's humble and obedient son and servant,

CHARLES.

Your Majesty's most humble slave and dog,

STEENIE.

James went so far as to swear, and to induce his Council to swear, to observe the Spanish articles of marriage relating to the liberty of faith of the Infanta and of any children of the marriage, and the other conditions laid down by the Pope in his dispensation.

XXIV. CHARLES AND BUCKINGHAM TO JAMES I

Madrid, July 29, 1623.

DEAR DAD AND GOSSIP,

After a long expectation of Gresley, he arrived yesterday morning, with the good news of your health, and the dispatch of our business. We are sorry that there arose in your conscience any scruples, but we are very confident, when we see Your Majesty, to give you very good satisfaction for all we have done; and had we had less help, we had done it both sooner and better; but we leave that till our meeting. Sir, we have not been idle in this interim; for we can now tell you certainly that, by the 29th of your August, we shall begin our journey, and hope to bring her with us; but if they will not suffer her to come till the spring, whether we shall be contracted or not, we humbly beseech Your Majesty to leave it to our discretions, who are upon the place, and see things at a nearer distance, and a truer glass than you and your Council can there; for marriage there shall be none, without her coming with us; and, in the meantime, comfort yourself with this, that we have already convinced the Count of Olivares in this point, that it is fit the Infanta should come with us before the winter. He is working underhand with the divines, and, under colour of the King's and Prince's journey, makes preparation for hers also: her household is a settling, and all other things for her journey; and the Count's own words are, he will throw us all out of Spain as soon as he can. There remains no more for you to do, but to send us peremptory commands to come away, and with all possible speed: we desire this, not that we fear we shall have need of it; but in case we have, that your son (who hath expressed much affection to the person of the Infanta) may press his coming away, under colour of your command, without appearing an ill lover. I, your baby, give you humble and infinite thanks for the care you have expressed, both to my person and honour. And I, your slave and dog, who have most cause, give you none at all, because you have sent me no news of my wife, and have given her leave to be sick, and I conclude it the more dangerous, because you dare not write me of it. We hope you have sent the rest of the navy towards us by this time; if you have not, we beseech you to use all the speed you can, as we shall do, to cast ourselves, with an increase of your fleet.

So we crave your blessing,

Your Majesty's most humble and obedient son and servant,
CHARLES.

Your Majesty's most humble slave and dog,
STEENIE.

The next few weeks convinced even Charles of the futility of staying any longer in Madrid. In the meantime there had been repeated quarrels, not only between Buckingham and Olivares, but also between the English and Spanish courtiers, and Sir Edmund Verney (who was later to die grasping the standard at Edgehill) struck a priest in the face. Philip thereupon informed Charles that if he wished to remain in Madrid he must dismiss all his Protestant attendants. This determined the Prince to be gone, but the appearance of a rupture was avoided by the pretence that Charles was returning to persuade the King to consent to toleration for the English Catholics, while Lord Bristol was left with a proxy for the celebration of the marriage.

XXV. CHARLES AND BUCKINGHAM TO JAMES I

Madrid, August 20, 1623.

DEAR DAD AND GOSSIP,

The cause why we have altered our secretary is, that I, your baby, will not let your dog trouble himself with writing, because he has been of late troubled with a great cold, with a little fit of an ague, for which he was drawn blood, but now, thanks be to God, he is perfectly well.

Cottington arrived here the fifth of this month late at night, whose coming, we hoped, would have made great alteration to the better in our business; but we find here that they believe the Marquis Inoyosa's intelligence better than all Your Majesty's real proceedings; but we beseech you to take no notice to the Marquis of Inoyosa of his juggling (for he has written hither, contrary to his professions) until we wait upon you. The cause why we have been so long in not writing to you, since Cottington's coming, is that we would try all possible means (before we would send you word) to see if we could move them to send the Infanta before winter. They, for form's sake, called the divines, and they stick to their old resolution; but we find by circumstances that conscience is not the true but seeming cause of the Infanta's stay.   To conclude, we have wrought what we can, but since we cannot have her with us that we desired, our next comfort is, that we hope shortly to kiss Your Majesty's hands.

Sir, we have been informed by my Lord of Bristol, that by the French ambassador's means, the Spanish ambassador has seen all the letters that we have written to you, and that you are betrayed in your bed-chamber. So craving your blessing, we rest

Your Majesty's most humble and obedient son and servant,
CHARLES.

SIR,

I have been the willinger to let your son play the secretary at this time of little need, that you may thereby see the extraordinary care he hath of me, for which I will not entreat you not to love him the worse, nor him that threatens you, that when he once gets hold of your bedpost again, never to quit it.

Your Majesty's most humble slave and dog,
STEENIE.

XXVI. CHARLES AND BUCKINGHAM TO JAMES I

Madrid, August 30, 1623.

DEAR DAD AND GOSSIP,

This day we take our leaves; to-morrow we begin our journey; we leave our businesses thus. The Pope being sick (as they say here), hath not given power for the delivery of the dispensation, upon the capitulations agreed upon, wherefore they not being able (though many divines say the contrary) to contract me your baby, until that power come from Rome, and they not having used us with those realities, as to encourage us to rely longer upon uncertainties, I, your baby, have thought fit to leave my promise to the King in my Lord of Bristol's hands, to deliver it when that power comes from Rome. As for the business of the Palatinate (now that we have pressed them to it), we have discovered these two impediments; first they say, they have no hope to accommodate it, without the marriage of your grandchild with the Emperor's daughter; but though we know you will like the proposition of the marriage, yet we know not how either you, or your son-in-law or daughter, will like it with this condition, that your grandchild be bred up in the Emperor's court.   The second is, that though they are content to restore him all his lands, and his son to both lands and honour, yet they will not engage themselves to restore himself to honours, but have left it to their mediation and courtesy; and how the first point will be obtained of the father, when they will discontent him in the latter, we leave you to judge.   For the jointure and temporal articles, we will be able (when we shall be so happy as to kiss Your Majesty's hands) to give you a perfect account; in the meantime we crave your blessing, and end

Your Majesty's humble and obedient son and servant,

CHARLES.

Your Majesty's most humble slave and dog,

STEENIE.

Charles and Buckingham travelled from Madrid to Santander, where they embarked upon the English ships, under the command of the Earl of Rutland, which they found waiting there for them.   From Segovia Charles wrote to Bristol to withhold the proxy until security had been given that the Infanta, even though betrothed, would not render the marriage impossible by going into a convent.

XXVII. TO THE EARL OF BRISTOL

BRISTOL,

You may remember that a little before I came from St. Lorenzo I spoke to you concerning a fear I had that the Infanta might be forced to go into a monastery after she is betrothed; which you know she may do with a dispensation.   Though at that time I was loath to preach it (because I thought it fit at the time of my parting, to eschew distastes or disputes as much as I could) yet since considering that if I should be betrothed before that doubt be removed and that upon ill-grounded suspicions or any other cause whatsoever they should take this way to break the marriage, the King my father, and all the world will justly condemn me for a rash-headed fool, not to foresee and prevent this in time. Wherefore I thought it necessary by this letter to command you not to deliver my proxy to the King of Spain until I may have sufficient security both from him and the Infanta that after I am betrothed a monastery may not rob me of my wife, and after you have got this security send with all possible speed to me, that if I find it is sufficient (as I hope I shall), I may send you order by the delivering of my proxy to dispatch the marriage. So not doubting but that you will punctually observe this command, I rest your loving friend,

CHARLES P.

Charles and Buckingham landed at Portsmouth on October 5th, and found public opinion greatly relieved that the union had not taken place.

One result of the journey to Spain was the disgrace of Lord Bristol, whom Buckingham succeeded in saddling with the responsibility for his own mistakes. The following letters show how this occurred.

XXVIII. TO THE EARL OF BRISTOL

1623, *October* 8. *From Royston*.

BRISTOL,

Your letter to the King and me concerning the doubt I made after I came from St. Lorenzo hath so satisfied us both that we think it fit no longer to stick upon it, but leave it to your discretion to take what security you shall think sufficient. The King likewise has thought good, in this interim of expectation for my mistress, to give you a command to try what the King of Spain will do concerning the business of the Palatinate before I be contracted, and his reason is (which I could not reply to) that having but two children he would be loath that one of them should have cause to weep when the other had reason to laugh, and I was the rather induced to yield unto it because the King may very well have a positive answer of this before Christmas, so that it will lose no time in that business I desire so much. Although this be a needless office because I am sure you will understand this more amply by the King's own letters, yet I have written this that you may know from me as well as from the King my father the intent of this direction, which I assure you is no way to break the marriage, but (in this dull interim of looking for my mistress) to put an end to the miseries of my sister and her children, which I should have done if I stayed this winter. I have no more to say at this time but to bid you commend my service to my mistress and to assure the King that I shall never forget the favours he did me while I was in his court. So farewell.

Your loving friend,
Charles P.

XXIX. To the Earl of Bristol

1623, November 14.

Bristol,

The false interpretation of the King's and my directions concerning the not delivering of my proxy, has made me in such haste to send away this bearer, that by this I can only give you a command without giving any reasons at this time, which is not to deliver my proxy until you hear further from the King and myself; make what shifts or fair excuses you will, but I command you as you answer it upon your peril, not to deliver my proxy till you hear further from hence. So hoping that you will obey this command punctually, I am your friend,

Charles P.

XXX. To the Earl of Bristol

1623, November 15, *Whitehall.*

Bristol,

Yesterday I had no more time than to send you a peremptory command, leaving the reasons for this day, the which you will find at large in Mr. Sec. Conway's dispatch; but because I see you have need of paraphrase upon the text, I have thought fit to write to you this letter. My father's meaning and mine is that fifteen days after the receipt of these you shall press with all fair means to have a speedy answer, then you shall take your leave and come away, and leave Wat Aston behind you. . . . But whatsoever answer you get you must not deliver the proxy till you make my father and me judge of it. As for the whole business you must deal freely with them, in as civil terms as you will, that except that King will promise some way underhand to help my father with his arms (in case mediation fail) to restore my brother-in-law to his honours and inheritances, there can neither be marriage nor friendship; and as to the breeding up my nephew in the Emperor's court, avoid it as handsomely as you can, but I assure you it shall never be. And if they will do all that my father desires they may not only be sure of an alliance, but of a hearty, sincere friendship. Make no replies, suffer no delays, and then I rest your friend,

CHARLES P.

Immediately on his return to England the Earl of Bristol was ordered to his country seat, and told to consider himself a prisoner. Buckingham communicated to Charles his own feelings towards the unfortunate diplomat as the following letter shows.

XXXI. TO THE MARQUESS OF BUCKINGHAM

STEENIE,

First I must thank you for the token you sent me; then that you employed so good a secretary to answer my letter. Now I must crave your pardon to trouble you a little, and it is this; Bristol stands upon his justification, and will by no means accept of my counsels; the King does hate to have him come to his trial, and I am afraid if you be not with us to help to charge him, and to set the King right, he may escape with too slight a censure; therefore I would have you to send to the King to put off Bristol's trial until you might wait on him; but for God's sake do not venture to come sooner than you may with the safety of your health, and with that condition, the sooner the better. If you will answer me, trouble not yourself, but do it by the secretary you used last. Take care of yourself for my sake, who is and ever shall be

Your true, loving, constant friend,
CHARLES P.

Even after he had ascended the throne Charles refused to restore Bristol to favour.

XXXII. TO THE EARL OF BRISTOL

January 21, 1626.

We have read your letter addressed to us by Buckingham, and we cannot but wonder that you should through forgetfulness make such a request to us of favour, as if you stood evenly capable of it; when you know what your behaviour in Spain deserved of us, which you are to examine by the observations we made, and know you well remember how, at our first coming into Spain, taking upon you to be so wise as to foresee our intentions to change our religion, you were so far from dissuading us that you offered your service and secrecy to concur in it, and in many other open conferences, pressing to show how convenient it was for us to be a Roman Catholic, it being impossible, in your opinion, to do any great action otherwise; how much wrong, disadvantage, and disservice you did to the treaty, and to the right and interest of our dear brother, and sister, and their children; what disadvantage, inconvenience, and hazard you entangled us in by your artifices putting off and delaying our return home. The great estimation you made of that state, and the vile price you set this kingdom at, still maintaining that we, under colour of friendship to Spain, did what was in our power against them, which (you said) they knew very well. And, last of all, your approving of those conditions, that our nephew should be brought up in the Emperor's court; to which Sir Walter Aston then said he durst not give his consent for fear of his head; you replying to him that, without some such great action, neither marriage nor peace could be had, etc.

34

Charles never again left the British Isles, and there can be little doubt but that his experiences in Madrid instilled into him a rooted mistrust of foreigners. The upshot of the failure of the negotiations for an Anglo-Spanish agreement was widespread resentment against Spain in England, and this feeling was shared to the full by Charles and Buckingham. An alliance was made with France, Charles was betrothed to Henrietta Maria, and steps were taken to recover the Palatinate. James unwillingly submitted, largely under the influence of Buckingham, to this reversal of his previous policy, and in the midst of it he died on March 27th, 1625.

CHAPTER II

THE BEGINNING OF THE REIGN
1625-1629

During the early years of his reign Charles was much under the influence of Buckingham, whom James had created a duke, and the minister's opinion was asked even upon the most personal matters. Whether the ascendancy of Buckingham was for good or ill is a moot point: until recently historians have been unanimous in adopting the latter point of view, but Mr. Belloc has now championed the minister and favourite. However this may be, there can be no doubt that Buckingham was the real ruler of England from the accession of Charles I in 1625 until his own murder by Felton in 1628.

One of the new King's first acts was to send Buckingham to Paris to escort Henrietta Maria to England, and also to use his best endeavours to induce Louis XIII and Richelieu to associate themselves with the anti-Spanish policy to which the British Government was now committed.

1. To Louis XIII

MY DEAR BROTHER,

My great affection continually reminds me that you have in your possession a pledge which I esteem most dearly, and I find the delay in her journey too insupportable to bear. To raise my hopes a little, I have sent my well-beloved cousin and councillor, the Duke of Buckingham, to you to ask you to hasten and facilitate the journey of my dear wife, whose happy arrival is to me a pre-occupation only to be understood by those who have fixed their desires upon things at once the most perfect and the most dear. . . .

Whitehall, May 11, 1625.

On May 1st Henrietta Maria, who was barely fifteen years of age, had been married by proxy to Charles outside the west door of Notre-Dame, and when she arrived in England her husband met her at Dover. At first all went well, but the marriage treaty had given the new Queen the right to bring a large French retinue, and the latter soon began to make trouble between husband and wife. The following letters not only tell the story of these quarrels, but also throw no inconsiderable light upon the character of Charles and his relations with the Queen and Buckingham.

II. To the Duke of Buckingham

STEENIE,

I wrote to you by Ned Clarke that I thought I would have cause enough in short time to put away the monsieurs, either by attempting to steal away my wife, or by making plots with my own subjects. For the first, I cannot say certainly whether it was intended, but I am sure it is intended; for the other, though I have good grounds to believe it, and am still hunting after it, yet seeing daily the maliciousness of the monsieurs, by making and fomenting discontentments in my wife, I could tarry no longer from advertising of you, that I mean to seek for no other grounds to cashier my monsieurs, having for this purpose sent you this other letter that you may, if you think good, advertise the Queen-Mother with my intention; for this being an action that may have a show of harshness, I thought it was fit to take this way, that she to whom I have had many obligations may not take it unkindly, and likewise I think I have done you no wrong in my letter, though in some place I may seem to chide you. I pray you send me word with what speed you may, whether you like this course or not, for I shall put nothing of this in execution until I hear from you; in the meantime, I shall think of the convenient means to do this business with the best mind, but I am resolute; it must be done, and that shortly. So, longing to see thee, I rest

Your loving, faithful, constant friend,

CHARLES R.

Hampton Court, November 20, 1625.

III. To the Duke of Buckingham

Hampton Court, November 20, 1625.

STEENIE,

You know what patience I have had with the unkind usages of my wife, grounded upon a belief that it was not in her nature, but made by ill instruments, and overcome by your persuasions to me, that my kind usages would be able to rectify those misunderstandings. I hope my ground may be true, but I am sure you have erred in your opinion; for I find daily worse and worse effects of ill offices done between us, my kind usages having no power to mend anything. Now, necessity urges me to vent myself to you in this particular, for grief is eased being told to a friend; and because I have many obligations to my mother-in-law (knowing that these courses of my wife are so much against her knowledge, that they are contrary to her advice) I would do nothing concerning her daughter that may taste of any harshness, without advertising her of the reasons and necessity of the thing; therefore I have chosen you for this purpose, because you, having been one of the chief causes that hath withheld me from these courses hitherto, you may well be one of my chief witnesses that I have been forced into these courses now. You must, therefore, advertise my mother-in-law, that I must remove all those instruments that are causes of unkindness between her daughter and me, few or none of the servants being free of this fault in one kind or other; therefore I would be glad that she might find a means to make themselves suitors to be gone; if this be not, I hope there can be no exceptions taken at me, to follow the example of Spain and Savoy in this particular. So, requiring a speedy answer of thee in this business (for the longer it is delayed, the worse it will grow), I rest

Your loving, faithful, constant friend,

CHARLES R.

The mention of Spain and Savoy refers to cases concerning those countries where the servants of foreign queens had been expelled in somewhat similar circumstances.

IV. TO THE DUKE OF BUCKINGHAM

STEENIE,

I have hitherto deferred writing to you, both because I wanted subject, and that I thought that you would be on your way towards me before my letters could reach you. Now I send this bearer to you, as well to answer your letter concerning the Turkish ambassador, as to entreat you not to stay upon uncertainty of winds, but come away as soon as all the army is shipped, which I hope will be before this can come to you. Your journey to my sister and France requires daily more haste than other; for though my uncle of late has had good luck, yet he needs present encouragement, and Mansfeld, without instant help, dissolves to nothing.   As for news, my wife begins to mend her manners; I know not how long it will continue, for they say it is by advice; but the best of all is, they, the monsieurs, desire to return home; I will not say this is certain, for you know nothing that they say can be so.   So hoping to see you shortly, I rest

Your loving, faithful, constant friend,

CHARLES R.

This letter, which is undated, was probably written in December, 1625, when Buckingham was in Holland.   Mansfeld, with some English troops, was trying to recover the Palatinate, while the uncle to whom the King refers was Christian IV of Denmark and Norway, who had recently intervened in the Thirty Years War, and had received a subsidy from his nephew.

v.To the Duke of Buckingham

STEENIE,

It is not unknown, both to the French King and his mother, what unkindnesses and distastes have fallen between my wife and me; which hitherto I have borne with great patience (as all the world knows), ever expecting and hoping an amendment; knowing her to be but young, and perceiving it to be the ill crafty counsels of her servants for advancing of their own ends, rather than her own inclination.   For, at my first meeting of her at Dover, I could not expect more testimonies of respect and love than she showed; as, to give one instance.   Her first suit was, that she being young, and coming to a strange country, both by her years and ignorance of the customs of the place, might commit many errors; therefore, that I would not be angry with her for her faults of ignorance, before I had, by my instructions, learned her to eschew them; and desired me, in these cases, to use no third person, but to tell her myself, when I found she did anything amiss.   I both granted her request and thanked her for it; but desired that she would use me as she had desired me to use her; which she willingly promised me, which promise she never kept.   For, a little after this, Madame St. George, taking a distaste because I would not let her ride with us in the coach when there were women of better quality to fill her room, claiming it as her due (which in England we think a strange thing) set my wife in such a humour of distaste against me as, from that very hour to this, no man can say that ever she asked me, two days together, with so much respect as I deserved of her; but, on the contrary, has put so many disrespects on me, that it were too long to set down all.

Some I will relate.   As I take it, it was at her first coming to Hampton Court I sent some of my Council to her with those orders that were kept in the Queen my mother's house, desiring she would command the Count of Tilliers that the same might be kept in hers.   Her answer was, that she hoped I would give her leave to order her house as she list herself.   Now if she had said that she would speak with me, not doubting to give me satisfaction in it, I could have found no fault with her, whatsoever she would have said of this to myself, for I could only impute it to ignorance.   But I could not imagine that she would have affronted me in such a thing publicly.   After I heard this answer, I took a time, when I thought we had both best leisure to dispute it, to tell her calmly both her fault in the public denial and her mistaking the business itself.   She, instead of acknowledging her fault and mistaking, gave me so ill an answer that I omit (not to be tedious) the relation of that discourse; having too much of that nature hereafter to relate.

Many little neglects I will not take the pains to set down; as, her eschewing to be in my company; when I have anything to speak to her, I must means [i.e. use as a mediator] her servant first, else I am sure to be denied; her neglect of the English tongue, and of the nation in general.   I will also omit the affront she did me, before my going to this last unhappy assembly of

Parliament, because there has been talk enough of that already. The author of it is before you in France.

To be short, omitting all other passages, coming only to that which is most recent in memory : I having made a commission to make my wife's jointure, to assign her those lands she is to live on, and it being brought to such a ripeness that it wanted but my consent to the particulars they had chosen; she, taking notice that it was now time to name the officers for her revenue, one night, when I was in bed, put a paper into my hand, telling me it was a list of those that she desired to be of her revenue. I took it, and said I would read it next morning; but withal told her that, by agreement in France, I had the naming of them. She said, there were both English and French in the note. I replied, that those English I thought fit to serve her I would confirm; but for the French, it was impossible for them to serve her in that nature. Then she said, all those in the paper had breviates from her mother and herself, and that she could admit no other. Then I said, it was neither in her mother's power nor hers to admit any without my leave; and that, if she stood upon that, whomsoever she recommended, should not come in. Then she bade me plainly take my lands to myself; for, if she had no power to put in whom she would in those places, she would have neither lands nor houses of me; but bade me give her what I thought fit in pension. I bade her then remember to whom she spoke; and told her she ought not to use me so. Then she fell into a passionate discourse, how miserable she was, in having no power to place servants, and that business succeeded the worse for her recommendation; which, when I offered to answer, she would not so much as hear me. Then she went on saying, she was not of that base quality to be used so ill. Then I made her both hear me, and end that discourse.

Thus, having had so long patience with the disturbance of that which should be one of my greatest contentments, I can no longer suffer those, that I know to be the cause and fomenters of these humours, to be about my wife any longer; which I must do, if it were but for one action which they made my wife do, which is, to make her go to Tyburn in devotion to pray : which action can have no greater invective made against it than the relation.   Therefore, you shall tell my brother, the French King, as likewise his mother, that this being an action of so much necessity, I doubt not but he will be satisfied with it; especially since he hath done the like himself, not staying until he had so much reason.   And, being an action that some may interpret to be of harshness to his nation, I thought good to give him an account of it; because that, in all things, I would preserve the good correspondency and brotherly affection that is between us. So I rest

Your loving, faithful, constant friend,

CHARLES R.

July 12, 1626.

Tyburn, near the north-east corner of Hyde Park, had been the scene of the execution of many Roman Catholic priests. Charles was informed that the Queen had made a pilgrimage to the place, and knelt to pray for the souls of those who had perished there.   Henrietta Maria denied the accusation.

VI. TO THE DUKE OF BUCKINGHAM

STEENIE,

I have received your letter by Dick Graeme.   This is my answer.   I command you send all the French away to-morrow out of the town.   If you can, by fair means (but stick not long in disputing), otherwise force them away; driving them away like so many wild beasts, until you have shipped them; and so the devil go with them!   Let me hear no answer but of the performance of my command.   So I rest

Your faithful, constant, loving friend,

CHARLES R.

Oaking, August 7, 1626.

This order was duly carried out, but Louis XIII was not in a position to resent it, for he had recently acted in precisely the same way towards his wife's Spanish retinue.   He therefore very wisely sent an envoy to make peace between Charles and Henrietta Maria, and he succeeded so well in his task that there were no further quarrels: indeed, for the future their married life was exceptionally happy.

45

Meanwhile Charles was having trouble with Parliament as well as with his wife, and it was destined to be both more lasting and more disastrous. Parliament met in June, 1625, and showed at once a desire for a spirited foreign policy, and a reluctance to vote the necessary funds. It only granted the King power to collect the Customs for one year, instead of for life, as had been the invariable rule with previous monarchs, and although this was to be but a temporary measure until the rates had been revised, it was nevertheless ominous of what was to come. The politicians then turned to religious matters, and attempted to dictate how the Church should be administered. Here, too, previous custom was entirely against their claim, which Elizabeth had never tolerated, and in August the King dissolved Parliament. In February, 1626, a new Parliament was summoned, but it proceeded to impeach Buckingham, and was dissolved in June. As it had refused to vote the necessary funds to carry on the government, the Council sent letters to all the Justices of the Peace that they should exhort their counties to make a free gift.

VII. To the Justices of Peace of the County of Lancaster

Westminster, July 7, 1626.

It is not unknown to you that, in February last, our High Court of Parliament was by us summoned and assembled to treat of the great and weighty affairs concerning the Church of England and the true religion therein established, and the defence and safety of the Kingdom, and that they there continued together until the 15th of June last. Within which time many things of good moment and much conducing to our honour and the honour and safety of this kingdom were propounded and begun to be handled. And, amongst other things, our Commons then assembled, taking into their serious considerations our present and important occasions, not for our own private use, but for the common safety of us and our people, did, with one unanimous consent, agree to give unto us a supply of four entire subsidies and three-fifteenths, and did, by order of that House, set down the days and times of payment of the same, which, their loving and free offer unto us, we did graciously accept and rely upon, and dispose of our affairs accordingly, and afterwards with much patience, even beyond the pressing necessity of our public affairs, continually did expect the real performance thereof, and we are assured the same had been performed accordingly, had not the disordered passion of some members of that House, contrary to the good inclination of the graver and wiser sort of them, so far misled themselves and others, that they neither did nor would intend that which concerned the public defence of the kingdom, for which they were specially called. Wherefore, when no gracious admonitions could stay them, though much against our heart, we have dissolved that Parliament. And the Parliament being now ended, and yet the necessity of a supply of money lying still upon us and pressing us, without which the common safety of us and our people cannot be defended and maintained, but is in imminent and apparent danger to be assailed and swallowed up by a vigilant and powerful enemy, we have been enforced to cast all the ways and means which honourably and justly we might take for supply of these important affairs, and many several courses have been propounded and offered unto us. And although no ordinary rules can prescribe a law to necessity, and the common defence and safety, and even the very subsistence of the whole might justly warrant us if out of our Royal prerogative and power we should take any ways more extraordinary or less indifferent to any part thereof; yet we, desiring nothing more (next to the love and favour of Almighty God, by whose gracious assistance we desire to govern ourself and all our actions) than the love of our people, which we esteem as our greatest riches, we have made choice of that way which may be most equal and acceptable unto them. And therefore we do desire all our loving subjects, in a case of this unavoidable necessity, to be a law unto themselves, and lovingly, freely, and voluntarily, to perform that which by law, if it had passed formally by an Act as was intended, they had been compellable unto, and so in a timely way to provide not only for ours, but for their own defence and for the common safety of all our friends and allies and of our lives and honours. The performance of which our request will not only give us an ample testimony of the dutiful and good affections of our people in general, but will give us just encouragement the more speedily to meet in Parliament.

We therefore desire you forthwith to meet together and to take such order as may best advance our service, and in our name to desire and exhort our people, according to such instructions as herewith we send unto you, that they would not fail freely to give unto us a full supply answerable to the necessity of our present occasions.

Instructions to the Justices of the Peace in the County of Lancaster

1. That speedily, upon the receipt of these our letters, you assemble together at some place convenient and take them and the matter thereby recommended unto you into your due considerations.

2. That when you are thus assembled, you call to mind the resolution in the Parliament lately dissolved, to have given us four subsidies and three-fifteenths and that the several days of payment were ordered for the same, and thereby the sum of money to have been raised thereby was, in the judgement of the Parliament, but competent, and the times of payment convenient for the present and pressing occasions. And we are confident that the same considerations will prevail with our people.

3. That you let them know how much it will avail to our affairs, and the affairs of our friends and allies, to assail our enemies on their own coasts, and that we have begun a preparation to that end, but want moneys to perfect the same. And that whilst we are in these consultations, we are advertised from all parts of powerful preparations made to assail us at home or in Ireland, or both.

4. That you put them in mind that nothing invites an enemy more to an invasion than an opinion that that part intended to be invaded is either insecure or distracted, and so unprovided for a resistance.

5. That therefore you, the Deputy Lieutenants, give present direction to have all the troops and bands of the county completed, mustered, trained, and so well furnished, that they may be prepared to march unto the rendezvous at an hour's warning, upon pain of death.

6. That you conclude upon a constant way of propounding and pursuing this our supply in your several divisions, to the inhabitants of the whole county.

7. That when you have first settled this work among yourselves, you agree how to divide yourselves, throughout the whole county, into so many parts and divisions as you in your judgements shall think fittest, and then that those who shall be there employed, deal effectually with the rest of the county in those several divisions.

8. That you agree in the nomination of such able persons as you shall think fit for the collecting and receiving of these moneys and paying the same over to our Exchequer.

9. That you assure them in our name and in our Royal word, which we will not break with our people, that we will wholly employ all the moneys which shall thus be given to us, to the common defence of the kingdom, and not to or for any other end whatsoever.

10. That (together with the moneys you collect) you send a perfect roll of the names of all those which do thus contribute and of those which shall refuse, if any such be, that we may be thereby informed who are well affected to our service and who are otherwise, and what moneys are given unto us, that so we may require an account of those who shall be trusted to receive it, and that it may afterward appear that we have expended it to those ends and purposes it is given.

And lastly, that all this be instantly performed, for that all delays will defeat and overthrow our greatest counsels and affairs.

In addition to the attempts to raise money, steps were also being taken to increase the standard of efficiency of the Militia, though without much effect, it is to be feared.

VIII. To the Lords of the Council

Westminster, January 14, 1626.

We having taken into consideration the providing for the safety of our dominions and people by all the ways that may be taken, we have found that the trained bands of this our kingdom are so considerable in strength in respect of their numbers, serviceable persons of men, and their own particular interest, as the well experiencing of them in the use of their arms and fitting them for the service would settle a great security at home and give terror to any of our enemies. We have therefore often recommended to our Lieutenants of our several counties the putting in execution of those plain and exact rules which were formerly conceived and sent now unto them in printed books. And being resolved to peruse the same to effect, we have caused a certain number of experienced soldiers to be sent from the Low Countries hither, to be distributed into several counties there to teach the captains and other officers and leaders of files in each company the true and modern use of their arms and order of soldiers, that the officers being well instructed may teach the soldiers.

The urgent need for money, and the advisability of strengthening the militia, were due to the exigencies of foreign policy, for Charles was now at war with France as well as with Spain. In 1625 an expedition had been sent to Cadiz without effecting anything, and in the following year Buckingham determined to attempt to placate his opponents at home by intervening on behalf of the Huguenots, who were besieged in La Rochelle by the forces of the French Government. Buckingham took command of the English forces himself, and effected a landing on the island of Rhé, opposite La Rochelle, in the hope of driving away the besiegers from that side of the city.

IX. TO THE DUKE OF BUCKINGHAM

Windsor, August 13, 1627.

STEENIE,

I have received the joyful news of your happy success in the taking of Rhé, by Dick Graeme. I pray God to give you as much contentment always, as I received then; and then, I assure you, you will be in no danger to die of melancholy. Beecher likewise gave me two letters from you, out of which I have taken such notes as to know what you desire and want, then burned them. After these, ere yesternight, I have received another; all which, by this occasion, you shall see some answer to, though I hope to please you better in my actions than my words. I have made ready a supply of victuals, munition, four hundred men for recruits, and £14,000 ready money, to be brought to you by Beecher, who, by the grace of God, shall set sail within these eight days. Two regiments, of a thousand men a-piece, victualled for three months, shall be embarked by the 10th of September. I have sent for as many officers of the Low Countries as may be had, of which, till my next, I can give you no perfect account. I hope, likewise, you shall have two thousand men out of Scotland, under the command of my Lord Morton and Sir William Balfour. So far for supplies, which by the grace of God I shall send speedily unto you, and you may certainly expect. Now, I shall give you my opinion in some things that Beecher has been talking with me, and that I have understood by your late dispatch. And, first, in case the French King should die, what were to be done upon it. My opinion is (and not without advice in it), that you are to prosecute the war, and by no means to be the first motioner of treaty, for it is both dishonourable and unsafe, considering what men of faith the French of late have proved themselves; but if they should offer, then to hearken, but not to believe too hastily. And believe it, this is the best way to gain our chief ends; for certainly making shows, or being desirous of a treaty, before they of themselves demand it, may much hurt us, no way help us. I have seen a draught of a manifesto which you have sent my Lord Conway, which, if you have not yet published, I would wish to alter one point in it, that whereas you seem to make the cause of religion the only reason that made me take arms, I would only have you declare it the chief cause, you having no need to name any other, so that you may leave those of the religion to think what they will: but I think it much inconvenient by a manifesto, to be tied only to that cause, of this war; for cases may happen that may force me to go against my declaration (being penned so), which I should be loath should fall out. I have set three main projects afoot (besides many small), mint, increasing of the customs, by imposing on the book of rates, and raising of a bank. The two first, I shall certainly go speedily through withal; the last is most difficult, but I have good hopes of it. So, going to bed, and wishing thee as much happiness and good success as thine own heart can desire, I rest

CHARLES R.

I cannot omit to tell you that my wife and I were never better together; she, upon this action of yours, showing herself so loving to me, by her discretion upon all occasions, that it makes us all wonder and esteem her.

x. To the Duke of Buckingham

Aldershot, August 25, 1627.

STEENIE,

Beecher staying longer at the sea-side than I expected, has given me this occasion of writing to you, which I do, rather to assure you, that upon all occasions I am glad to remember you, and that no distance of place, nor length of time, can make me slacken, much less diminish my love to you, than that I have any business to advertise you of. I know, too, that this is nothing but what you know already; yet, imagining that we (like usurers) love sometimes to look on our riches, I think it is not unacceptable to you to bid you look on that I esteem to be the greatest riches, and now hardest to be found, true friendship, there being no style more justly to be given to any man, than that to me of being

Your faithful, loving, constant friend,
CHARLES R.

xi. To the Duke of Buckingham

Whitehall, September 2, 1627.

STEENIE,

Having received a letter from you by this bearer, I cannot let him return empty; and indeed I should much condemn myself, if I did let any occasion slip, without remembering my love to you. At this time I have not much to say, but to congratulate with you for your escape from that treacherous blow, which was meant you; for which I give God greater thanks than for your victory, hoping to have oft cause of rejoicing for the one, no more for the other; and upon this occasion I pray you take my counsel, that for my sake, you will trust as little as may be any Papistical French rascal. Your recommendations of Halie and Coningham came too late at this time, but you may assure them that I shall not fail to remember them with the first occasion. So praying for your good success in all things, and (with your wife) hoping and longing for your safe return, I rest

Your loving, faithful, constant friend,

CHARLES R.

The ' treacherous blow ' was the attempted assassination of Buckingham by a French Catholic with a three-edged knife.

XII. TO THE DUKE OF BUCKINGHAM

Theobalds, September 20, 1627.

STEENIE,

I have received yours by this bearer D'Albier, whom I have dispatched as soon as was possible, and to whose relation I shall need to add little, for I think he deserves the character that you put on him, and I assure you, it rejoices me not a little, to hear him (being a stranger and a soldier) give so just a description of your inclination (which I know to be true); that making me believe the rest he says concerning your proficiency in the trade you have so happily begun, which, though I never doubted, yet I am glad to see that truth forces all men to approve my judgement of you. Within a week after you have received this, I hope Holland shall deliver you another from me; therefore now I haste to end, only I must chide you (if it be true that I hear), that you hazard yourself too boldly. This I must command you to mend and take care of; there being more inconveniences in it than I (almost dare write) or fit for you to hear, but it is enough, that you are willed to preserve yourself for his sake, that is and ever shall be

Your loving, faithful, constant friend,

CHARLES R.

This bearer will (tell) you that I approve all your designs, and be confident of what succours these froward times can

53

yield, which though they cannot be according to mind, yet, by God's grace, shall be enough for your fortune to maintain a just cause.

XIII. To the Duke of Buckingham

Hampton Court, October 1, 1627.

STEENIE,

I have received your dispatch by Jack Ashburnham, by which I have understood the necessity in which you are, and I am much grieved and ashamed that I must make an apology for our slowness here in giving you supplies; the cause whereof is, the hardness of getting mariners, and the slow proceeding of the commissioners of the navy (which all commissioners are subject to), money being more readily furnished than I could have expected in these necessitous times; but for that our best answer is (as the schoolboy says) pardon this, and we shall do so no more; and now, by the grace of God, you shall have no more cause to complain of us, for now we know how to prevent those faults, which we, without some experience, could hardly foresee. Holland, within two or three days, will attend you with supplies, wherefore at this time I shall say little more, but concerning the instructions you sent me for Ned Clarke, and Will Hayden's place of the Ordnance. For the first, the King of Denmark's ambassadors being here, for an accommodation between France and me, I have sent them away well enough satisfied, yet without discovering my intentions; so that I hope my uncle will be content with my proceedings with France; Ned Clarke likewise having instructions correspondent to the answer that was given the Denmark ambassadors; so that I think it needless, or rather hurtful, to discover any main intent in this business, because divulging of it (which this may cause) in my mind, must needs hazard it.

John Hayden has his brother's place already passed unto him, so that you must excuse me, at this time, for Colonel Brett, yet because I see you have so great a care for him, I assure you that, at the next occasion, I shall remember him with as good a turn (though I did not know him, as I do, to be an honest sufficient man) if it were only because I see you esteem him. Lastly, for

God's sake be not disheartened with our by-past slowness, for, by the grace of God, it is all past. This I say not, that I fear thy constant stout heart can slack in an honest cause, but that some rascal may cast doubts in the army as if I neglected you; which I imagine is likely enough to fall out, since some villains stick not to divulge it; and it is possible those who were the cause of your consultation of leaving the siege, and coming home (for the resisting of which I give thee a thousand thanks), may mutter such things. Now I pray God to prosper me, but as I shall stick to thee in all occasions, and, in this action, as I shall show myself,

Your loving, faithful, constant friend,

CHARLES R.

XIV. TO THE DUKE OF BUCKINGHAM

Whitehall, October 13, 1627.

STEENIE,

Since I have understood by Jack Ashburnham your necessities for fault of timely supplies, I still stand in fear (until I shall hear from you) that these may come too late, but I hope that God is more merciful to me, than to inflict so great a punishment on me. Holland can tell you all occurrences here, which I may use for a good excuse of a short letter; but in case his gladness to see you (I judge him by himself) may make him forget some things, I will remember those I have most care of. The Denmark ambassadors, since their taking leave of me, having demanded a private audience there moved unto me to send you powers to treat with France, in case they could procure them to begin; their reason for this was gaining of time, which they said, otherwise must be needs lost: but my answer was, that it was no ways honourable for me to send powers to treat, before I knew France's disposition to treat, it being necessary for my honour that they should begin, not I. After some dispute, they found my reasons good, they ending with this request (which I could not refuse, but was glad of), that they might advertise you from time to time of their proceedings with the French King, and to give them some contentment at their farewell, I told them, that in case they made a peace between me and France,

55

the army that you command should be ready to serve my uncle, if he desired it. Now, honest rascal, though I refused, being demanded, to send thee powers to treat, yet thou (knowing my well-grounded confidence of thee) mayst easily judge the warrant dormant power thou hast in this, as in anything else, where confidence may be placed on any man; but for fear that thy modesty in this particular might hinder thee to remember thy power of trust, which I have given thee, I thought not amiss to write as I have written.

Gerbier's treaty is at an end, wherein he has showed both his honesty and sufficiency, but mightily abused by the King of Spain's ministers. So referring you to Holland, I rest (though not in quiet until I shall see you safe and happily returned)

Your loving, faithful, constant friend,

CHARLES R.

Meanwhile Buckingham was meeting with disaster. The French had resisted all attempts to dislodge them from St. Martin, the chief town of Rhé, and their reinforcements were pouring into the island. On October 27th Buckingham tried to carry St. Martin by storm, but the scaling-ladders were too short, and the assault failed. It was thereupon determined to evacuate Rhé, but Marshal Schomberg fell upon the English as they were marching to the ships, and inflicted heavy casualties. To Buckingham's credit it should be observed that, whatever his shortcomings as a general, his personal bravery was never in question.

The allusion to ' some design ' in the following letter is to an attack on Calais which had been suggested to compensate for the failure before La Rochelle.

xv. TO THE DUKE OF BUCKINGHAM

Whitehall, November 6, 1627.

STEENIE,

I pray God that this letter be useless or never come to your hands, this being only to meet you at your landing in England, in case you should come from Rhé, without perfecting your work, happily begun, but I must confess, with grief, ill seconded. A letter you sent by Jack Epslie is the cause of this, wherein you have taught me patience, and how to seek the next best in misfortunes. This is therefore to give you power (in case you should imagine that you have not enough already) to put in execution any of those designs you mentioned to Jack Epslie, or any other that you should like of. So that I leave it freely to your will, whether, after your landing in England, you will set forth again to some design, before you come hither; or else that you will first come to ask my advice, before you undertake a new work; assuring you that, with whatsomever success you shall come to me, you shall be ever welcome, one of my greatest griefs being that I have not been with you in this time of suffering, for I know we would have much longer on this subject, for fear of losing myself in it. To conclude, you cannot come so soon as you are welcome, and, unfeignedly in my mind, you have gained as much reputation, with wise and honest men, in this action, as if you had performed all your desires. I have no more to say at this time, but conjure thee, for my sake, to have a care of thy health, for every day I find new reasons to confirm me in being

Your loving, faithful, constant friend,

CHARLES R.

The blame for the failure of the expedition cannot fairly be laid at the door of the King but must be shared between the politicians, who wanted war but would not tax themselves to pay for it, and Buckingham, who displayed in foreign affairs a levity more suited to a later age. Charles and his minister were, however, by no means daunted by their lack of success, and in the following year (1628) another expedition was fitted out to relieve La Rochelle. Before it sailed Buckingham was, on August 23rd, murdered at Portsmouth by one John Felton.

Five months before the murder of Buckingham another Parliament had been summoned, and its first act was to pass the Petition of Right, which was as follows:—

To THE KING'S MOST EXCELLENT MAJESTY

Humbly show unto our Sovereign Lord the King, the Lords Spiritual and Temporal, and Commons in Parliament assembled.

that whereas it is declared and enacted by a statute made in the time of the reign of King Edward I, commonly called *Statutum de Tallagio non Concedendo*, that no tallage or aid shall be laid or levied by the King or his heirs in this realm, without the good will and assent of the archbishops, bishops, earls, barons, knights, burgesses, and other the freemen of the commonalty of this realm; and by authority of Parliament holden in the five-and-twentieth year of the reign of King Edward III, it is declared and enacted, that from thenceforth no person should be compelled to make any loans to the King against his will, because such loans were against reason and the franchise of the land; and by other laws of this realm it is provided, that none should be charged by any charge or imposition called a benevolence, nor by such like charge; by which statutes before mentioned, and other the good laws and statutes of this realm, your subjects have inherited this freedom, that they should not be compelled to contribute to any tax, tallage, aid, or other like charge not set by common consent, in Parliament.

II.   Yet nevertheless of late divers commissions directed to sundry commissioners in several counties, with instructions, have issued; by means whereof your people have been in divers places assembled, and required to lend certain sums of money unto Your Majesty, and many of them, upon their refusal so to do, have had an oath administered unto them not warrantable by the laws or statutes of this realm, and have been constrained to become bound and make appearance and give utterance before your Privy Council and in other places, and others of them have been therefore imprisoned, confined, and sundry other ways molested and disquieted; and divers other charges have been laid and levied upon your people in several counties by Lord Lieutenants, Deputy Lieutenants, commissioners for musters, Justices of Peace and others, by command or direction from Your Majesty, or your Privy Council, against the laws and free customs of the realm.

III.   And whereas also by the statute called 'The Great Charter of the Liberties of England', it is declared and enacted, that no freeman may be taken or imprisoned or be disseised of his freehold or liberties, or his free customs, or be outlawed or exiled, or in any manner destroyed, but by the lawful judgement of his peers, or by the law of the land.

IV.   And in the eight-and-twentieth year of the reign of King Edward III, it was declared and enacted by authority of Parliament, that no man, of what estate or condition that he be, should be put out of his land or tenements, nor taken, nor imprisoned, nor disherited, nor put to death without being brought to answer by due process of law.

V.   Nevertheless, against the tenor of the said statutes of your realm to that end provided, divers of your subjects have of late been imprisoned without any cause showed; and when for their deliverance they were brought before your Justices by Your Majesty's writs of *habeas corpus*, there to undergo and receive as the court should order, and their keepers commanded to certify the causes of their detainer, no cause was certified, but that they were detained by Your Majesty's special command, signified by the lords of your Privy Council, and yet were returned back to several prisons, without being charged with anything to which they might make answer according to the law.

VI.   And whereas of late great companies of soldiers and mariners have been dispersed into divers counties of the realm, and the inhabitants against their will have been compelled to receive them into their houses, and there to suffer them to sojourn against the laws and customs of this realm, and to the great grievance and vexation of the people.

VII.   And whereas also by authority of Parliament, in the five-and-twentieth year of the reign of King Edward III, it is declared and enacted, that no man shall be forejudged of life or limb against the form of the Great Charter and the law of the land; and by the said Great Charter and other the laws and statutes of this your realm, no man ought to be adjudged to death but by the laws established in this your realm, either by the customs of the same realm, or by Acts of Parliament : and whereas no offender of what kind soever is exempted from the proceedings to be used, and punishments to be inflicted by the laws and statutes of this your realm; nevertheless of late time divers commissions under Your Majesty's Great Seal have issued forth, by which certain persons have been assigned and appointed commissioners with power and authority to proceed within the land, according to the justice of martial law, against such soldiers or mariners, or other dissolute persons joining with them, as should commit any murder, robbery, felony, mutiny, or other outrage or misdemeanour whatsoever, and by such summary course and order as is agreeable to martial law, and as is used in armies in time of war, to proceed to the trial and condemnation of such offenders, and them to cause to be executed and put to death according to the law martial.

VIII.   By pretext whereof some of Your Majesty's subjects have been by some of the said commissioners put to death, when and where, if by the laws and statutes of the land they had deserved death, by the same laws and statutes also they might, and by no other ought to have been judged and executed.

IX.   And also sundry grievous offenders, by colour thereof claiming an exemption, have escaped the punishments due to them by the laws and statutes of this your realm, by reason that divers of your officers and ministers of justice have unjustly refused or forborne to proceed against such offenders according to the same laws and statutes, upon pretence that the said offenders were punishable only by martial law, and by authority of such commissions as aforesaid: which commissions, and all other of like nature, are wholly and directly contrary to the said laws and statutes of this your realm.

X.   They do therefore humbly pray Your Most Excellent Majesty, that no man hereafter be compelled to make or yield any gift, loan, benevolence, tax, or such like charge, without common consent by Act of Parliament; and that none be called to make answer, or take such oath, or to give attendance, or be confined, or otherwise molested or disquieted concerning the same or for refusal thereof; and that no freeman, in any such manner as is before mentioned, be imprisoned or detained; and that Your Majesty would be pleased to remove the said soldiers and mariners, and that your people may not be so burdened in time to come; and that the aforesaid commissions, for proceeding by martial law, may be revoked and annulled; and that hereafter no commissions of like nature may issue forth to any person or persons whatsoever to be executed, as aforesaid, lest by colour of them any of Your Majesty's subjects be destroyed or put to death contrary to the laws and franchise of the land.

XI.   All which they most humbly pray of Your Most Excellent Majesty as their rights and liberties, according to the laws and statutes of this realm; and that Your Majesty would also vouchsafe to declare, that the awards, doings, and proceedings, to the prejudice of your people in any of the premises, shall not be drawn hereafter into consequence or example; and that Your Majesty would be also graciously pleased, for the further comfort and safety of your people, to declare your Royal will and pleasure, that in the things aforesaid all your officers and ministers shall serve you according to the laws and statutes of this realm, as they tender the honour of Your Majesty, and the prosperity of this kingdom.

The attitude of Charles to the Petition may be gathered from the following message to the House of Lords:—

xvi. TO OUR TRUSTY AND RIGHT WELL-BELOVED THE LORDS SPIRITUAL AND TEMPORAL OF THE HIGHER HOUSE OF PARLIAMENT

CHARLES R.

We being desirous of nothing more than the advancing of the good, peace, and prosperity of our people, have given leave to free debates of the highest points of our prerogative Royal, which, in the times of our predecessors, Kings and Queens of this realm, were ever restrained, as matters that they would not have disputed; and in other things we have been willing so far to descend to the desires of our good subjects, as might fully satisfy all moderate minds, and free them from all just fears and jealousies; which those messages that we have heretofore sent unto the Commons House will well demonstrate to the world.   And yet we find it still insisted on, that, in no case whatsoever, should it never so nearly concern matters of state and government, we or our Privy Council have power to commit any man without the cause showed; whereas it often happens that should the cause be showed, the service itself would thereby be destroyed and defeated: and the cause alleged must be such as may be determined by our judges of our courts of Westminster in a legal and ordinary way of justice; whereas the cause may be such as those judges have not capacity of judicature, nor rules of law, to direct and guide their judgements, in cases of that transcendent nature; which happening so often, the very inter-mitting of the constant rules of government, for so many ages, within this kingdom practised, would soon dissolve the very frame and foundation of our monarchy. Wherefore, as to our Commons we made fair propositions, which might equally prefer the just liberties of the subjects; so, My Lords, we have thought good to let you know, that, without overthrow of sovereignty, we cannot suffer this power to be impeached. Notwithstanding, to clear our conscience and just intentions, this we publish, that it is not in our heart, nor will we ever extend our regal power (lent unto us from God) beyond that just rule of moderation, wherein the safety of our people shall be our only aim. And we do hereby declare our Royal pleasure and resolution to be, which God willing we shall ever constantly maintain, that neither we nor our Privy Council shall or will, at any time hereafter, com-mit or command to prison, or otherwise restrain, the person of any, for the not lending of money unto us, or for any other cause which in our conscience doth not concern the State, the public good, and safety of us and our people.

We will not be drawn to pretend any cause, which, in our judgement, is not expressed (which base thought we hope no man will imagine can fall into our Royal breast); and that, in all causes of this nature which shall hereafter happen, we shall, upon the humble petition of the party, or address of our judges unto us, readily and really express the true cause of their com-mitment or restraint, so soon as with conveniency and safety the same is fit to be disclosed and expressed.

And that, in all causes criminal of ordinary jurisdiction, our judges shall proceed to the deliverance or bailment of the prisoner, according to the known and ordinary rules of the law of this land, and according to the statute of *Magna Charta* and those other six statutes insisted on; which, we do take knowledge, stand in full force, and which we intend not to abrogate or weaken, against the true intention thereof.

This we have thought fit to signify unto you the rather for shortening of any long debate upon this question; the season of the year so far advanced, and our great occasions of state, not lending us many days for longer continuance of this session of Parliament.   Given under our signet, at our Palace of Westminster the 12th Day of May, in the Fourth Year of our reign.

Parliament, however, would not hear of any compromise, and on June 7th the King gave his assent to the Petition of Right.

Parliament met again in January of the next year (1629), but immediately questioned the King's right to the Customs, and proceeded to interfere once more in the government of the Church.   After disorderly scenes, during which the Speaker of the House of Commons was forcibly held down in the chair by the Opposition, the third Parliament of Charles came to an end in March, 1629.   On the 10th of that month the King issued a proclamation giving his reasons for the action which he had taken.

XVII

Howsoever princes are not bound to give account of their actions, but to God alone; yet for the satisfaction of the minds and affections of our loving subjects, we have thought good to set down thus much by way of declaration, that we may appear to the world in the truth and sincerity of our actions, and not in those colours in which we know some turbulent and ill-affected spirits (to mask and disguise their wicked intentions, dangerous to the State) would represent us to the public view.

We assembled our Parliament the seventeenth day of March, in the third year of our reign, for the safety of religion, for securing our kingdoms and subjects at home, and our friends and allies abroad; and therefore at the first sitting down of it we declared the miserable afflicted estate of those of the reformed religion, in Germany, France, and other parts of Christendom; the distressed extremities of our dearest uncle, the King of Denmark, chased out of a great part of his dominions; the strength of that party which was united against us; that (besides

the Pope, and the House of Austria, and their ancient con-
federates) the French King professed the rooting out of the
Protestant religion; that, of the princes and states on our party,
some were overrun, others diverted, and some disabled to give
assistance : for which, and other important motives, we propounded a speedy supply of treasure, answerable to the necessity
of the cause.

These things in the beginning were well resented by the
House of Commons, and with much alacrity and readiness they
agreed to grant a liberal aid : but before it was brought to any
perfection, they were diverted by a multitude of questions raised
amongst them touching their liberties and privileges, and by
other long disputes, that the Bill did not pass in a long time;
and by that delay our affairs were put into a far worse case than
at the first, our foreign actions then in hand being thereby disgraced and ruined for want of timely help.

In this, as we are not willing to derogate from the merit
and good intentions of those wise and moderate men of that
House (to whose forwardness we attribute it, that it was
propounded and resolved so soon) : so we must needs say, that
the delay of passing it, when it was resolved, occasioned by
causeless jealousies, stirred up by men of another temper, did
much lessen both the reputation and reality of that supply : and
their spirit, infused into many of the commissioners and
assessors in the country, hath returned up the subsidies in such
a scanty proportion, as is infinitely short, not only of our great
occasions, but of the precedents of former subsidies, and of the
intentions of all well-affected men in that House.

In those large disputes, as we permitted many of our high
prerogatives to be debated, which in the best times of our
predecessors had never been questioned without punishment or
sharp reproof, so we did endeavour to have shortened those
debates, for winning of time, which would have much advantaged
our great affairs both at home and abroad.   And therefore both
by speeches and messages we did often declare our gracious and
clear resolution to maintain, not only the Parliament, but all our
people, in the ancient and just liberties without either violation
or diminution; and in the end, for their full satisfaction and

security, did by an answer, framed in the form by themselves desired, to their Parliamentary Petition, confirm their ancient and just liberties and rights, which we resolve with all constancy and justice to maintain.

This Parliament, howsoever, besides the settling our necessary supply and their own liberties, they wasted much time in such proceedings, blasting our government, as we are unwilling to remember, yet we suffered them to sit, until themselves desired us to appoint a time for recess, not naming either adjournment or prorogation.

Whereupon, by advice of our Council, we resolved to prorogue and make a session; and to that end prefixed a day, by which they might (as was meet in so long a sitting) finish some profitable and good laws; and withal, gave order for a gracious pardon to all our subjects; which, according to the use of former Parliaments, passed the Higher House, and was sent down to the Commons. All which being graciously intended by us, was ill-entertained by some disaffected persons of that House, who by their artifices in a short time raised so much heat and distemper in the House—for no other visible cause but because we had declared our resolution to prorogue, as our Council advised, and not to adjourn, as some of that House (after our resolution declared, and not before) did manifest themselves to affect—that seldom hath greater passion been seen in that House, upon the greatest occasions. And some glances in the House, but upon open rumours abroad, were spread, that by the answer to the Petition we had given away, not only our impositions upon goods exported and imported, but the Tonnage and Poundage— whereas in the debate and hammering of that Petition, there was no speech or mention in either House concerning those impositions, but concerning taxes and other charges, within the land; much less was there any thought thereby to debar us of Tonnage and Poundage, which both before and after the answer to that Petition the House of Commons, in all their speeches and treaties, did profess they were willing to grant; and at the same time many other misinterpretations were raised of that Petition and answer, by men not well distinguishing between well-ordered liberty and licentiousness; as if by our answer to that Petition we had let loose the reins of our government : and in this distemper, the House of Commons laying aside the pardon (a thing never done in any former Parliament) and other business, fit to have been concluded that session, some of them went about to frame and contrive a remonstrance against our receiving of Tonnage and Poundage, which was so far proceeded in the night before the prefixed time for concluding the session, and so hastened by the contrivers thereof, that they meant to have put it to the vote of the House the next morning, before we should prorogue the session : and therefore finding our gracious favours in that session, afforded to our people, so ill-requited, and such sinister strains made upon our answer to that Petition, to the diminution of our profit, and (which was more) to the danger of our government : we resolved to prevent the finishing of that remonstrance, and other dangerous intentions of some ill-affected persons, by ending the session the next morning, some few hours sooner than was expected, and by our own mouth to declare to both Houses the cause thereof; and for hindering the spreading of those sinister interpretations of that Petition and answer, to give some necessary directions for settling and quieting our government until another meeting; which we performed accordingly the six-and-twentieth of June last.

The session thus ended, and the Parliament risen, that intended remonstrance gave us occasion to look into the business of Tonnage and Poundage : and therefore, though our necessities pleaded strongly for us, yet we were not apt to strain that point too far, but resolved to guide ourself by the practice of former ages, and examples of our most noble predecessors; thinking those counsels best warranted, which the wisdom of former ages, concurring with the present occasions did approve; and therefore gave order for a diligent search of records : upon which it was found, that although in the Parliament holden in the first year of the reign of King Edward the Fourth, the subsidy of Tonnage and Poundage was not granted unto that King, but was first granted unto him by Parliament in the third year of his reign; yet the same was accounted and answered to that King, from the first day of his reign, all the first and second years of his reign, and until it was granted by Parliament : and that in the succeeding times of King Richard the Third, King Henry the Seventh, King Henry the Eighth, King Edward the Sixth, Queen Mary, and Queen Elizabeth, the subsidy of Tonnage and Poundage was not only enjoyed by every one of those Kings and Queens, from the death of each of them deceasing, until it was granted by Parliament unto the successor; but in all those times (being for the most part peaceable, and not burdened with like charges and necessities, as these modern times) the Parliament did most readily and cheerfully, in the beginning of every of those reigns, grant the same, as a thing most necessary for the guarding of the seas, safety and defence of the realm, and supportation of the Royal dignity : and in the time of our Royal father of blessed memory, he enjoyed the same a full year, wanting very few days, before his Parliament began; and above a year before the Act of Parliament for the grant of it was passed : and yet when the Parliament was assembled, it was granted without difficulty.   And in our own time we quietly received the same three years and more, expecting with patience, in several Parliaments, the like grant thereof, as had been made to so many of our predecessors; the House of Commons still professing that multitude of other businesses, and not want of willingness on their part, had caused the settling thereof to be so long deferred : and therefore, finding so much reason and necessity, for the receiving of the ordinary duties in Custom House, to concur with the practice of such a succession of Kings and Queens, famous for wisdom, justice, and government; and nothing to the contrary, but that intended remonstrance, hatched out of the passionate brains of a few particular persons; we thought it was so far from the wisdom and duty of a House of Parliament, as we could not think that any moderate and discreet man (upon composed thoughts, setting aside passion and distemper) could be against receiving of Tonnage and Poundage; especially since we do, and still must, pursue those ends, and undergo that charge, for which it was first granted to the Crown; it having been so long and constantly continued to our predecessors, as that in four several Acts of Parliament for the granting thereof to King Edward the Sixth, Queen Mary, Queen Elizabeth, and our blessed father, it is in express terms mentioned, to have been had and enjoyed by the several Kings, named in those Acts, time out of mind, by authority of Parliament : and therefore upon these reasons we held it agreeable to our kingly honour, and necessary for the safety and good of our kingdom, to continue the receipt thereof, as so many of our predecessors had done.   Wherefore when a few merchants (being at first but one or two), fomented, as it is well known, by those evil spirits, that would have hatched that undutiful remonstrance, began to oppose the payment of our accustomed duties in the Custom House, we gave order to the officers of our Customs to go on, notwithstanding that opposition, in the receiving of the usual duties; and caused those that refused to be warned to attend at the Council Board, that by the wisdom and authority of our Council they might be reduced to obedience and duty; where some of them, without reverence or respect to the honour and dignity of that presence, behaved themselves with such boldness and insolency of speech, as was not to be endured by a far meaner assembly, much less to be countenanced by a House of Parliament, against the body of our Privy Council.

And as in this we did what in reason and honour was fit for the present, so our thoughts were daily intentive upon the reassembling of our Parliament, with full intention on our part to take away all ill understanding between us and our people, whose love as we desired to continue and preserve, so we used our best endeavours to prepare and facilitate the way to it; and to this end, having taken a strict and exact survey of our government, both in the Church and commonwealth, and what things were most fit and necessary to be reformed : we found in the first place that much exception had been taken at a book entitled *Appello Cæsarem*, or an *Appeal to Cæsar,* and published in the year 1625 by Richard Montague, then Bachelor of Divinity, and now Bishop of Chichester; and because it did open the way to those schisms and divisions which have since ensued in the Church, we did, for remedy and redress thereof, and for the satisfaction of the consciences of our good people, not only by our public proclamation, call in that book, which ministered matter of offence, but to prevent the like danger for hereafter, reprinted the Articles of Religion, established in the time of

Queen Elizabeth of famous memory, and by a declaration before those Articles, we did tie and restrain all opinions to the sense of those Articles, that nothing might be left for private fancies and innovations. For we call God to record, before whom we stand, that it is, and always hath been, our heart's desire to be found worthy of that title, which we account the most glorious in all our Crown, Defender of the Faith. Neither shall we ever give way to the authorizing of anything, whereby any innovation may steal or creep into the Church, but to preserve that unity of doctrine and discipline, established in the time of Queen Elizabeth, whereby the Church of England hath stood and flourished ever since.

And as we were careful to make up all breaches and rents in religion at home, so did we, by our proclamation and commandment, for the execution of laws against Priests and Popish Recusants, fortify all ways and approaches against that foreign enemy; which, if it have not succeeded according to our intention, we must lay the fault where it is, in the subordinate officers and ministers in the country, by whose remissness Jesuits and Priests escape without apprehension, and Recusants, from those convictions and penalties which the law and our commandment would have inflicted on them : for we do profess, that, as it is our duty, so it shall be our care, to command and direct well; but it is the part of others to perform the ministerial office, and when we have done our office we shall account ourself, and all charitable men will account us innocent, both to God and men; and those that are negligent we will esteem as culpable both to God and us, and therefore will expect that hereafter they give us a better account.

And, as we have been careful for the settling of religion and quieting the Church, so were we not unmindful of the preservation of the just and ancient liberties of our subjects, which we secured to them by our gracious answer to the Petition in Parliament, having not since that time done any act whereby to infringe them : but our care is, and hereafter shall be, to keep them entire and inviolable, as we would do our own right and sovereignty, having for that purpose enrolled the Petition and answer in our courts of justice.

Next to the care of religion and of our subjects' rights, we did our best for the provident and well-ordering of that aid and supply, which was granted us last session, whereof no part hath been wastefully spent, nor put to any other use, than those for which it was desired and granted, as upon payment of our fleet and army; wherein our care hath been such as we chose rather to discontent our dearest friends and allies, and our nearest servants, than to leave our soldiers and mariners unsatisfied, whereby any vexation or disquiet might arise to our people. We have also, with part of those moneys, begun to supply our magazines and stores of munition, and to put our navy into a constant form and order. Our fleet likewise is fitting, and almost in a readiness, whereby the narrow seas may be guarded, commerce maintained, and our kingdom secured from all foreign attempts. These acts of ours might have made this impression in all good minds, that we were careful to direct our counsels, and dispose our actions, as might most conduce to the maintenance of religion, honour of our government, and safety of our people. But with mischievous men once ill-affected, *seu bene seu male facta premunt*; and whatsoever once seemed amiss is ever remembered, but good endeavours are never regarded.

Now all these things that were the chief complaints the last session, being by our princely care so seriously reformed, the Parliament reassembled the twentieth of January last. We expected, according to the candour and sincerity of our own thoughts, that men would have framed themselves for the effecting of a right understanding between us and our people; but some few malevolent persons, like empirics and lewd artists, did strive to make new work, and to have some disease on foot, to keep themselves in request, and to be employed and entertained in the cure. And yet to manifest how much offences have been diminished, the committees for grievances, committees for courts of justice, and committees for trade, have, since the sitting down of the Parliament, received few complaints, and those such as they themselves have not thought to be of that moment or importance, with which our ears should be acquainted.

No sooner therefore was the Parliament set down but these ill-affected men began to sow and disperse their jealousies, by

casting out some glances and doubtful speeches, as if the subject
had not been so clearly and well dealt with, touching the
liberties, and touching the Petition answered the last Parliament.
This being a plausible theme, thought on for an ill purpose,
easily took hold on the minds of many that knew not the practice.   And thereupon the second day of the Parliament, a committee was appointed to search whether the Petition and our
answer thereunto were enrolled in the Parliament roll, and in
the courts at Westminster, and in what manner the same was
done.   And a day also was then appointed, on which the House,
being resolved into a committee, should take into consideration
those things wherein the liberty of the subject had been invaded,
against the Petition of Right.   This, though it produced no
other effect of moment or importance, yet was sufficient to raise
a jealousy against our proceedings, in such as were not well
acquainted with the sincerity and clearness of them.   There
followed another of less skill; for although our proceeding
before the Parliament, about matters of religion, might have
satisfied any moderate men of our zealous care thereof (as we are
sure it did the most), yet, as bad stomachs turn the best things
into their own nature for want of good digestion, so those distempered persons have done the like of our good intents by a
bad and sinister interpretation; for, when they did observe that
many honest and religious minds in that House did complain of
those dangers that did threaten the Church, they likewise took
the same word in their mouth, and their cry likewise was
Templum Domini, Templum Domini, when the true care of
the Church never came into their hearts; and what the one did
out of zeal unto religion, the other took up as a plausible theme
to deprave our government, as if we, our clergy and Council,
were either senseless or careless of religion; and this wicked
practice hath been to make us seem to walk before our people
as if we halted before God.

Having by these artifices made a jealous impression in the
hearts of many, and a day being appointed to treat of the grant
of Tonnage and Poundage, at the time prefixed, all express great
willingness to grant it.   But a new strain is found out, that it
could not be done without great peril to the right of the subject,

unless we should disclaim any right therein, but by grant in Parliament, and should cause all those goods to be restored, which, upon commandment from us or our Council, were stayed by our officer until those duties were paid, and consequently should put ourselves out of the possession of the Tonnage and Poundage before they were granted; for else, it was pretended, the subject stood not in fit case to grant it. A fancy and cavil raised of purpose to trouble the business; it being evident that all the Kings before-named did receive that duty, and were in actual possession of it before, and at the very time, when it w̧as granted to them by Parliament. And although we, to remove all difficulties, did from our own mouth, in those clear and open terms that might have satisfied any moderate and well-disposed minds, declare that it was our meaning, by the gift of our people, to enjoy it, and that we did not challenge it of right, but took it *de bene esse*, showing thereby not the right, but the necessity by which we were to take it (wherein we descended, for their satisfaction, so far beneath ourself, as we are confident never any of our predecessors did the like, nor was the like ever required or expected from them). Yet for all this, the Bill of Tonnage and Poundage was laid aside, upon pretence they must first clear the right of the subject therein; under colour whereof, they entertain the complaints, not only of John Rolle, a member of their House, but also of Richard Chambers, John Fowkes, and Bartholomew Gilman, against the officers of our Customs, for detaining their goods upon refusal to pay the ordinary duty, accustomed to be paid for the same. And upon these complaints they send for the officers of the Customs, enforcing them to attend day after day by the space of a month together; they cause them to produce their letters patents under our Great Seal, and the warrants made by our Privy Council for levying of those duties. They examine the officers upon what questions they please, thereby to entrap them for doing our service and commandments. In these and other their proceedings, because we would not give the least show of interruption, we endured long with much patience both these and sundry other strange and exorbitant encroachments and usurpations, such as were never before attempted in that House.

We are not ignorant how much that House hath of late years endeavoured to extend their privileges, by setting up general committees for religion, for courts of justice, for trade, and the like; a course never heard of until of late : so as, where in former times the Knights and Burgesses were wont to communicate to the House such business as they brought from their countries; now there are so many chairs erected, to make inquiry upon all sorts of men, where complaints of all sorts are entertained, to the unsufferable disturbance and scandal of justice and government, which, having been tolerated a while by our father and ourself, hath daily grown to more and more height; insomuch that young lawyers sitting there take upon them to decry the opinions of the judges; and some have not doubted to maintain that the resolutions of that House must bind the judges, a thing never heard of in ages past : but in this last assembly of Parliament they have taken on them much more than ever before.

They sent messengers to examine our Attorney-General (who is an officer of trust and secrecy) touching the execution of some commandments of ours, of which, without our leave first obtained, he was not to give account to any but ourself. They sent a captious and directory message to the Lord Treasurer, Chancellor, and Barons of the Exchequer, touching some judicial proceedings of theirs in our Court of Exchequer.

They sent messengers to examine upon sundry questions, our two Chief Justices and three other of our judges, touching their judicial proceedings at the Gaol Delivery at Newgate, of which they are not accountable to the House of Commons.

And whereas suits were commenced in our Court of Star Chamber, against Richard Chambers, John Fowkes, Bartholomew Gilman, and Richard Phillips, by our Attorney-General, for great misdemeanours; they resolved that they were to have privilege of Parliament against us for their persons, for no other cause but because they had petitions depending in that House; and (which is more strange) they resolved that a signification should be made from that House, by a letter to issue under the hand of their Speaker unto the Lord Keeper of our Great Seal, that no attachments should be granted out against the said

Chambers, Fowkes, Gilman, or Phillips, during their said privilege of Parliament. Whereas it is far above the power of that House to give direction to any of our courts at Westminster to stop attachments against any man, though never so strongly privileged; the breach of privilege being not in the court that grants, but in the party or minister that puts in execution such attachments. And therefore, if any such letter had come to the Lord Keeper, as it did not, he should have highly offended us if he had obeyed it. Nay, they went so far as they spared not the honour of our Council Board, but examined their proceedings in the case of our customers, interrogating what this or that man of our Council said in direction of them in the business committed to their charge. And when one of the members of that House, speaking of our counsellors, said we had wicked counsel; and another said that the Council and judges sought to trample under feet the liberty of the subject; and a third traduced our Court of Star Chamber for the sentence given against Savage, they passed without check or censure by the House. By which may appear, how far the members of that House have of late swollen beyond the rules of moderation and the modesty of former times; and this under pretence of privilege and freedom of speech, whereby they take liberty to declare against all authority of Council and courts at their pleasure.

They sent for our Sheriff of London to examine him in a cause whereof they had no jurisdiction; their true and ancient jurisdiction extending only to their own members, and to the conservation of their privileges, and not to the censure of foreign persons and causes, which have no relation to their privileges, the same being but a late innovation. And yet upon an enforced strain of a contempt, for not answering to their satisfaction, they commit him to the Tower of London, using that outward pretext for a cause of committing him, the true and inward cause being, for that he had showed himself dutiful to us and our commandments in the matter concerning our Customs.

In these innovations (which we will never permit again) they pretended indeed our service, but their drift was to break, by this means, through all respects and ligaments of government,

74

and to erect a universal over-swaying power to themselves, which belongs only to us, and not to them.

Lastly, in their proceedings against our customers, they went about to censure them as delinquents, and to punish them for staying some goods of some factious merchants in our storehouse, for not paying those duties which themselves had formerly paid, and which the customers, without interruption, had received of all other merchants many years before, and to which they were authorized both by our Great Seal and by several directions and commandments from us and our Privy Council.

To give some colour to their proceeding herein, they went about to create a new privilege (which we will never admit), that a Parliament-man hath privilege for his goods against the King; the consequence whereof would be, that he may not be constrained to pay any duties to the King during the time of privilege of Parliament. It is true, they would have this case to have been between the merchants and our farmers of our Customs, and have severed them from our interest and commandment, thereby the rather to make them liable to the censure and punishment of that House. But on the other side, we holding it both unjust and dishonourable to withdraw ourself from our officers in anything they did by our commandment, or to disavow anything that we had enjoined to be done; upon Monday, the twenty-third of February, sent a message unto them by Secretary Coke, thanking them for the respect they had showed in severing the interest of our farmers from our own interest and commandment. Nevertheless we were bound in honour to acknowledge a truth, that what was done by them was done by our express commandment and direction; and if, for doing thereof, our farmers should suffer, it would highly concern us in honour. Which message was no sooner delivered unto them, but in a tumultuous and discontented manner they called Adjourn, Adjourn; and thereupon, without any cause given on our part, in a very unusual manner, adjourned unto the Wednesday following.

On which day, by the uniform wisdom of our Privy Council, we caused both Houses to be adjourned until the second day of March, hoping that in the meantime a better and more right understanding might be begotten between us and the members of that House, whereby the Parliament might come to a happy issue.

But understanding by good advertisement that their discontent did not in that time digest and pass away, we resolved to make a second adjournment until the tenth of March, which was done, as well to take time to ourself to think of some means to accommodate those difficulties, as to give them time to advise better; and accordingly we gave commandment for a second adjournment in both Houses, and for cessation of all business till the day appointed, which was very dutifully obeyed in the Higher House, no man contradicting or questioning it. But when the same commandment was delivered in the House of Commons by their Speaker, it was straightway contradicted; and although the Speaker declared unto them it was an absolute right and power in us to adjourn as well as to prorogue or dissolve, and declared and read unto them divers precedents of that House to warrant the same; yet our commandment was most contemptuously disobeyed, and some rising up to speak said they had business to do before the House should be adjourned.

Whilst the Duke of Buckingham lived he was entitled to all the distempers and ill events of former Parliaments, and therefore much endeavour was used to demolish him, as the only wall of separation between us and our people. But now he is dead, no alteration was found amongst those envenomed spirits which troubled then the blessed harmony between us and our subjects, and still continue to trouble it. For now under the pretence of public care of the commonwealth they suggest new and causeless fears, which in their own hearts they know to be false; and devise new engines of mischief, so to cast a blindness upon the good affections of our people, that they may not see the truth and largeness of our heart towards them. So that now it is manifest, the Duke was not alone the mark these men shot at, but was only as a near minister of ours taken up, on the by, and in their passage to their more secret designs; which were only to cast our affairs into a desperate condition to abate the powers of our Crown, and to bring our government into obloquy, that in the end all things may be overwhelmed with anarchy and confusion.

We do not impute these disasters to the whole House of Commons, knowing that there were amongst them many religious, grave, and well-minded men; but the sincerer and better part of the House was overborne by the practices and clamours of the other, who, careless of their duties, and taking advantage of the times and our necessities, have enforced us to break off this meeting; which, had it been answered with like duty on their parts as it was invited and begun with love on ours, might have proved happy and glorious both to us and this whole nation.

We have thus declared the manifold causes we had to dissolve this Parliament, whereby all the world may see how much they have forgotten their former engagements at the entry into the war, themselves being persuaders to it; promising to make us feared by our enemies and esteemed by our friends, and how they turned the necessities grown by that war to enforce us to yield to conditions incompatible with monarchy.

And now that our people may discern that these provocations of evil men (whose punishments we reserve to a due time) have not changed our good intentions to our subjects, we do here profess to maintain the true religion and doctrine established in the Church of England, without admitting or conniving at any backsliding either to Popery or schism. We do also declare that we will maintain the ancient and just rights and liberties of our subjects, with so much constancy and justice that they shall have cause to acknowledge that under our government and gracious protection they live in a more happy and free estate than any subjects in the Christian world. Yet let no man hereby take the boldness to abuse that liberty, turning it to licentiousness; nor misinterpret the Petition by perverting it to a lawless liberty, wantonly or frowardly, under that or any other colour, to resist lawful and necessary authority. For as we well maintain our subjects in their just liberties, so we do and will expect that they yield as much submission and duty to our royal prerogatives, and as ready obedience to our authority and commandments, as hath been promised to the greatest of our predecessors.

And for our ministers, we will not that they be terrified by those harsh proceedings that have been strained against some of them. For, as we will not command anything unjust or dishonourable, but shall use our authority and prerogatives for the good of our people; so we will expect that our ministers obey us, and they shall assure themselves we will protect them.

As for our merchants, we let them know we shall always endeavour to cherish and enlarge the trade of such as be dutiful, without burthening them beyond what is fitting; but the duty of five in the hundred for guarding of the seas, and defence of the realm, to which we hold ourselves still obliged (and which duty hath continued without interruption so many succession of ages), we hold no good or dutiful subject will deny it, being so necessary for the good of the whole kingdom : and if any factious merchant will affront us in a thing so reasonable, and wherein we require no more, nor in no other manner, than so many of our predecessors have done, and have been dutifully obeyed, let them not deceive themselves, but be assured that we shall find honourable and just means to support our estate, vindicate our sovereignty, and preserve the authority which God hath put into our hands.

And now having laid down the truth and clearness of our proceedings, all wise and discreet men may easily judge of those rumours and jealous fears that are maliciously and wickedly bruited abroad; and may discern, by examination of their own hearts, whether (in respect of the free passage of the Gospel, indifferent and equal administration of justice, freedom from oppression, and the great peace and quietness which every man enjoyeth under his own vine and fig-tree) the happiness of this nation can be paralleled by any of our neighbour countries; and if not, then to acknowledge their own blessedness, and for the same be thankful to God, the author of all goodness.

CHAPTER III

PERSONAL GOVERNMENT

1629-1640

Charles now determined to do without Parliament, since that body appeared set upon obstructing his policy in every detail. In adopting this course he had, it should be observed, precedent on his side, for since the accession of the Tudors in 1485, Parliament had met at irregular intervals. In the reign of his father seven years at a stretch had elapsed without one, and in ten years not a single statute had been enacted. Furthermore, the monarch was still the head of the government; he appointed and dismissed the ministers, presided in Council, and dispatched the current business of the State. There was thus nothing unconstitutional about the line Charles was taking, and there is no evidence that it roused the least discontent in the country. What was in doubt was whether it would prove practicable, particularly from the financial point of view, although peace was at once made with both France and Spain in the interests of economy. Before, however, turning to a consideration of the King's attitude towards the major problems of the day, it is not without interest to see Charles dealing with matters of less importance. The following letter, for instance, not only testifies to his well-known fondness for pictures, but throws a curious light upon the way in which sales were conducted at this time.

I

Whereas we understand that an excellent collection of paintings is to be sold in Venice, which are known by the name of Bartolomeo della Nave's collection; we are desirous that our beloved servant, Mr. William Petty, should go thither to make the bargain for them; we ourselves being resolved to go a fourth share in the buying of them, so it exceed not the sum of eight hundred pounds sterling; but that our name be concealed in it. And, if it shall please God that the same collection be bought and come safely hither, then we do promise, in the word of a King, that they shall be divided with all equality in this manner, *videlicet*—that they shall be equally divided into four parts by some men skilful in paintings, and then everyone interested in the shares, or some for them, shall throw the dice severally; and, whosoever throws most, shall choose his share first, and so in order, every one shall choose after first, as he casts most, and shall take their shares freely to their own uses, as they shall fall to them.

In witness whereof we have set our hand, this eighth day of July in the tenth year of our reign.

In the seventeenth century it was still by no means unusual for monarchs to take an active interest in the matrimonial affairs of their subjects, and Charles was no exception.

11. To Sir Gervaise Clifton and Sir Thomas Hutchinson

Hampton Court, October 16, 1634.

Trusty and well-beloved we greet you well. Whereas in our princely favour to Sir John Suckling, we have formerly granted our letters of recommendation concerning a marriage between him and the daughter of Sir Henry Willoughby, who after the receipt of them gave such civil admission as we required, and also promised (as we are advertised) that if his daughter's affection could be gained, he would give his consent likewise, which we are assured is obtained, and also we are informed that the liberty of speaking with her is now debarred unto Sir John Suckling by her father, which we taking into our consideration have thought fit again to signify our pleasure unto him, by our second letter (that he send us the cause of this change) which we send by this gentleman, Mr. Philip Willoughby, whom we desire you to accompany with Sir John Suckling, that Sir Henry Willoughby, receiving by him our pleasure, which we have commanded to be delivered to him, we may be certified from you how his daughter's affection stands at present, to the end that if he cannot show just cause against Sir John Suckling, we may insist upon our former recommendation, especially if you find it agrees with the young gentlewoman's affection. And thus not doubting of your care herein, we bid you farewell.

III. TO THE EARL OF PEMBROKE

May, 1636.

MY LORD,

I cannot use a better argument of my care of you and your family, than by taking into consideration that which mostly concerns you, and that is the marriage of your son, the Lord Herbert, which, though perhaps at this time may seem unseasonable, considering he is not yet out of his mourning and true sorrow for the loss of his late dear and virtuous lady; yet, because afflictions must have an end, and those that wish well to persons in his condition cannot do a better office than to minister occasions of diversion, I have thought fit to propose this unto you, leaving the time and other circumstances to yourself. The person that I would recommend unto you is Mrs. Dorothy Savage, daughter of the Lady Savage, whose birth and virtues are so well known, that there can be no doubt but when such a couple as your son and she shall come together, the conjunction will be very happy. I know your son so dutiful (and he owes to you, considering how noble a father you have been to him) that he will not so much as think upon bestowing himself without your knowledge and liking, and therefore you shall do well of yourself to sound his affections, and if you find him well inclined, further it as much as you can, which I shall take very well; and you may be confident I will be ever cherishing my own work, both for your own and my Lady Savage's sake, who shall know nothing of this until you shall think fit; but I would have my lady, your wife, know and take to herself what I write to you; and, howsoever this succeed, I will never be unmindful of yours and your son's continual readiness to do me service, and you shall ever find me, etc.

The state of the Militia was still far from satisfactory, and although the foreign policy of Charles was pacific, he did not neglect any precautions where national defence was concerned.

IV. TO THE EARL OF SUFFOLK

Windsor Castle, September 21, 1629.

The abuses and neglects of the trained bands of the several counties are by connivance and want of due care grown so customary, as the directions of the State for reformation are commonly received for matters of form only, and so slightly executed as the wished and necessary effects are not at all produced. And since so essential a part of the strength and safety of the kingdom consists in those bands, and in having them well chosen, well armed and well disciplined, and that neither the serious recommendations from us nor the imminent dangers of the times can serve for sufficient admonition, we are resolved to take a strict account ourselves of the performance of each man's duty in that so important service. Our will and pleasure is that you cause a general muster to be taken of all the trained bands, horse and foot, under your lieutenancies and that you make equal impartial and indifferent charge, according to the value of each man's lands and means, whether the owners be resident or not for finding horse and foot, and see the horse and arms so charged and sufficient men to ride the horses. Those that are to be enrolled in the trained lists are to be of gentry, freeholders, good farmers, and their sons, that are like to be resident in the country and ready to serve with the arms they bear and are trained in at the musters, and that the meaner sort of people and servants whose residence cannot be expected to be constant be avoided, at least where any servant is enrolled it shall not be in his master's power to change or put him away without the licence of you, because by such changes the benefit of training and teaching the use of arms is utterly lost.

In 1634 Charles issued a Proclamation stating the Government's need for saltpetre, and empowering any three or more Justices of the Peace to ' enter, break open, and work for it in the lands or possessions of us or any of our subjects in England and Wales and all privileged places, and to make saltpetre and thereof powder '. The Justices were also authorized to take carts, paying sixpence a mile for their use, and to commandeer sea coal, outhouses, barns, etc., as required, but always to pay a fair price for them. Private property was thus not so sacred as it became after the Revolution of 1688, and the interests of the nation still prevailed over those of individuals. It was actions such as these that naturally determined the rich landed gentry, of whom Parliament was composed, to reduce the power of the monarchy.

The following letter also throws some light upon the methods of benevolent despotism during the years of the King's personal rule.

v. To the Commissioners of Sewers on the north-east side of
the River of Witham, Co. Lincoln

Abthorpe, July 20, 1634.

Sir Anthony Thomas, knight, together with our loving subject John Worsopp, esquire, having many years attempted the general work of draining the Fens and surrounded grounds in our county of Lincoln and elsewhere. And lately undertaken that particular level on the north and north-east side of the river of Witham, called (as we are informed) the east and west fens, north fens, Earls fen, Armtree fen, and Wildmore fen commons, and the adjacent several drowned grounds, have by God's blessing, and by and through their own extraordinary labour and sedulity, and their and their friends' disbursements and adventures of great sums of money expended, now lately accomplished the draining of the said grounds, and making of them dry and fit for arable, or meadow, or pasture, to the improvement (as is alleged) of forty-five thousand acres of land, and the bettering of many thousands more; the which we well understand to be no small enrichment of those countries; and being thereof certainly advertised by sight of an Act or Ordinance of Sewers, expressing a declaration under some of your hands and seals, that the said undertaken work is now done by the said Sir Anthony Thomas and John Worsopp, within the time limited; we therefore in our gracious respect towards our said well deserving subjects, that have approved themselves therein real performers of so great a work, both for their remuneration and for example and encouragement to others, do will and require you, that you fail not to do to them speedy justice in and by an equal and most indifferent partition and setting forth by metes and bounds of such parts, portions and allotments of these drained lands, as your former Acts, Orders and Decrees of Sewers did grant, promise and appoint to them for recompense of their said undertaken work of draining; and that you forthwith decree the same unto the said Sir Anthony Thomas and John Worsopp their heirs and assigns for ever to be holden of us, our heirs and successors, as of our honour of Bullingbrook in our said county of Lincoln, with such privileges, liberties and immunities as you shall think fit.   And you are also to require all those, which pretend interest to any of the said lands, that they give ready obedience to your order, and quietly permit the said Anthony Thomas and John Worsopp to enjoy their allotments peaceably and without interruption, according to their agreement, as they tender our displeasure and will answer the contrary at their perils.   Given under our signet.   At our court at Abthorpe the twentieth day of July in the tenth year of our reign.

In all matters affecting the Church the King took a keen personal interest.   In 1633 William Laud was appointed Archbishop of Canterbury, and Charles and he lost no opportunity of giving religion what they believed to be its proper place in the national life.

VI. TO THE LORD MAYOR OF YORK

Right trusty and well-beloved, and trusty and well-beloved, we greet you well.

Whereas, for the preservation of the solemnity of divine service in some of our cathedral churches, and for the good of those inhabitants of those cities, we have required the Mayor and aldermen and their companies to frequent those holy places upon Sundays and holidays, with all due reverence, and that they be there at the beginning of divine service, and at their going-out and coming-in, and while they are there, carry themselves so as becometh them, in obedience to the canons of the Church and the customs of those cathedrals requiring also the Mayors of those cities, that they shall not use the ensigns of their authority within our said cathedral churches, that hereafter the distinct liberties and privileges granted by our Royal progenitors to those several bodies may be inviolably kept.   We, therefore, casting the same gracious eye upon our cathedral and metropolitan Church of Saint Peter, in our city of York, to have it regulated in like manner, do hereby require you, according to your several duties, to take care for the due performance of all the said orders in that church; and further, that as well you the Lord Mayor, and also the Recorder, and aldermen, at some solemn times in every year, shall receive the holy communion in the said cathedral church of York, to manifest your conformity to the orders established in the Church.

Given under our signet at our court at Greenwich, 2nd of July, in the 13th year of our reign, 1634.

To our right trusty and well-beloved Recorder and aldermen of our said city.

The following letters show both the King's interest in ecclesiastical affairs, and his determination to put an end to all abuses.

VII. TO THE DEAN AND CHAPTER OF WELLS

January 29, 1634.

Whereas our late dear father, King James of blessed memory, was pleased by his letters to recommend unto you Edward Abbott, chief chantor of that church, to be chosen residentiary there, since which time ourself likewise have been graciously pleased to write our letters to you in favour of him for that purpose; notwithstanding all which, we understand he hath not yet obtained any place of resident there. We have thought good, by this our special letters, to let you know that although we lately thought fit that Robert Creighton should be preferred before the said Abbott, it was neither of dislike of the person of the said Abbott, nor of opinion of any disability or unfitness in him, but because you then certified us that the residentiaryship then vacant did, by the express words of our charter, belong to the treasurership of that church, which we had then bestowed upon the said Creighton. Now forasmuch as we hold the said Edward Abbott very fit for that preferment, and to the end he may be no longer delayed, we are now again graciously pleased to recommend him unto you to be chosen into the next residentiary place in that church which shall become vacant, upon the death, surrender or other avoidance of any prebend residentiary, at large there, according to the custom of that church, which we do the more earnestly require you because the former letters written in favour of him have been heretofore without success.

We doubt not of your conformity to this our pleasure, both in regard of this our princely recommendation and of the merits of the said Edward Abbott, wherein you shall do a service very acceptable to us. Provided always, and our will and pleasure is, that this shall be no prejudice nor wrong to any dignity in that church which now hath a residentiaryship annexed to it.

At our Palace of Westminster.

VIII. To William Piers, Bishop of Bath and Wells

June 22, 1634.

We have of late taken the state of our several Bishoprics into our princely consideration, that we may be the better able to preserve that livelihood which as yet is left unto them. Upon this deliberation, we find that of later times there hath not risen a greater inconvenience than by turning leases of one and twenty years into lives, for by that means the present Bishop puts a great fine into his own purse, to enrich himself, his wife and children, and leaves all the succeeding Bishops, of what deserts soever, to us and the Church, destitute of all that growing means which else would come in to help them. By which course, should it continue, scarce any Bishop could be able to live, and keep house according to his place and calling. We know the statute makes it alike lawful for a Bishop to let his lease for one and twenty years or three lives, but time and experience have made it apparent that there is a great deal of difference between them, especially in Church leases, where men are commonly in great years before they come to those places. These are therefore to will and command you, upon peril of our utmost displeasure and what shall follow thereon, that, notwithstanding any statute or any other pretence whatsoever, you presume not to let any lease belonging to your Bishopric into lives which is not in lives already; and further, that where any fair opportunity is offered you, if any such be, you fail not to reduce such as are in lives into years.* And we do likewise will and require you that these our Royal letters remain upon record, both with your own register and with the register of the Dean and Chapter of your cathedral church, and that by them notice be given to all your successors respectively (whom we will that these letters shall concern as much as yourself) that they presume not to break any of these our commands in the least manner, as you and they will answer it at your and their uttermost perils.

At our Manor at Greenwich.

IX. TO THE DEAN AND CHAPTER OF WELLS

June 22, 1634.

[In terms similar to the last, *mutatus mutandis*, down to the asterisk.]

And we do likewise will and require that these our letters may remain upon record in your own register books and in the registry of the Lord Bishop of that diocese, that he may take notice of these our commands unto you, and give us and our Royal successors knowledge if you presume in any sort to disobey them. And further, whereas in our late instructions we have commanded all our Bishops respectively not to let any lease after we have named any of them to a better Bishopric, but did not in those instructions name the Deans, who yet were intended by us; these are therefore to declare unto you that no Dean shall presume to renew any lease, either into lives or years, after such time as we have nominated him either to a better Deanery or a Bishopric, having observed that, at such times of remove, many men care not what or how they let, to the prejudice of the Church and their successors. And this is our express command to you, your Chapter and your successors, which in any case we require both you and them strictly to observe, upon pain of our high displeasure, and as you and they will answer the contrary at your and their utmost perils.

At our Manor of Greenwich.

X. TO THE BISHOP OF BATH AND WELLS

October 6, 1634.

[Reciting his letters of June 22 last.]

All which we have done for the great good and advancement of the Church, as we doubt not but in future times will plainly appear. Now forasmuch as we have been informed that some, more affecting their present private gain than the future good of the Church, whereof they are members, have misinterpreted those our princely letters, and do conceive that our meaning is to prohibit only the letting of such leases into lives as are granted by the Dean and Chapter of any church by common consent, and that every particular Dean, Archdeacon or Prebend, who hath any *corpus* allotted to his dignity, might notwithstanding dispose of it for lives without breach of our Royal command, as if we would direct our letters to a body in general and not intend to include every several member thereof. These are therefore to will and require you that you fail not to signify this explanation of our princely pleasure to your several Archdeacons and to the Dean and Chapter of your cathedral church, that they may impart it to every Prebend, which is, that we do not only lay these our commands upon them and their successors in general, but likewise upon every particular member of that church whom they may any way concern, from the highest to the meanest officer in the same, including the vicars choral, in what church soever any such body is.

At our honour of Hampton Court.

XI. To the Dean and Chapter of Wells

June 22, 1636.

Whereas our trusty and well-beloved Robert Creighton, one of the Canon residentiaries of that church, is to be employed in a service which we have commanded him to undertake, by reason whereof he cannot keep his residence there, as by the statutes of that church he is enjoined : We do therefore hereby dispense with the said statute in this particular, and do give him license to attend the said charge, requiring you to take order that he be not any way prejudiced by his non-residence there during the time of this his employment, but that he may receive the profits and benefits of his place of Canon residentiary as fully and absolutely as if he were resident there, the said statute, or any other matter or thing whatsoever, to the contrary in any wise notwithstanding. And these our letters shall be your sufficient warrant and discharge in this behalf.

At our honour of Hampton Court.

In later years Pepys heard Dr. Creighton preach ' a most admirable, good, learned, and most severe sermon '. He was consecrated Bishop of Bath and Wells in 1670.

In spite of the fact that the country was now at peace the revenue, in the absence of a Parliament to vote direct taxation, did not meet the expenditure. Charles had, therefore, to devise various means of raising money, and he took care that they should be such as would bear most heavily upon those who, as there was no direct taxation, were paying no taxes at all. One of these was distraint of knighthood, which dated from the days of Edward I, and in January, 1630, the King summoned all freeholders of £40 a year upwards to take up their knighthood or compound for not having done so. This produced a good sum, but not before the matter had been tested in the Court of Exchequer, and further pressure had been applied.

XII. To the Earl of Westmorland, Lord Montagu, and others

Palace of Westminster, March 22, 1631.

Whereas we have formerly directed our commissions with instructions and letters unto you for compounding with such our subjects as are to make fine unto us for not appearing at our coronation for receiving the order of knighthood, which took not that effect which we expected: We notwithstanding, still continuing our princely intentions to our loving subjects, have thought good for their ease, and for avoiding of their further trouble, to renew the said commissions, which together with our instructions we do herewith send unto you : Not doubting but such as have been hitherto backward in this service will now, upon the late public declaration in our Court of Exchequer by counsel learned in the laws of our right to these fines, cheerfully conform themselves to render us our due as by law they are bound to do.

Another method of increasing the revenue at this time (1634) was by the levying of ship money, which by old practice had long been paid by the maritime counties. In 1635 Charles made the whole kingdom liable.

XIII

CAROLUS REX, ETC.

To the Mayor, commonalty, and citizens of our city of
London, and to the sheriffs of the same city, and good men in
the said city and in the liberties, and members of the same, greet-
ing: Because we are given to understand that certain thieves,
pirates, and robbers of the sea, as well Turks, enemies of the
Christian name, as others, being gathered together, wickedly
taking by force and spoiling the ships, and goods, and
merchandises, not only of our subjects, but also the subjects of
our friends in the sea, which hath been accustomed anciently to
be defended by the English nation, and the same, at their
pleasure, have carried away, delivering the men in the same into
miserable captivity : and forasmuch as we see them daily preparing all manner of shipping farther to molest our merchants, and
to grieve the kingdom, unless remedy be not sooner applied,
and their endeavours be not more manly met withal; also the
dangers considered which, on every side, in these times of war
do hang over our heads, that it behoveth us and our subjects to
hasten the defence of the sea and kingdom with all expedition or
speed that we can; we willing by the help of God chiefly to
provide for the defence of the kingdom, safeguard of the sea,
security of our subjects, safe conduct of ships and merchandises
to our kingdom of England coming, and from the same kingdom to foreign parts passing; forasmuch as we, and our
progenitors, Kings of England, have been always heretofore
masters of the aforesaid sea, and it would be very irksome unto
us if that princely honour in our times should be lost or in any
thing diminished.   And although that charge of defence which
concerneth all men ought to be supported by all, as by the laws
and customs of the kingdom of England hath been accustomed
to be done : notwithstanding we considering that you constituted
in the sea-coasts, to whom by sea as well great dangers are
imminent, and who by the same do get more plentiful gains for
the defence of the sea, and conservation of our princely honour
in that behalf, according to the duty of your allegiance against
such attempts, are chiefly bound to set to your helping hand; we

command firmly, enjoining you the aforesaid Mayor, commonalty and citizens, and sheriffs of the said city, and the good men in the same city and in the liberties, and members of the same, in the faith and allegiance wherein you are bound unto us, and as you do love us and our honour, and under the forfeiture of all which you can forfeit to us, that you cause to be prepared and brought to the port of Portsmouth, before the first day of March now ensuing, one ship of war of the burden of nine hundred tons, with three hundred and fifty men at the least, as well expert masters, as very able and skilful mariners; four other ships of war, every of them of the burden of five hundred tons, and every of them with two hundred men at the least, as well expert masters, as very able and skilful mariners : and one other ship of war of the burden of three hundred tons, with a hundred and fifty men, as well expert masters, as very able and skilful mariners : and also every of the said ships with ordnance, as well greater as lesser, gunpowder, and spears and weapons, and other necessary arms sufficient for war, and with double tackling, and with victuals, until the said first of March, competent for so many men; and from that time, for twenty-six weeks, at your charges, as well in victuals as men's wages and other things necessary for war, during that time, upon defence of the sea in our service, in command of the admiral of the sea, to whom we shall commit the custody of the sea, before the aforesaid first day of March, and as he, on our behalf, shall command them to continue; so that they may be there the same day, at the farthest, to go from thence with our ships, and the ships of other faithful subjects, for the safeguard of the sea, and defence of you and yours, and repulse and vanquishing of whomsoever busying themselves to molest or trouble upon the sea our merchants, and other subjects, and faithful people coming into our dominions for cause of merchandise, or from thence returning to their own countries. Also we have assigned you, the aforesaid Mayor and aldermen of the city aforesaid, or any thirteen, or more of you, within thirteen days after the receipt of this writ, to assess all men in the said city, and in the liberties, and members of the same, and the landholders in the same, not having a ship, or any part of the aforesaid ships, nor serving in the same, to contribute to the expenses, about the necessary provision of the premises; and to assess and lay upon the aforesaid city, with the liberties and members thereof, viz. upon every of them according to their estate and substances, and the portion assessed upon them; and to nominate and appoint collectors in this behalf. Also we have assigned you, the aforesaid Mayor, and also the Sheriffs of the city aforesaid, to levy the portions so as aforesaid assessed upon the aforesaid men and landholders, and every of them in the aforesaid city, with the liberties and members of the same, by distress and other due means; and to commit to prison all those whom you shall find rebellious and contrary in the premises, there to remain until we shall give further order for their delivery. And moreover we command you, that about the premises you diligently attend, and do, and execute those things with effect, upon peril that shall fall thereon : but we will not, that under colour of our aforesaid command, more should be levied of the said men than shall suffice for the necessary expenses of the premises; or that any who have levied money for contribution to raise the aforesaid charges, should by him detain the same, or any part thereof; or should presume, by any manner of colour, to appropriate the same to other uses; willing, that if more than may be sufficient shall be collected, the same may be paid out among the contributors, for the rate of the part to them belonging.

Witness myself, at Westminster the twentieth day of October, in the tenth year of our reign.

Since the murder of Buckingham the King had been his own minister, but with the passage of time he came to rely in many matters upon Thomas Wentworth, who had been one of the leaders of the Opposition. In 1628 he was raised to the peerage and made President of the Council of the North; four years later he was appointed Lord Deputy of Ireland, but did not go there until July, 1633. Charles revealed his thoughts and policy more clearly to Wentworth than to any other of his advisers with the exception of Buckingham.

xiv. To Lord Wentworth

London, April 17, 1634.

WENTWORTH,

The great dispatch that your brother brought me has given me so much satisfaction, that I could not but testify it by my own hand.   Though I know you will find my public letters enough to your contentment, and full enough to make this short, yet there is one general and one particular that I will name to you, to take care of, to wit, the Parliament and Arundel; in a word, to content them both, so far as may not be to my prejudice.   As for Arundel, I need say no more; but as for that Hydra, take good heed, for you know that here I have found it as well cunning as malicious.   It is true that your grounds are well laid, and, I assure you, that I have a great trust in your care and judgement; yet my opinion is, that it will not be the worse for my service, though their obstinacy make you to break them, for I fear they have some ground more than it is fit for me to give.   This I would not say, if I had not confidence in your courage and dexterity; that, in that case, you would set me down there an example what to do here.   So I rest,

> Your assured friend,
> CHARLES R.

xv. To Lord Wentworth

Hampton Court, October 23, 1634.

WENTWORTH,

Before I answer any of your particular letters to me, I must tell you, that your last public dispatch has given me a great deal of contentment, and especially for keeping off the envy [i.e. ill will] of a necessary negative from me, of those unreasonable graces that the people expected from me, not in one particular dissenting from your opinion (that is of moment, as I remember) but concerning the tallow, and that but *ad referendum* neither.

Now I will begin concerning your suit, though last come to my hands; and the first for the form, that is to say, in coming to me not only primarily but solely without so much as acquaint-

ing anybody with it, the bearer being as ignorant as any.   This
I do not only commend, but recommend you to follow always
hereafter at least in what concerns your own particular; for, to
servants of your quality (and some degrees under too), I allow
of no mediators, though friends are commendable; for the
dependence must come merely from me and to me; and as for the
matter, I desire you not to think that I am displeased with the
asking, though for the present I grant it not.   For I acknowledge
that noble minds are always accompanied with lawful ambitions;
and be confident that your services have moved me more than
it is possible for any eloquence or importunity to do.   So that
your letter was not the first proposer of putting marks of favour
on you; and I am certain that you willingly stay my time, now
you know my mind so freely, that I may do all things *a mi modo*;
and so I rest,

Your assured friend,
CHARLES R.

Wentworth had written to Charles asking for an earldom.

XVI. To LORD WENTWORTH

London, January 22, 1635.

WENTWORTH,

The accounts that you give me are so good, that if I should
answer them particularly, my letters would rather seem pane-
gyrics than dispatches; so leaving them I come to those things
wherein you require directions.   And although I shall refer
myself to secretary Coke for an answer of those things that are
in the public dispatches, yet concerning two of them I must
express my own sense, to wit, the not continuing of the
Parliament and the guard of the coast.   For the first, my reasons
are grounded upon my experience of them here; they are of the
nature of cats, that ever grow cursed with age, so that if you
will have good of them, put them off handsomely when they
come to any age; for young ones are ever most tractable; and,
in earnest, you will find that nothing can more conduce to the
beginning of a new than the well ending of a former Parliament:
wherefore, now that we are well, let us content ourselves there-
with.

I have read and considered your proposition for the guarding of the Irish coast, and (upon one condition) like it very well; that they should be subordinate and accountable to the Admiralty here : for (by your favour) I do not hold it fit to sever the jurisdiction of the sea. So that if you can make it good with this condition, I shall esteem it a very good service; only I pray let us not imitate the King of Spain in the sea of discipline.

Concerning Fort Inoland, since my last to you . . . speaking with me about Irish affairs, put me in mind of some engagements I had to . . . about this. But whether it were absolute or on condition of his finding it on his own charge, I do not now well remember; wherefore, go on to put it into my hands, and then, as I shall find my engagement and the fitness of the thing, I shall dispose of it accordingly; only see that none in the meantime, upon whatsoever pretence, snatch it up.

As for the reserved rent you put upon the new plantations, I like it well, and that no undertaker should have too great a proportion. But now I desire that you send me particularly the number of acres I am this time to dispose of, as also, by way of articles, the conditions that I am to tie every undertaker to perform.

For the tallow, I can assure you that, for anything I know, you are misinformed, for I never heard you taxed to have a private end in it; but indeed I think you are mistaken in the business; but I leave the disputing part of it to others.

Lastly, I forgot in my last to satisfy you that what I did concerning the stopping of the horse and foot companies that last fell, was not by court importunity, for the truth is, that I intend it for Jacob Astley. I say this to no other end than to clear you that there was no practice in the thing to your disadvantage, as likewise to desire you to put me in mind when anything shall fall in that kingdom fit for me to give such a man; for I have had this long time a desire to call him home to my service. So having answered, as I think, all your dispatch, I assure you likewise that I shall not fail to answer your services in being really

Your most assured friend,

CHARLES REX.

Wentworth had wished to prorogue, rather than to dissolve, the Irish Parliament, which he had already persuaded to make substantial grants to the Crown.   Soon afterwards, he asked the King's permission to pay a visit to England.

XVII. To Lord Wentworth

Lyndhurst, September 3, 1636.

WENTWORTH,

Certainly I should be much to blame not to admit so good a servant as you are to speak with me, since I deny it to none there is not a just exception against, yet I must freely tell you, that the cause of th: desire of yours, if it be known, will rather hearten than discourage your enemies; for, if they can once find that you apprehend the dark setting of a storm, when I say no, they will make you leave to care for anything in a short while but for your fears.   And, believe it, the marks of my favours that stop malicious tongues are neither places nor titles, but the little welcome I give to accusers, and the willing ear I give to my servants.   This is not to disparage those favours (for envy flies most at the fairest mark) but to show their use; to wit, not to quell envy, but to reward service; it being truly so, when the master without the servant's importunity does it otherwise, men judge it more to proceed from the servant's wit, than the master's favour.

I will end with a rule that may serve for a statesman, a courtier, or a lover—never make a defence or apology before you be accused.   .And so I rest,

Your assured friend,

CHARLES R.

Early in 1637 Charles was considering another attempt to recover the Palatinate for his brother-in-law, and he wrote to ask the advice of Wentworth, who was strongly opposed to any foreign adventures.

XVIII. To Lord Wentworth

Theobalds, June 1, 1637.

WENTWORTH,

I thought it not necessary to reply to yours of the 31st of March, because the occasion is not, as I think, very near; but I would not be too long without writing to you, and the rather to tell you, that I am now resolved to take the lands, and not the money, from the Londoners. For I will not lose, for the use of a little present money, so good a bargain, though I confess I imagined the lands were more worth than I find by your letters that they are.

Now to end with that purpose, I begin withal, I thank you for your considerations concerning war and peace; but, by your favour, you mistake the question. For it is not whether I should declare war to the House of Austria or not, but whether I shall join with France and the rest of my friends to demand of the House of Austria my nephew's restitution, and so hazard (upon refusal) a declaration of war. Howsoever, your conclusion is very good, and I shall follow the advice therein, with as much judgement as God has given me. And so I rest,

Your assured friend,
CHARLES R.

The citizens of London had been prosecuted in the Star Chamber for having failed to fulfil the conditions upon which the county of Londonderry had been granted to them by James I, and were sentenced to forfeiture and a fine of £70,000. The King remitted the latter all but £12,000.

XIX. To Lord Wentworth

Woodstock, August 30, 1638.

WENTWORTH,

Though I am in debt to you for three letters, yet there is little to answer, most of them being narrations, and for that which concerns the army, because your dispatch to secretary Coke made me direct him fully in that particular, I refer you to him; so that I conceive there rests nothing but the particular of the Earl of Antrim to answer, whose professions have been so free and noble at this time, that (as I have promised) indeed, he deserves to be recommended unto you, which at his coming over to you, I wish you to take notice of to him. But to have the command of a magazine of arms, I leave to you and the council there to judge how far you will trust any one of that kind, of his profession in religion. To conclude this, I would have you favour and countenance him as much as any one of his profession in religion. There is one other at this time which I am to recommend unto you of a far different humour, to wit, the Lord Castle Stewart, whom really I leave you to judge whether he or his suit be fit to be favoured, or not; only this, his mother's son deserves to be countenanced if his comportments merit not the contrary. So farewell.

Your assured friend,
CHARLES REX.

The Scottish War (vide infra) *was now beginning, and the problem of possible assistance from Ireland for the King was being mooted for the first, but by no means the last, time.*

xx. To Lord Wentworth

WENTWORTH,

Some months ago I wrote to know of you what assistance I might expect from thence to curb the rebels in Scotland. The expectation of which (because I found by your answer, to be so difficult to be had, and likewise of no great consequence being had) I have relinquished so far, as not to build much upon those hopes; yet I have thought upon one particular, wherein I think you may do me no small service to the aforesaid end, to wit, the securing of Carlisle, for the doing of which, five hundred men, well provided, will serve. Wherefore I desire you to send me word, first if you can do this? then, how soon? with caution of highest secrecy; for you must find some other pretext for the providing and transporting of those men. I would know, likewise, what cannon you could spare or lend to this purpose. So expecting a speedy and I hope a good answer of this letter, I rest,

Your assured friend,
CHARLES REX.

If this be feasible, lose no time in providing all things necessary, that you may be ready at the first warning from me.

XXI. To Lord Wentworth

Whitehall, November 21, 1638.

WENTWORTH,

Though your letter of the 11th of this month was long, yet was it neither tedious nor unpleasing to me (for good council and cheerful obeying of my commands cannot but be always acceptable to me), nor will it require a long answer, you have set this business in so good a way; for I fully approve of all your ways of preparation—to wit, the way of levy, the pretence of it, the distribution of the companies, and the arms and the port you have named for their landing. But for the pay of the common soldier, it must not be augmented; for I must keep all the men I use in this service under one establishment, which I have resolved to be after the Holland pay; yet something may be done for them by way of conduct money, considering their long march. I give you willing leave to raise five hundred new foot to supply the want of others, and thank you for your willing undertaking of this new charge. Now for the leading of these men, I am so far from altering, that I thank you for naming Sir Frank Willoughby; and in the general command of those parts, I assure you, I shall not forget my Lord Clifford.

Now, having answered your letter, I have little more to say at this time, but to mention Sir Jacob Astley to you in two respects: the first, to tell you that I have trusted him with all the secrets of this business, and have appointed him sergeant-major-general for the northern parts. The other is, that in respect I mean to use his service in this kingdom, I have made him refuse that employment you appointed for him there, to show that I will give no man dispensation to live from his charge, and so I rest

Your assured friend,

CHARLES REX.

I must not forget to tell you, that as I am glad to hear you have so good store of gunpowder; so that when you want, I expect you should furnish yourself from hence.   C.R.

As I cannot expect you can be sooner ready than two months, so I hope at that time to find you ready at furthest.   C.R.

XXII. To Lord Wentworth

Whitehall, January 25, 1639.

WENTWORTH,

This is to advertise you, that at last I have taken a resolution concerning Carlisle and Berwick (which by the grace of God I will not alter. For the first, I need only to set you down the time, the way be so well laid already, that I will not change it), which is, the first of April next for your five hundred men to be in Carlisle. For by that time I am confident both to have twelve hundred men in Berwick, and to be ready to march, at a day's warning, with ten thousand foot and fifteen hundred horse to relieve either place. Only this I must add to my former directions that your men may bring with them bread and cheese for sixteen days after their landing, with this *quære*, whether Carlisle may not be conveniently victualled from Ireland or no? I do not mean that the Irish exchequer should pay for it. For you know that Westmorland, Cumberland, and Northumberland are ill stored with those provisions. Lastly, I should be glad if you could find some way to furnish the Earl of Antrim with arms, though he be a Roman Catholic; for he may be of much use to me at this time to shake loose upon the Earl of Argyll, of which particulars none of my secretaries at this time are acquainted with, wherefore the answer of this must come immediately to

Your assured friend,

CHARLES R.

XXIII. To Lord Wentworth

February 25, 1639.

WENTWORTH,

Yours of the 10th of this month came to my hands this morning, but for the present I shall only answer one part of it —to wit, concerning the five hundred which are to go to Carlisle. You know that it is fit that Berwick and it should be possessed at the same time. Now, I thought I might have done it by the 1st of April; but I find it will be the 8th before this of Berwick can be performed; therefore I will not have you embark your men neither sooner nor later than the 28th of this next month.   So thanking you for all the ways of your hearty expression to my service at this time, I rest

Your assured friend,

CHARLES R.

This letter, it may be noted, did not reach Wentworth until March 14th, so imperfect were the means of communication at that time.

XXIV. To Lord Wentworth

Berwick, June 22, 1639.

If this young lord be as diligent with you as he hath been with me, you will have no cause to complain of his negligence; and indeed I like him so well, that I cannot but recommend him to your care, who assuring me that he means to settle his fortunes there, I think it would be well done to admit him to be a planter upon the same conditions as others.   So much for him.

There is a Scottish proverb that bids you put two locks on your door, when you have made friends with a foe; so now upon this pacification, I bid you have a most careful eye upon the north of Ireland.   Not that I think this caution is needful in respect of you, but to let you see I have a care of that kingdom, though I have too much trouble with these.   So I rest

Your assured friend,

CHARLES R.

The 'young lord' was probably Lord Grandison, a grand-nephew of Buckingham.

XXV. To Lord Wentworth

Berwick, June 30, 1639.

WENTWORTH,

Though it add something to my trouble, yet I am content to see that men so much desire to carry my letters to you, it both declaring their estimation and knowledge of that that I have to you : and indeed this is the chief cause of my writing at this time, this gentleman not willing to go without a line from me, the better to assure you, that though he be a Scottishman, yet he is no Covenanter, nor ever was; which indeed is not the ordinary.

As for my affairs here, I am far from thinking that at this time I shall get half of my will, though I mean, by the grace of God, to be in person both at Assembly and Parliament; for which I know many wise men blame me, and it may be you among the rest: and I confess, not without many weighty and considerable arguments, which I have neither time to repeat nor confute; only this, believe me, nothing but my presence at this time in that country can save it from irreparable confusion: yet I will not be so vain as absolutely to say that I can. Wherefore my conclusion is, that if I see a great probability, I go, otherwise not, but return to London, or take other counsels. And so I rest

Your assured friend,
CHARLES R.

In the end Charles did not open the Parliament at Edinburgh in person.

XXVI. TO LORD WENTWORTH

Berwick, July 23, 1639.

WENTWORTH,

Henry Bruce hath delivered yours of the 3rd of July, and likewise had full discourse with me of all those affairs; and though I esteem him a better soldier than a statesman, yet he has made me some propositions in the polite way, somewhat mixed with the martial, not to be despised, yet not to be hastily embraced without such a good commentary as you are able to make on them.

This cause only I confess were too slight to draw you, though but for a time, from your weighty charge; but I have much more, and indeed too much to desire your attendance and counsel for some time, which I think not fit to express by letter more than this. The Scots' Covenant begins to spread too far: yet for all this, I will not have you take notice that I have sent for you, but pretend some other occasion of business, as to be present at the Chancellor's appeal, or what you will else; whom since I have named, I must tell you freely, I would wish you would send him over without delay, if he have performed most, though not all (his friends pretend all) which I enjoined him to do before his departure; if yet he stood not in some high contempt, which if it be, were most fit to be made clearly appear. It is very well done to go on with the Scotsman's oath. So I rest

Your most assured friend,
CHARLES R.

Wentworth arrived in England in November, 1639, and two months later was created Earl of Strafford, raised to the position of Lord Lieutenant of Ireland, and invested with the Order of the Garter. His health, however, was none too good, and he was often hampered by illness at a critical moment.

XXVII. TO THE EARL OF STRAFFORD

Whitehall, April 12, 1640.

STRAFFORD,

Having seen divers letters of my Lord of Canterbury concerning the state of your health, and in this I must require you not to hazard to travel before you may do it with safety to your health, and in this I must require you to be your own judge, but be content to follow the advice of those that are about you, whose affections and skill you shall have occasion to trust unto; if I did know that this care of your health were necessary for us both at this time, I would have deferred my thanks to you for your service lately done, until I might have seen you. So, praying God for your speedy recovery, I rest

Your assured friend,
CHARLES R.

Strafford had been back to Dublin, and the ' service lately done' was his obtaining from the Irish Parliament a grant of four subsidies, and a promise of two more, if required. On his return he had been obliged by illness to stop at Lichfield.

It was the course of events in Scotland that had compelled Charles to summon Strafford to his aid in England. In the seventeenth century it was not yet realized by any section of opinion that two countries under the same monarch could have

*different forms of religion, and Charles endeavoured to bring the
Scottish Church, which was Presbyterian, into line with the
Church of England. The result was the National Covenant,
which was very widely signed, and by which the signatories
bound themselves not to accept any religious innovations, though
at the same time declaring their loyalty to the throne. Charles
appointed the Marquess of Hamilton to negotiate.*

XXVIII.To the Marquess of Hamilton

Greenwich, June 11, 1638.

HAMILTON,

Though I answered not yours of the 4th, yet I assure you
that I have not been idle; so that I hope by the next week I
shall send you some good assurance of the advancing of our
preparations. This I say, not to make you precipitate anything
(for I like of all you have hitherto done, and over, of that which
I find you mind to do); but to show you that I mean to stick
to my grounds, and that I expect not anything can reduce that
people to obedience, but only force.

I thank you for the clearness of your advertisements, of all
which none troubles me so much as that (in a manner) they have
possessed themselves of the castle of Edinburgh, and likewise I
give Stirling as good as lost. As for the dividing of my declaration, I find it most fit in that way as you have resolved it; to
which I shall add, that I am content you forbear the latter part
thereof, until you hear that my fleet hath set sail for Scotland.
In the meantime, your care must be how to dissolve the multitude; and, if it be possible, to possess yourself of my castles of
Edinburgh and Stirling (which I do not expect) and to this end,
I give you leave to flatter them with what hopes you please, so
you engage not me against my grounds (and, in particular, that
you consent neither to the calling of Parliament nor General
Assembly, until the Covenant be disavowed and given up).
Your chief end being now to win time, that they may not commit public follies, until I be ready to suppress them. And that
it is (as you well observe) my own people, which by this means
will be for a time ruined; so that the loss must be inevitably mine;
and this if I could eschew (were it not with a greater) were well.

But, when I consider that not only now my crown, but my reputation for ever, lies at stake, I must rather suffer the first that time will help, than this last, which is irreparable.

This I have written to no other end than to show you that I will rather die than yield to these impertinent and damnable demands (as you rightly call them), for it is all one, as to yield to be no King in a very short time. So wishing you better success than I can expect, I rest,

Your assured, constant friend,
CHARLES R.

Postscript.—As the affairs are now, I do not expect that you should declare the adherers to the Covenant traitors, until (as I have already said) you have heard from me that my fleet hath set sail for Scotland, though your six weeks should be elapsed. In a word, gain time by all the honest means you can, without forsaking your grounds.

Hamilton was not without hope of effecting a peaceful settlement, and asked Charles to suspend his preparations to use force.

XXIX. TO THE MARQUESS OF HAMILTON

Theobalds, June 13, 1638.

HAMILTON,

The dealing with multitudes makes diversity of advertisements no way strange; and certainly the alteration from worse to less ill, cannot be displeasing. Wherefore, you may be confident I cannot but approve your proceedings hitherto; for certainly you have gained a very considerable point in making the heady multitude begin to disperse, without having engaged me in any unfitting thing.

I shall take your advice in staying the public preparations for force; but in a silent way (by your leave) I will not leave to prepare, that I may be ready upon the least advertisement. Now, I hope there may be a possibility of securing my castles; but I confess it must be done closely and cannily. One of the chief things you are to labour in now, is to get a considerable number of sessioners and advocates to give their opinion that the Covenant is at least against law, if not treasonable. This, you have my approbation in several shapes, wherefore you need not doubt but that I am

Your assured, constant friend,

CHARLES R.

XXX. TO THE MARQUESS OF HAMILTON

Greenwich, June 20, 1638.

HAMILTON,

I do not wonder, though I am very sorry for your last dispatch; to which I shall answer nothing concerning what you have done, or mean to do, because I have approved all, and still desire you to believe I do so, until I shall contradict it with my own hand. What now I write is, first to show you in what estate I am, and then to have your advice in some things. My train of artillery consisting of 40 piece of ordnance (with the appurtenances) all drakes (half and more of which are to be drawn with one or two horses apiece), is in good forwardness, and I hope will be ready within six weeks; for I am sure there wants neither money, nor materials to do it with. I have taken as good order as I can for the present, for securing of Carlisle and Berwick; but of this you shall have more certainly by my next. I have sent for arms to Holland, for 14,000 foot and 2,000 horse : for my ships they are ready, and I have given order to send three for the coast of Ireland immediately, under pretence to defend our fishermen. Last of all, which is indeed most of all, I have consulted with the Treasurer and Chancellor of the Exchequer, for money for this year's expedition; which I estimate at two hundred thousand pounds sterling, which they doubt not but to furnish me; more I have done, but these are the chief heads. Now for your advice, I desire to know whether you think it fit that I should send six thousand land-men with the fleet that goes to the Firth, or not; for since you cannot secure me my castle of Edinburgh, it is a question whether you can secure the landing of those men, and if with them you can make yourself master of Leith, to fortify and keep it : of this I desire you to send me your resolution with all speed. I leave it to your consideration whether you will not think it fit to see if you can make all the guns of the castle of Edinburgh unserviceable for anybody, since they cannot be useful for me. Thus you may see, that I intend not to yield to the demands of those traitors the Covenanters, who I think will declare themselves so by their actions, before I shall do it by my Proclamation; which I shall not be sorry for, so that it be without the personal hurt of you, or any other of my honest servants, or the taking of any English place. This is to show you, that I care not for their affronting or disobeying my Declaration, so that it got not to open mischief, and that I may have some time to end my preparations. So I rest

Your assured, constant friend,

CHARLES R.

XXXI. To the Marquess of Hamilton

Greenwich, June 25, 1638.

HAMILTON,

I must needs thank you that you stand so close and constantly to my grounds, and you deserve the more since your fellow-counsellors do rather dishearten than help you in this business, for which I swear I pity you much. There are two things in your letter that require answer, to wit, the answer to their petition, and concerning the explanation of their damnable Covenant; for the first, the telling you that I have not changed my mind in this particular, is answer sufficient, since it was both foreseen by me, and fully debated betwixt us two before your downgoing; and for the other, I will only say, that so long as this Covenant is in force (whether it be with, or without, explanation), or anything else to win time, which now I see is one of your chiefest cares, wherefore I need not recommend it to you. Another I know is, to show the world clearly that my taking of arms is to suppress rebellion, and not to impose novelties, but that they are the seekers of them; wherefore if upon the publishing of my Declaration a protestation should follow, I should think it would rather do right than wrong to my cause : and for their calling a Parliament or Assembly without me, I should not much be sorry, for it would the more loudly declare them traitors, and the more justify my actions; therefore in my mind my

Declaration would not be long delayed : but this is a bare opinion and no command.   Lastly, my resolution is to come myself in person, accompanied like myself, sea-forces nor Ireland shall not be forgotten; the particulars of which I leave to the Comptroller's relation, as I do two particulars to the Archbishop of Canterbury, which you forgot to mention in my letter : and so I rest

Your assured, constant friend,

CHARLES R.

XXXII. TO THE MARQUESS OF HAMILTON

Greenwich, June 29, 1638.

HAMILTON,

Yours of the 24th (though it be long) requires but a short answer, it being only to have leave to come up, which is grounded upon so good reason, that I cannot but grant it.   Some considerations in the meantime I think fit to put to you; first, to take heed how you engage yourself in the way of mediation to me; for though I would not have you refuse to bring up to me any demands of theirs to gain time, yet I would not have you promise to mediate for anything that is against my grounds; for if you do, I must either prejudice myself in the granting, or you in denying : then, I would have you take care, that no subscriptions be urged upon any, especially of Council or Session : lastly, that you leave such encouragement to these few, that have not yet forsaken my cause, that they may be assured (as well as I) that your up-coming is neither to desert them nor it.   And thus certainly if (as you write) you get the mutinous multitude once dispersed, you will have done me very good service; for I am confident that my Declaration published before your coming away (according to the alterations that I have given you leave to make), will give some stop to their madnesses : however your endeavours have been such, that you shall be welcome to

Your assured, constant friend,

CHARLES R.

XXXIII. TO THE MARQUESS OF HAMILTON

Greenwich, July 9, 1638.

HAMILTON,

I hope that this will find you on the way hitherward; wherefore remitting all business till I speak with you, these lines are only to hearten you in your journey, for I think that it will be very much for my service. So desiring you to make as much haste as the weather will permit, I rest

Your assured, constant friend,

CHARLES R.

Hamilton came to London with a demand from the Covenanters for a General Assembly from which the Bishops should be excluded, and for a Parliament. Charles agreed to the meeting of a General Assembly and the convocation of Parliament, but he would not accept the Covenant. Hamilton returned to Edinburgh with this answer, but no settlement was reached, and both sides had recourse to arms. The following letter is typical of many written by Charles at this time.

XXXIV. TO THEOPHILUS, EARL OF SUFFOLK, LORD-LIEUTENANT OF CAMBRIDGE, SUFFOLK, AND DORSET

Palace at Westminster, February 18, 1639.

The great and considerable forces lately raised in Scotland, without order or warrant from us, by the instigation of some factious persons ill affected to monarchical government, who seek to cloak their too apparent rebellious designs under pretence of religion, albeit we have often given them good assurance of our resolution constantly to maintain the religion established by the laws of that kingdom, have moved us to take into our Royal care to provide for the preservation and safety of this our kingdom of England, which is by the tumultuous proceedings of those factious spirits in apparent danger to be annoyed and invaded; wherefore, upon serious debate and mature advice with our Privy Council we have resolved to repair in person to the northern parts of this our kingdom with a Royal army. And this being for the defence and safety of this our kingdom, unto which all our good subjects are obliged, we have appointed that a select number of foot shall be presently taken out of our trained bands, and brought to our city of York, or such other rendezvous as the General of our army shall appoint, there to attend our person and standard; of which number we require and command that you cause to be forthwith selected out of the trained bands in our county of Cambridge 400, in our county of Suffolk 1,500, and in our county of Dorset 700, of the most able men, which, together with their arms complete, you are to cause to be presently put in readiness, and to be weekly exercised. [Here follow directions as to the admission of substitutes, the charges of the journey, etc.] And our will and command is that you cause to be forthwith selected out of the troop of horse in Cambridge 40 horse, in Suffolk 150 horse, and in Dorset 50 horse, to be armed, and exercised weekly, so as to be ready to march to the rendezvous.

A campaign, often called the First Bishops' War, took place in which the King had the worst of it. Lack of money compelled Charles to negotiate, and peace was made in 1639 by the Treaty of Berwick, though neither party observed its terms. Largely for financial reasons the King then summoned Parliament, but to no purpose, and in a further campaign (the Second Bishops' War) he was again defeated by the Scots. On November 3rd, 1640, the Long Parliament met.

CHAPTER IV

THE LONG PARLIAMENT AND THE CIVIL WAR
1640-1646

*One of the first actions of the House of Commons was to attack
Strafford. The latter knew that the King's opponents had been
in negotiation with the Covenanters, and he wished Charles to
strike at once by accusing them, and particularly Pym, of treason.
While the King hesitated, Pym persuaded the House of Commons
to impeach Strafford, and when that procedure proved too slow
for the revolutionary party, a Bill of Attainder was passed, by a
majority of less than one-half of the members, on April 21st,
1641.*

1. TO THE EARL OF STRAFFORD

Whitehall, April 23, 1641.

STRAFFORD,

The misfortune that is fallen upon you by the strange mistaking and conjuncture of these times, being such that I must lay
by the thought of employing you hereafter in my affairs; yet I
cannot satisfy myself in honour or conscience without assuring
you (now in the midst of your troubles), that upon the
word of a king you shall not suffer in life, honour, or fortune.
This is but justice, and therefore a very mean reward from a
master to so faithful and able a servant as you have showed yourself to be; yet it is as much as I conceive the present times will
permit, though none shall hinder me from being

Your constant, faithful friend,

CHARLES R.

*It appeared as if the House of Lords would reject the Bill,
but Pym organized demonstrations outside Parliament which
overawed the Upper House, and the third reading was passed by
twenty-six votes to nineteen. This forced the King to give way,
but he made one last effort to save Strafford's life by sending the
Prince of Wales in person to Parliament with the following letter.*

11.TO THE HOUSE OF LORDS

Whitehall, May 11, 1641.

My Lords,

I did yesterday satisfy the justice of the kingdom, by the passing of the Bill of Attainder against the Earl of Strafford; but mercy being as inherent and inseparable to a king as justice, I desire, at this time, in some measure, to show that likewise, by suffering that unfortunate man to fulfil the natural course of his life in a close imprisonment; yet so that, if ever he make the least offer to escape, or offer directly or indirectly to meddle in any sort of public business, especially with me, by either message or letter, it shall cost him his life, without further process. This, if it may be done without a discontentment to my people, would be an unspeakable contentment to me. To which end, as in the first place, I by this letter do earnestly desire your approbation, and, to endeavour it the more, have chosen him to carry it that of all your House is most dear to me; so I desire that, by a conference, you would endeavour to give the House of Commons contentment likewise; assuring you that the exercising of mercy is no more pleasing to me, than to see both Houses of Parliament content, for my sake, that I should moderate the severity of the law in so important a case. I will not say that your complying with me in this my intended mercy shall make me more willing, but certainly it will make me more cheerful, in granting your just grievances. But, if no less than his life can satisfy my people, I must say *Fiat Justitia*. Thus again earnestly recommending the consideration of my intention unto you, I rest,

Your unalterable and affectionate friend,

CHARLES R.

If he must die, it were a charity to reprieve him until Saturday.

The King's appeal was without effect, and Strafford was executed.

Events now began to move fast. The Court of Star Chamber was abolished; ship money was declared illegal; and the various provisions of the Petition of Right were re-affirmed. The next

step was to attempt to overthrow the Church of England, and to wrest the control of the Militia from the Crown.

III. To Mr. Nicholas

Edinburgh, October 18, 1641.

I hear it is reported, that I am resolved, at my return, to alter the form of the Church government in England to this here; therefore I command you to assure all my servants there, that I am constant for the doctrine and discipline of the Church of England, as it was established by Queen Elizabeth and my father; and resolve (by the grace of God) to live and die in the maintenance of it.

Nicholas was clerk to the Council. Charles had gone to Scotland to see what support he could get there.

At this point the political situation was further complicated by the outbreak of a rebellion in Ireland, for the question at once rose as to whether the King or the Parliament was to deal with it. Charles announced his intention of taking personal command, but Parliament replied that it did not approve of the project.

IV. To both Houses of Parliament

April 25, 1642.

We are so troubled and astonished to find the unexpected reception and misunderstanding of our message of the eighth of April, concerning our Irish journey, that, being so much disappointed of the approbation and thanks we looked for to that declaration, we have great cause to doubt whether it be in our power to say or do anything which shall not fall within the like interpretation. But, as we have in that message called God to witness the sincerity of the profession of our only ends for the undertaking that journey, so we must appeal to all our good subjects, and the whole world, whether the reasons alleged against that journey be of weight to satisfy our understanding, or the counsel presented to dissuade us from it be full of that duty as is like to prevail over our affections.

For our resolving of so great a business without the advice of our Parliament, we must remind you how often, by our messages, we made the same offer, if you should advise us thereunto : To which you never gave us the least answer; but, in your late declaration, told us, that you were not to be satisfied with words; so that we had reason to conceive you rather avoided (out of regard to our person) to give us counsel to run that hazard, than that you disapproved the inclination.   And what greater comfort or security can the Protestants of Christendom receive, than by seeing a Protestant King venture and engage his person for the defence of that profession and the suppression of Popery; to which we solemnly protested in that message never to grant a toleration upon what pretence soever, or an abolition of any of the laws there in force against the professors of it?   And when we consider the great calamities and unheard-of cruelties our poor Protestant subjects in that kingdom have undergone for the space of near or full six months; the growth and increase of the strength of those barbarous rebels, and the evident probability of foreign supplies (if they were not speedily suppressed); the very slow succours hitherto sent them from hence; that the officers of several regiments, who have long time been allowed entertainment from you for that service, have not raised any supply or succour for that kingdom; that many troops of horse have long lain near Chester untransported; that the Lord Lieutenant of Ireland, on whom we relied principally for the conduct and managing of affairs there, is still in this kingdom, notwithstanding our earnestness expressed that he should repair to his command; and when we consider the many and great scandals raised upon ourself by report of the rebels, and not sufficiently discountenanced here, notwithstanding so many professions of ours; and had seen a book, lately printed by the order of the House of Commons, intituled, *A Remonstrance of divers remarkable Passages concerning the Church and Kingdom of Ireland,* wherein some examinations are set down, which (how improbable or impossible soever) may make an impression in the minds of many of our weak subjects; and lastly, when we duly weigh the dishonour which will perpetually lie upon this kingdom, if full and speedy relief be not dispatched thither; we could nor cannot think of a better way to discharge our duty to Almighty God, for the defence of the true Protestant profession, or to manifest our affection to our three kingdoms for their preservation, than by engaging our person in this expedition, as many of our Royal progenitors have done, even in foreign parts, upon causes of less importance and piety, with great honour to themselves and advantage to this kingdom, and therefore we expected at least thanks for such our inclination.

For the danger to our person, we conceive it necessary and worthy of a king to adventure his life to preserve his kingdom; neither can it be imagined that we will sit still, and suffer our kingdoms to be lost, and our good Protestant subjects to be massacred, without exposing our own person to the utmost hazard, for their relief and preservation; our life, when it was most pleasant, being nothing so precious to us, as it is, and shall be, to govern and preserve our people with honour and justice.

For any encouragement to the rebels because of the reports they raised, we cannot conceive that the rebels are capable of a greater terror than by the presence of their lawful King in the head of an army to chastise them : Besides, it will be an unspeakable advantage to them, if any report of theirs could hinder us from doing anything which were fit for us to do if such reports were not raised; this would quickly teach them, in this jealous age, to prevent by such reports any other persons coming against them, whom they had no mind should be so employed.

We marvel that the adventurers, whose advantage was a principal motive (next the reason before mentioned) to us, should so mistake our purpose, whose interest we conceive must be much improved by the expedition we hope (by God's blessing), to use in this service, this being the most probable way for the speedy conquest of the rebels : Their lands are sufficiently secured by Act of Parliament.

We think not ourself kindly used that the addition of so few men to your levies (for a guard to our person in Ireland) should be thought fit for your refusal; and much more that (having used so many cautions in that message, both in the smallness of the number, in our having raised none until your answer, in their being to be raised only near their place of shipping, in their being there to be armed, and that not till they were ready to be shipped, in the provision by the oaths that none of them should be Papists; all which appears sufficient to destroy all grounds of jealousy of any force intended by them in opposition to the Parliament, or favour to any malignant party) any suspicion should notwithstanding be grounded upon it.

Neither can it be understood that, when we recommended the managing of that war to you, that we intended to exclude ourself, or not to be concerned in your counsels, that if we found any expedient (which in our conscience or understanding we thought necessary for that great work) we might not put it in practice. We look upon you as our great council, whose advice we always have and will (with great regard and deliberation) weigh and consider: But we look upon ourself as neither deprived of our understanding, or divested of any right we had if there were no Parliament sitting. We called you together by our own writ and authority (without which you could not have met), to give us faithful counsel about our great affairs : But we resigned not up our own interest and freedom; we never subjected ourself to your absolute determination; we have always weighed your counsels as proceeding from a body entrusted by us; and, when we have dissented from you, we have returned you the reasons which have prevailed with our conscience and understanding, with that candour as a prince should use towards his subjects, and that affection which a father can express to his children. What application hath been used to rectify our understanding by reasons, or motives have been given to persuade our affections, we leave all the world to judge; and then we must tell you, howsoever a major part may bind you in matter of opinion, we hold ourself (and we are sure the law and the constitution of the kingdom hath always held the same) as free to dissent (till our reason be convinced for the general good) as if you delivered no opinion.

For our journey itself, the circumstances of your petition are such, as we know not well what answer to return, or whether we were best to give any. That part which pretends to carry reason with it, doth no way satisfy us; the other which is rather reprehension and menace than advice, cannot stagger us. Our answer therefore is, that we shall be very glad to find the work of Ireland so easy as you seem to think it; which did not so appear by any-thing known to us when we sent our message.   And though we will never refuse or be unwilling to venture our person, we are not so weary of our life as to hazard it impertinently; and there-fore, since you seem to have received advertisements of some late and great successes in that kingdom, we will stay some time, to see the event of those, and not pursue this resolution till we have given you a second notice : But if we find the miserable condition of our poor subjects of that kingdom, be not speedily relieved, we will (with God's assistance) visit them with succours, as our particular credit and interest can supply us with, if you refuse to join with us.   And we doubt not but the levies we shall make (in which we will observe punctually the former and all other cautions, as may best prevent all fears and jealousies, and to use no power but what is legal) will be so much to the satisfaction of our subjects, as no person will dare presume to resist our com-mands; and if they should, at their peril.   In the meantime, we hope our forwardness so remarkable to that service shall be notorious to all the world, and that all scandals laid on us in that business shall be clearly wiped away.

We were so careful that our journey into Ireland should not interrupt the proceedings of Parliament, nor deprive our subjects of any acts of justice, or further acts of grace, for the real benefit of our people, that we made a free offer of leaving such power behind, as should not only be necessary for the peace and safety of the kingdom, but fully provided for the happy progress of the Parliament; and therefore we cannot but wonder, since such power hath been always left here by commission for the govern-ment of this kingdom when our progenitors have been out of the same during the sitting of Parliaments : and since yourselves desired that such a power might be left here by us at our last going into Scotland, what law of the land have you to dispense with you from submitting to such authority legally derived from us in our absence, and to enable you to govern this kingdom by your own mere authority?

For our return towards London, we have given you so full an answer in our late declaration, and in answer to your petition presented to us at York the 26th of March last, that we know not what to add, if you will not provide for our security with you, nor agree to remove to another place, where there may not be the same danger to us.

We expected that (since we have been so particular in the causes and grounds of our fears) you should have sent us word that you had published such declarations against future tumults and unlawful assemblies and taken such courses for the suppressing of seditious sermons and pamphlets, that our fears of that kind may be laid aside, before you could press our return.

To conclude, we could wish that you would (with the same strictness and severity) weigh and examine your messages and expressions to us, as you do those you receive from us; for we are very confident, that, if you examine our rights and privileges by what our predecessors have enjoyed, and your own addresses by the usual courses of your ancestors, you will find many expressions in this petition warranted only by your own authority, which indeed we forbear to take notice of, or give answer to, lest we should be tempted (in a just indignation) to express a greater passion than we are yet willing to put on. God in His good time (we hope) will so inform the hearts of all our subjects, that we shall recover from the mischief and danger of this distemper, on whose good pleasure we will wait with all patience and humility.

Both the King and his enemies were now preparing for the war which had become inevitable. The following documents illustrate the line taken by Charles at this time.

v. By the King

A Proclamation, forbidding all His Majesty's Subjects, belonging to the Trained Bands or Militia of this Kingdom, to rise, march, muster or exercise by virtue of any Order or Ordinance of one or both Houses of Parliament, without Consent or Warrant from His Majesty, upon Pain of Punishment according to the Laws.

Whereas, by the statute made in the seventh year of King Edward the First, the Prelates, Earls, Barons, and commonalty of this realm, affirmed in Parliament, that to the King it belongeth, and his part it is by his Royal Seignory, straitly to defend wearing of armour, and all other force against the peace, at all times when it shall please him, and to punish them which do the contrary according to the laws and usages of the realm; and hereunto all subjects are bound to aid the King, as their sovereign lord, at all seasons when need shall be : And whereas we understand that, expressly contrary to the said statute, and other good laws of this our kingdom, under colour and pretence of an ordinance of Parliament, without our consent, or any commission or warrant from us, the trained bands and militia of this kingdom have been lately, and are intended to be put in arms, and drawn into companies, in a warlike manner, whereby the peace and quiet of our subjects is, or may be, disturbed : we, being desirous, by all gracious and fair admonitions, to prevent that some malignant persons in this our kingdom do not by degrees seduce our good subjects from their due obedience to us and the laws of this our kingdom, subtly endeavouring, by a general combustion or confusion, to hide their mischievous designs and intentions against the peace of this our kingdom, and, under a specious pretence of putting our trained bands into a posture, draw and engage our good subjects in a warlike opposition against us, as our town of Hull is already by the treason of Sir John Hotham, who at first pretended to put a garrison into the same only for our security and service :

We do therefore, by this our proclamation, expressly charge and command all our sheriffs, and all colonels, lieutenant-colonels, sergeant-majors, captains, officers, and soldiers, belonging to the trained bands of this our kingdom, and likewise all high and petty constables, and other our officers and subjects whatsoever, upon their allegiance, and as they tender the peace of this our kingdom, not to muster, levy, raise, or march, or to summon or warn, upon any warrant, order, or ordinance, from one or both our Houses of Parliament (whereto we have not, or shall not, give our express consent), any of our trained bands, or other forces, to rise, muster, march, or exercise, without express warrant under our hand, or warrant from our sheriff of the county, grounded upon a particular writ to that purpose under our great seal : And in case any of our trained bands shall rise or gather together contrary to this our command, we shall then call them in due time, to a strict account, and proceed legally against them, as violators of the laws, and disturbers of the peace of the kingdom.

Given at our court at York, the 27th day of May, 1642.

VI. To Lord Willoughby of Parham

CHARLES REX.

Right trusty and well-beloved, we greet you well.   Though we could not but rest much unsatisfied that our last gracious letter could work no better effects in you, but that you remain still obstinate in pursuing those illegal commands you have received from both Houses; yet, since we perceive that you have some colourable excuse for this your great error, upon the mistaking of what was the opinion of the Lord Keeper and the Lord Chief Justice Banks upon this particular, the one having voted clearly against it, and the other having never declared his opinion therein, it having never been sought, and to this hour having done nothing in the prosecution thereof, as by their several letters will most clearly appear unto you : Therefore we are pleased once again to lay our commands upon you, that, seeing the grounds whereon you build your error hath been thus mistaken by you, we cannot but observe unto you the strange exorbitant power which the two Houses at this time, misled by a few factious, malicious spirits, pretend to arrogate to themselves, and by which the Militia (as they call it) is put in execution; it being so supreme and absolute, that our consent is not thought necessary for the execution of anything they judge to be convenient for the welfare of the kingdom, of which as we hope you are ignorant, so doubt not but, it being made known unto you by us, it will be more than a sufficient ground to make you desist from those illegal, undutiful, upon so much knowledge by warning, and (therefore) unsafe ways.

Given at our court at York, the 7th of June, 1642.

VII. To the Earl of Warwick

CHARLES R.

Right trusty and right well-beloved cousin and counsellor, we greet you well.   We have herewith sent you, under our Great Seal, a duplicate of our revocation of the grant of the office of the Lord High Admiral of England, heretofore passed by us to our right trusty and right well-beloved cousin and counsellor the Earl of Northumberland, to hold during our pleasure, whereby you may perceive that, he being thus legally discharged of the said office, all the commissions, powers, and instructions, formerly given by him, are void; wherefore we do, by these our letters, expressly charge and command you, upon your allegiance, and as you tender the peace of our kingdom, forthwith to give over and relinquish the command you have, or pretend to have, in any of our ships of our fleet, and forthwith to leave our ship *The James*, and our said fleet, to be commanded by such person as we have or shall appoint to take charge hereof; and in regard it is notoriously known, that, by the laws of the land, it is no less than high treason for any person whatsoever to detain any of our ships contrary to our express commands, we doubt not your ready obedience herein; for which this shall be your sufficient warrant and discharge.

Given at our court at York, the 28th of June, 1642.

VIII. To the Principal Officers of the Navy

CHARLES R.

Trusty and well-beloved, we greet you well.   Whereas we have discharged the Earl of Northumberland from the office of Lord High Admiral; and whereas we have likewise commanded the Earl of Warwick, upon his allegiance, to deliver the possession of our ship *The James*, and the rest of our fleet to Sir John Pennington, to whom we have given warrant to take the charge and command of our fleet; and whereas the said Earl of Warwick, notwithstanding our said command, doth rebelliously withhold from us our said ship and fleet : We do therefore, by these our letters, will and command you, upon your allegiance, not to obey any order, ordinance, or warrant whatsoever, which shall be sent unto you, or any of you, from one or both our Houses of Parliament, or from the said Earl of Warwick, or any other, for any stores or provisions, or for any business whatsoever concerning our said fleet, navy, or ships; and that you take special care, that no moneys or provisions of any kind whatsoever be issued or expended by you, or any of you, or any officer subordinate to you, for the use of any of the ships belonging to our fleet now at sea, without warrant from us, or such as we shall appoint commissioners for our admiralty and navy; and herein we require your exact obedience, as you tender the forfeiture of your places, and will answer the contrary; for which this shall be your warrant.

Given at our court at York, the 7th day of July, 1642.

IX. To the Mayor of Boston

Lincoln, July 13, 1642.

Charles R.

Trusty and well-beloved, we greet you well. Whereas we understand that, contrary to our proclamation and the laws of the land, divers of the trained bands, and others belonging to that our town, do frequently assemble, train, and exercise, in a warlike manner, without any order from us, or delivered from any authority given by us; our will and command is, that presently upon sight hereof, you take effectual order, not only to suppress and hinder any such meeting, training, or exercising; but that you punish, according to law, such as you shall find are refractory and disobedient to this our command, and certify their names to us, or one of our principal Secretaries of State, together with the particulars of such their offences; and of the due performance of this our command, we expect a speedy account of you; for which this shall be your warrant.

Charles raised his standard at Nottingham on August 22nd.

x. To both Houses of Parliament

Nottingham, August 25, 1642.

CHARLES R.

We have, with unspeakable grief of heart, long beheld the distractions of this our kingdom. Our very soul is full of anguish, until we may find some remedy to prevent the miseries which are ready to overwhelm this whole nation with a civil war. And though all our endeavours, tending to the composing of those unhappy differences betwixt us and our two Houses of Parliament (though pursued by us with all zeal and sincerity) have been hitherto without that success we hoped for; yet such is our constant and earnest care to preserve the public peace, that we shall not be discouraged from using any expedient which, by the blessing of the God of mercy, may lay a firm foundation of peace and happiness to all our subjects. To this end observing that many mistakes have arisen by the messages, petitions, and answers, betwixt us and our two Houses of Parliament, which happily may be prevented by some other way of treaty, wherein the matters in difference may be more clearly understood and more freely transacted, we have thought fit to propound to you, that some fit persons may be by you enabled to treat with the like number to be authorized by us, in such a manner, and with such freedom of debate, as may best tend to that happy conclusion which all good men desire, the peace of the kingdom; when, as we promise, in the word of a king, all safety and encouragement to such as shall be sent to us, if you shall choose the place where we are for the treaty (which we wholly leave to you), presuming of the like care of the safety of those we shall employ, if you shall name another place; so we assure you and all our good subjects that (to the best of our understanding) nothing shall be therein wanting, on our part, which may advance the true Protestant religion, oppose Popery and superstition, secure the law of the land (upon which is built as well our just prerogative as the propriety and liberty of the subject), confirm all just power and privileges of Parliament, and render us and our people truly happy, by a good understanding betwixt us and our two Houses of Parliament. Bring with you as firm resolution to do your duty; and let all our good people join with us in our prayers to Almighty God, for His blessing upon this work. If this proposition shall be rejected by you, we have done our duty so amply, that God will absolve us from the guilt of any of that blood which must be spilt.   And what opinion soever other men may have of our power, we assure you nothing but our Christian and pious care to prevent the effusion of blood hath begot this motion; our provision of men, arms, and money, being such as may secure us from further violence, till it please God to open the eyes of our people.

XI. To the Earl of Newcastle

Shrewsbury, September 23, 1642.

NEWCASTLE,

This is to tell you that this rebellion is grown to that height, that I must not look what opinion men are who at the time are willing and able to serve me.   Therefore I do not only permit, but command you to make use of all my loving subjects' services, without examining their consciences (more than their loyalty to me), as you shall find most to conduce to the upholding of my just regal power.   So I rest

Your most assured, faithful friend,

CHARLES R.

Newcastle had been appointed to command the Royal troops in the North of England.

The first serious clash between the opposing forces took place at Edgehill on October 23rd.

XII. To Prince Rupert

NEPHEW,

I have given order as you have desired so that I doubt not but all the foot and cannon will be at Edgehill betimes this morning, where you will also find

Your loving uncle and faithful friend,

CHARLES R.

xiii. To the Earl of Newcastle

Oxford, November 2, 1642.

NEWCASTLE,

Your endeavours are so really faithful and lucky in my service, that though I pretend not to thank you in words, yet I cannot but tell you of (though I cannot all) the sense I have of them, when, as now, I have time and opportunity for it. This bearer will tell you of the defeat the rebels have received, which referring to him, I will tell you of four thousand pounds I have sent you, for which do not too much thank me, for it may be, you should not have had it if I had known how it might have been speedily and safely conveyed hither, yet I think very well employed. That I have designed of you is to make what haste you can to come to join your forces with mine, for I suppose and hope that my wife will be come to you before you can be ready to march. I write this, that you may be ready when she comes, or if (as it is possible) she should take another course, you might make haste without her; the certainty of which (I mean my wife's journey) you will know within few days or hours after the return of this bearer.

This is all for this time. So I rest

Your most assured, constant friend,

CHARLES R

The 'defeat' of the rebels refers to the battle of Edgehill. The Queen had gone abroad in February.

xiv. To the Earl of Newcastle

Oxford, December 15, 1642.

NEWCASTLE,

The services I have received from you hath been so eminent, and is likely to have so great an influence upon all my affairs, that I need tell you that I shall never forget it, but always look upon you as a principal instrument in keeping the crown upon my head. The business of Yorkshire I account almost done, only I put you in mind to make yourself master (according as formerly but briefly I have written to you) of all the arms there, to ask them from the trained bands by several divisions to desire them from the rest of my well-affected subjects, and to take them from the ill-affected, especially Leeds and Halifax. I have no greater need than of arms, nor means to supply myself than from you, and therefore I recommend to you the getting as many as you can from all the parts you may, and even from Newcastle (whither for future supplies I have ordered great store to be sent), into some safe magazine there. My next greatest want is dragooners, which I want the more because it is the rebels' (indeed only) strength, their foot having no inclination to winter marches; wherefore, if you could get there horse and arms so, and send these presently to me, they might be of very great advantage. You have likewise neighbours in Derbyshire, Cheshire, and Lancashire, who, for their good service, stand now in great need of your assistance, which I shall desire you to give, as far as will suit with my other service; and that you may do it the more effectually, I have given order that a commission be drawn for you to command all the countries beyond Trent. Lastly, I will put you in mind that some of your forces extended to Nottingham and Newark would make Lincolnshire extremely right, and restore those good subjects of mine who are now banished. So, desiring to hear often from you, I rest

Your most assured, constant friend,
CHARLES R.

xv. TO THE EARL OF NEWCASTLE

Oxford, December 29, 1642.

NEWCASTLE,

I thank you for your letter of the 25th December, and in particular for sending for my wife with that earnestness that you have done. I give you free leave to disobey my warrants for issuing arms, for what I have done in that was in supposition that you had enough for yourself and your friends, but having not, I confess charity begins at home. I wonder to hear you say that there are few arms in that country; for when I was there, to my knowledge there was twelve thousand of the trained bands (except some few Hotham got into Hull) complete, besides those of particular men; therefore, in God's name, inquire what is become of them, and make use of them all, for those who are well-affected will willingly give or lend them to you, and those who are not, make no bones to take them from them.   As for your invitation to several places, do therein as you shall find best for my service, without looking to the little commodities of particular persons or shires; for though I may propose many things to your consideration, yet I shall not impose anything upon you; as, for example, I hear General King is come; now I desire you to make use of him in your army.   I am sure you have not good commanders to spare no more than arms, yet I confess there may be such reasons that may make this desire of mine impossible.   I know Newport has that place he expected, to which I will only say that I wish you an abler in his room. You have had a little trial already; yet (according to my rule) I do not command, but earnestly desire you to see if you can comply with this my desire.   My conclusion is to assure you that I do not only trust in your fidelity, which (as Charles Chester said of Queen Elizabeth's faults) all the world takes on, but likewise to your judgement in my affairs; and you may be confident that nothing shall alter me from being

Your most assured, constant friend,

CHARLES R.

I promise you to be weary of a treaty as you can desire.   I pray you let me hear from you as oft as you may.

The allusion to a treaty in the above letter is to the negotiations which began at this time between Charles and the Parliament, but one of the latter's conditions was the abolition of Episcopacy, to which the King would not agree.

One of the most notable events of the following year, 1643, was the settlement of Ireland.   The insurgents had gained possession of practically the whole kingdom, and had established what amounted to a provisional government at Kilkenny, though they still acknowledged Charles.   As both the King and the Irish had a common enemy in the English Parliament, it was only natural that negotiations should take place between them.

131

XVI. To the Marquess of Ormonde

Oxford, January 12, 1643.

ORMONDE,

Although I have not yet had any answer of Sergeant-Major Warren's message (of which this bearer knows nothing, nor do I desire he should, because neither is it needful, nor do men ordinarily labour so heartily in any business that they begin not themselves), nevertheless I could not but make this dispatch, fearing lest the delay of the business might make it fruitless unto me.   And that honour and public safety may go along with my particular interests, I here send you a memorial, whereby to govern yourself in this; which I permit you to communicate according to your discretion.   For the rest, I have given so full instructions to this trusty bearer, that I need say no more, but that I am

Your most assured, constant friend,

CHARLES R.

Memorial for the Irish Treaty

There is danger that the Irish rebels in their propositions for peace may desire :

1. A toleration of the Romish religion, or an abrogation of the penal statutes concerning religion (which in effect is the same thing).   This is so contrary to the laws of this and that kingdom, to His Majesty's several professions, would be so generally distasteful to the subjects of England, and would give such an advantage to the King's enemies here, that it may not be granted without apparent danger of ruin to the King's affairs.   The penal statutes in Ireland are not strict, and more than such a conveniency in the execution of them (as was before the rebellion) may not be admitted.

2. That Ireland should not be obliged by any statutes made in England, which shall not be confirmed by their Parliament, nor be commanded by orders of the Parliament of England. They may have much to say for themselves in this point;

but this caution must be observed, both in respect of the precedent, and the influence it may have upon His Majesty's affairs here; what shall be agreed unto concerning the same, be admitted by way of declaration of what is their right, not as granted *de novo*.

3. That Poynings' Law, and many of the statutes now in force in Ireland, be repealed, under pretence that they were made when a great part of Ireland had none to answer for them in that Parliament there. If this reason be admitted, the whole frame of government of that kingdom will be shaken; besides the ill consequence there and here, that such an innovation should be agreed to in the close of a rebellion.

4. That the Parliament there should have a proposing power, without the approbation of the King and his Privy Council here. This crosseth an express Act of Parliament in Ireland, and is contrary to that policy which hath for many ages preserved that kingdom in peace. The consequence of it is far greater than may appear *prima facie*.

5. That the native Irish may be restored to their plantation lands, which they pretend have been unjustly taken from them. This point must be very tenderly handled : no retrospect may be admitted farther than from the beginning of the King's reign; neither is it proper to conclude anything positively for the present. It may be proper to refer it to the examination of some fit commissioners, whereby the conclusions may be subsequent to the present treaty; and then it may be more easy for His Majesty to give satisfaction either to his British subjects (the late possessors of these lands) or to the Irish pretenders to the same.

6. That they may be governed by Irish officers and Ministers of State. If this be propounded as exclusive to the British, it may not be granted neither in honour or safety; but if it be desired only to enable the Irish in such capacities, the more way may be given, because it will always be in His Majesty's choice, whom he will entrust with those charges; and if some of the more subordinate ministers be Irish, so long as they shall be controllable by the major part of the English, the danger will be less, and by degrees His Majesty may with

more safety reduce the frame of the government to its former condition.

Oxford, January 12, 1643.

XVII. TO THE MARQUESS OF ORMONDE

Oxford, February 2, 1643.

ORMONDE,

I am glad to see by yours of the 18th January that you are ready to put those propositions in execution which I made to you by Sergeant-Major Warren, assuring you that that service shall not be hindered by the arrival of a more powerful head. And I earnestly desire you (for many reasons, which I have not time now to set down) to send me word with all speed the particulars of this business, as, how, when, and in what measure it will be done; as likewise what use you will make of Mr. Burke's dispatch in relation to it. Accommodation is much spoken of here, I having yesterday received propositions from both Houses of Parliament; but those that see them will hardly believe that the propounders have any intention of peace : for certainly no less power than His, who made the world of nothing, can draw peace out of these articles. Therefore I leave you to judge what hope there is for you to receive supplies from hence, which you should not want, were it in the power of

Your most assured, constant friend,

CHARLES R.

I have sent you a cipher that you may write the more freely.

XVIII. TO THE MARQUESS OF ORMONDE

Oxford, March 12, 1643.

ORMONDE,

I have received such an account of Antrim and Daniel O'Neill's negotiation with the Irish, as gives me an expectation, that, with your help and co-operation, they may do me very eminent good service. I have commanded Digby to inform you exactly of all particulars : only one thing I thought necessary earnestly to give you in charge myself; which is, that you will unite yourself in a strict and entire correspondence with Antrim, and contribute all your power to further him in those services which he hath undertaken; for I find that almost that whole kingdom is so much divided betwixt your two interests, that if you join in the ways, as well as in the end, for my service, you will meet with small difficulties there; which I no way doubt, being thus recommended by

Your assured friend,
CHARLES R.

XIX. TO THE MARQUESS OF ORMONDE

CHARLES R.

Right trusty and right well-beloved cousin and counsellor, we greet you well. Since our two Houses of Parliament here (to whose care at their instance we left it to provide for the support of our army in Ireland, and the relief of our good subjects there) have so long failed our expectation, whereby our said army and subjects are there reduced to very great extremities; we have thought good (for preservation of our good subjects there) to resume the care of them again to ourself; and to the end that we may the better understand, as well the state of that our kingdom (as it is now reduced) as the cause of levying the arms that are at present there held against our authority; we have thought fit by these our letters to command and authorize you (the Lieutenant-General of our army there), with all secrecy and convenient expedition, to treat with our subjects (who have there taken up arms against us and our authority), and to agree with them for a present cessation of arms for one year, in as advantageous and beneficial a manner as you in your wisdom and good affection to us (whereof we have had very good experience) shall conceive to be for our honour, and to conduce most to our service; the particulars whereof we cannot prescribe unto you, being we are not well informed of the true state of our or their army or forces, or of the condition of the country, or any other thing, whereupon to fix a judgement, but shall remit the same entirely to you, promising hereby in the word of a king, that we shall under our great seal ratify and confirm whatsoever you, upon such treaty, shall conclude and agree unto, and set under your hand on our behalf in this business; for which these our letters shall be your sufficient warrant.

Given at our court at Oxford, 23rd April, 1643.

xx. To the Marquess of Ormonde

Oxford, April 23, 1643.

ORMONDE,

I have sent you herewith a command and power to make a cessation with the rebels; which, though it be not so formally legal as I could wish, yet I desire you earnestly to put those my commands in execution; and as soon as that is done, Ormonde must bring over the Irish Army to Chester, as I have given this trusty bearer, Sir Patrick Wemyss, full instruction; wherefore not having time to write more, I refer you to him, and rest

Your most assured, constant friend,

CHARLES R.

After some negotiation an armistice for one year on the basis of the status quo *was concluded on September 15th; and in this way the first period of the Irish Rebellion came to an end.*

On the whole, fortune favoured the King during the year 1643, and the two following letters are significant of his chivalry towards his opponents, and his scrupulous regard for legality.

xxi. To the Mayor of Newbury

September 21, 1643.

Our will and command is, that you forthwith send into the towns and villages adjacent, and bring thence all the sick and hurt soldiers of the Earl of Essex's army; and though they be rebels, and deserve the punishment of traitors, yet out of our tender compassion upon them as being our subjects, our will and pleasure is, that you carefully provide for their recovery, as well as for those of our own army, and then to send them to Oxford.

The first battle of Newbury was fought on September 20th.

XXII. TO THE GOVERNOR OF DARTMOUTH

Oxford, December 13, 1643.

Whereas divers ships and vessels of good value are brought in, as we understand, to our port of Dartmouth, which our and other ships have taken from the rebels and their adherents; and whereas it is like that many more will be hereafter brought in thither, concerning which it is fit that there be a legal proceeding before they be any way disposed of.   Our pleasure and command therefore is, that you take effectual order that not only the said ships already brought in, but all that shall be hereafter, be first legally adjudicated by the judge of our Admiralty there who is or shall be for the time being, before you or any others whatsoever, offer to dispose of such ships, vessels, and prizes, or anything belonging to them, or of any their goods, and commodities aboard.   Which rule we will and command you punctually to observe and cause to be observed for the avoiding of injustice, and the prejudice that would ensue to our service by the contrary.

The marriage suggested in the next letter did not take place.

XXIII. TO PRINCE MAURICE

Oxford, July 4, 1643.

NEPHEW MAURICE,

Though Mars be now most in vogue, yet Hymen may be sometimes remembered.   The matter is this.   Your mother and I have been somewhat engaged concerning a marriage between your brother Rupert and Mademoiselle de Rohan, and now her friends press your brother to a positive answer, which I find him resolved to give negatively; therefore, I have thought fit to know if you will not by your engagement take your brother handsomely off.   I have not time to argue the matter; but, to show my judgement, I assure you that if my son James were of a fit age, I would want of my will but he should have her; and, indeed, the total rejecting of this alliance may do us some prejudice, whether you look to these or German affairs, the performance of which is not expected until the times shall be reasonably settled, though I desire you to give me an answer as soon as you can (having now occasion to send to France), because delays are sometimes as ill as denials. So, hoping and praying God for good news from you, I rest

> Your loving uncle and faithful friend,
>
> CHARLES R.

The Scots had remained neutral up to this point, but the King's successes made them alarmed in view of their own insurrection previously. Both Parliament and King accordingly began to angle for Scottish support.

XXIV. TO THE EARL OF MAR

Oxford, April 21, 1643.

CHARLES R.

Right trusty and right well-beloved cousin and counsellor, we greet you well. Since nothing on earth can be more dear unto us than the preservation of the affections of our people, and amongst them none more than of those of our native kingdom; which as the long and uninterrupted government of us and our predecessors over them doth give us just reason in a more near and special manner to challenge from them, so may they justly expect a particular tenderness from us in everything which may contribute to their happiness. But knowing what industry is used (by scattering seditious pamphlets and employing private agents and instruments to give bad impressions of us and our proceedings and under pretence of a danger to religion and government) to corrupt their fidelities and affections, and to engage them in an unjust quarrel against us, their King, we cannot therefore but remove these jealousies and secure their fears from all possibility of any hazard to either of these from us. We have therefore thought fit to require you to call together your friends, vassals, tenants and such others as have any dependency upon you, and in our name to show them our willingness to give all the assurance they can desire or we possibly grant (if more can be given than already is) of preserving inviolable all those graces and favours which we have of late granted to that our kingdom; and that we do faithfully promise never to go to the contrary of anything there established either in ecclesiastical or civil government, but that we will inviolably keep the same according to the laws of that our kingdom. And we do wish God so to bless our proceedings and posterity as we do really make good perform this promise. We hope this will give so full satisfaction to all who shall hear of this our solemn protestation, that no such persons as study division, or go about to weaken the confidence betwixt us and our people, and justly deserve the name and punishment of incendiaries, shall be sheltered from the hand of justice; and all such others as shall endeavour peace and unity and obedience to us and our laws may expect that protection and increase of favour from us which their fidelity deserves. So expecting your care hereof, we bid you heartily farewell.

The Parliament was more successful in its blandishments than the King, and a Scottish army entered England in support of the former in January, 1644.

CHAPTER V

THE LONG PARLIAMENT AND THE CIVIL WAR

1640-1646

(continued)

(continued)

The intervention of the Scots proved to be the turning-point in the war, for Newcastle was unable to maintain his position in Yorkshire, and so the plan of a joint advance upon London from the North and West had to be abandoned.

i. To the Earl of Newcastle

Oxford, April 5, 1644.

Newcastle,

By your last dispatch I perceive that the Scots are not the only, or (it may be said) the enemies you contest withal, at this time; wherefore I must tell you a word (for I have not time to make long discourses), you must as much condemn the impertinent or malicious tongues and pens of those that are, or profess to be your friends, as well as you despise the sword of an equal enemy. The truth is, if either you, or my Lord E———, then leave my service, I am sure (at least) all the North (I speak not all I think) is lost. Remember all courage is not in fighting, constancy in a good cause being the chief, and the despising of slanderous tongues and pens being not the least ingredient. I'll say no more, but let nothing dishearten you from doing that which is most for your honour and good of (the thought of leaving your charge being against book)

Your most assured, real, constant friend,

Charles R.

ii. To the Earl of Newcastle

Oxford, April 11, 1644.

Newcastle,

You need not doubt of the care I have of the North, and in particular of your assistance against the Scots' invasion, but you must consider that we, like you, cannot do always what we would; besides our task is not little that we struggle with, in

143

which, if we fail, all you can do will be to little purpose; wherefore you may be assured of all assistance from hence that may be, without laying ourselves open to eminent danger, the particulars of which I refer you to my Lord Digby, and rest

Your most assured, real, constant friend,

CHARLES R.

Rupert was sent to the North to retrieve the situation, and in particular to raise the siege of York. At first he was singularly successful, for he compelled the Parliamentary forces before Newark to capitulate, and then captured Stockport, Bolton, and Liverpool.

III. To Prince Rupert

Ticknell, June 14, 1644.

NEPHEW,

First, I must congratulate with you for your good successes, assuring you that the things themselves are no more welcome to me than that you are the means. I know the importance of supplying you with powder, for which I have taken all possible ways, having sent both to Ireland and Bristol, as from Oxford this bearer is well satisfied that it is impossible to have at present : but if he tell you that I may spare them from hence, I leave you to judge, having but thirty-six left; but what I can get from Bristol (of which there is not much certainty, it being threatened to be besieged), you shall have.

But now I must give you the true state of my affairs, which, if their condition be such as enforces me to give you more peremptory commands than I would willingly do, you must not take it ill. If York be lost, I shall esteem my crown little less, unless supported by your sudden march to me, and a miraculous conquest in the South, before the effects of the northern power can be found here; but if York be relieved, and you beat the rebel armies of both kingdoms which are before it, then, but otherwise not, I may possibly make a shift (upon the defensive) to spin out time, until you come to assist me : wherefore I command and conjure you, by the duty and affection which I know you bear me, that (all new enterprises laid aside) you immediately march (according to your first intention) with all your force to the relief of York; but if that be either lost, or have freed themselves from the besiegers, or that for want of powder you cannot undertake that work, you immediately march with your whole strength to Worcester, to assist me and my army; without which, or your having relieved York by beating the Scots, all the successes you can afterwards have most infallibly will be useless to me. You may believe nothing but an extreme necessity could make me write thus to you; wherefore, in this case, I can noways doubt of your punctual compliance with

Your loving uncle and faithful friend,

CHARLES R.

Rupert obeyed the King's instructions, but he and Newcastle were defeated at Marston Moor on July 2nd, and the North was lost to the Royalists.

Meanwhile, Charles made yet another effort at negotiation.

IV. TO THE LORDS AND COMMONS OF PARLIAMENT ASSEMBLED AT WESTMINSTER

Evesham, July 4.

We being deeply sensible of the miseries and calamities of this our kingdom, and of the grievous sufferings of our poor subjects, do most earnestly desire that some expedient may be found out, which, by the blessing of God, may prevent the further effusion of blood, and restore the nation to peace, from the earnest and constant endeavouring of which, as no discouragement given us on the contrary part shall make us cease, so no success of ours shall ever divert us. For the effecting thereof we are most ready and willing to condescend to all that shall be for the good of us and our people whether by way of conformity which we have already granted, or such further concessions as shall be requisite to the giving of a full assurance of all the performance of all our most real professions, concerning the maintenance of the true reformed Protestant religion established in this kingdom, with due regard to the ease of tender consciences, the just privileges of Parliament, and the liberty and prosperity

L

145

of the people, according to the laws of the land; as also by granting a general pardon without, or with exceptions, as shall be
thought fit.   In order to which blessed peace we do desire and
propound to the Lords and Commons of Parliament assembled
at Westminster, that they appoint such and so many persons as
they shall think fit, sufficiently authorized by them to attend us
at our army, upon safe conduct to come and return (which we
do hereby grant), and conclude with us how the premises, and
all other things in question betwixt us and them, may be fully
settled, whereby all unhappy mistaking between us and our
people being removed, there may be a present cessation of arms,
and as soon as may be, a total disbanding of all armies, the
subject have his due, and we restored to our rights.   Wherein,
if this our offer shall be accepted, there shall be nothing wanting
on our part which may make our people secure and happy.

*In the West fortune was favouring the King, who was driving
the Earl of Essex before him.*

v.To the Earl of Essex

Liskeard, August 6, 1644.

Essex,

I have been very willing to believe, that whenever there
should be such a conjuncture as to put it in your power to effect
that happy settlement of this miserable kingdom (which all good
men desire), you would lay hold of it.   That season is now
before you, you having it at this time in your power to redeem
your country and the crown, and to oblige your King in the
highest degree (an action certainly of the greatest piety, prudence,
and honour), such an opportunity as, perhaps, no subject before
you hath ever had, or after you shall ever have; to which there
is no more required, but that you join with me, heartily and
really, in the settling of those things which we have both professed
constantly to be our only aims.   Let us do this : and if any shall
be so foolishly unnatural as to oppose their King's, their country's,
and their own good, we will make them happy (by God's blessing), even against their wills.   The only impediment can be

want of mutual confidence; I promise it you on my part, as I have endeavoured to prepare it on yours, by my letter to Hertford from Evesham.   I hope this will perfect it, when (as I here do) I shall have engaged to you, on the word of a king, that you, joining with me in that blessed work, I shall give both to you and your army such eminent marks of my confidence and value, as shall not leave a room for the least distrust amongst you, either in relation to the public or yourself, unto whom I shall then be

Your faithful friend,

C.R.

If you like of this, hearken to this bearer, whom I have fully instructed in particulars, but this will admit of no delay.

Essex forwarded this letter to the Parliament, observing that it was his business to fight, not to negotiate.   On August 31st his army capitulated at Lostwithiel, and Charles allowed the men to go home after the confiscation of their arms.   Had he wished, he could have imposed far harsher terms, and his moderation robbed him of the fruits of his most complete victory.

VI. TO THE PARLIAMENT

It having pleased God in so eminent a manner lately to bless our armies in these parts with success, we do not so much joy in that blessing for any other consideration, as for the hopes we have it may be a means to make others lay to heart, as we do, the miseries brought and continued upon our kingdoms by this unnatural war, and that it may open your ears, and dispose your minds to embrace those offers of peace and reconciliation which have been so often and earnestly made unto you by us, and from the constant and firm endeavours of which we are resolved never to desist; in pursuance whereof we do, upon this occasion, conjure you to take into consideration our too long neglected message of the 4th of July, from Evesham, which we again renew unto you; and that you will speedily send such an answer thereunto, as may show unto our poor subjects some light of deliverance from their present calamities by a happy accommodation, towards which we do here engage the word of a king to make good all these things which we have therein promised, and really to endeavour a happy conclusion of this treaty; and so God direct you in the ways of peace.

Given at our court at Tavistock, September 8, 1644.

VII. TO THE MARQUESS OF NEWCASTLE

CHARLES R.

Right trusty and entirely beloved cousin and counsellor, we greet you well. The misfortune of our forces in the North, we know, is repented as sadly by you, as the present hazard of the loss of so considerable a portion of this our kingdom deserves: which also affects us the more, because in that loss so great proportion falls upon yourself, whose loyalty and eminent merit we have ever held, and shall still, in a very high degree of our Royal esteem. And albeit the distracted condition of our affairs and kingdom will not afford us means at this present to comfort you in your sufferings, yet we shall ever retain so gracious a memory of your merit, as when it shall please God, in mercy, to restore us to peace, it shall be one of our principal endeavours to consider how to recompense those that have, with so great affection and courage as yourself, assisted us in the time of our greatest necessity and troubles; and, in the meantime, if there be anything wherein we may express the reality of our good intentions to you, or the value we have of your person, we shall most readily do it upon any occasion that shall be ministered; and so we bid you heartily farewell.

Given at our court at Oxford, the 28th day of November, 1644.

By His Majesty's command,

EDW. NICHOLAS.

Newcastle retired to the Continent after the battle of Marston Moor.

To contemporaries the success of the King in Cornwall seemed to offset his failure in Yorkshire, and there appeared, at the beginning of 1645, to be little chance of the war ending in other than a stalemate. In these circumstances a further effort was made to terminate it by some negotiations, which were held

at Uxbridge, when Charles put forward the following pro-
positions.

VIII

1. That His Majesty's own revenue, magazines, towns, forts and ships, which have been taken or kept from him by force, be forthwith restored unto him.

2. That whatsoever hath been done or published contrary to the known laws of the land, or derogatory to His Majesty's legal and known power and rights, be renounced and recalled; that no seed may remain for the like to spring out of for the future.

3. That whatsoever illegal power hath been claimed or exercised by or over his subjects, as imprisoning or putting to death their persons without law, stopping their Habeas Corpuses, and imposing upon their estates without Act of Parliament, etc., either by both or either House, or any committee of both or either, or by any persons appointed by any of them, be disclaimed, and all such persons so committed be forthwith discharged.

4. That as His Majesty hath always professed his readiness to that purpose, so he will most cheerfully consent to any good Acts to be made for the suppression of Popery, and for the firmer settling of the Protestant religion established by law; as also that a good Bill may be framed for the better preserving of the Book of Common Prayer from scorn and violence; and that another Bill may be framed for the ease of tender consciences, in such particulars as shall be agreed upon. For all which His Majesty conceives the best expedient to be, that a National Synod be legally called with all convenient speed.

5. That all such persons, as upon the Treaty shall be excepted and agreed upon on either side out of the general pardon, shall be tried *per pares*, according to the usual course and known law of the land, and that it be left to that either to acquit or condemn them.

6. And to the intent that this Treaty may not suffer interruption by any intervening accidents, that a cessation of arms

and free trade for all His Majesty's subjects may be agreed upon with all possible speed.

Given at the Court at Oxford, the 21st day of January, 1645.

IX. TO THE MARQUESS OF ORMONDE

Oxford, January 9, 1645.

ORMONDE,

Upon the great rumours and expectations which are now of a peace, I think it necessary to tell you the true state of it, lest mistaken reports from hence might trouble my affairs there.

The rebels here have agreed to treat, and most assuredly one of the first and chiefest articles they will insist on, will be to continue the Irish war; which is a point not popular for me to break on; of which you are to make double use; first, to hasten (with all possible diligence) the peace there, the timely conclusion of which will take off that inconvenience, which otherwise I may be subject to, by the refusal of that article upon any other reason. Secondly, by dexterously conveying to the Irish the danger there may be of their total and perpetual exclusion from those favours I intend them, in case the rebels here clap up peace with me upon reasonable terms, and only exclude them, which possibly were not advisable for me to refuse, if the Irish peace should be the only difference betwixt us, before it were perfected there. These, I hope, are sufficient grounds for you to persuade the Irish diligently to dispatch a peace upon reasonable terms, assuring them that you having once engaged to them my word in the conclusion of a peace, all the earth shall not make me break it. But not doubting of a peace, I must again remind you to press the Irish for their speedy assistance to me here, and their friends in Scotland, my intention being to draw from thence into Wales (the peace once concluded) as many as I can of my armed Protestant subjects, and desire that the Irish would send as great a body as they can to land about Cumberland; which will put those northern counties into a brave condition. Wherefore you must take speedy order to provide all the shipping you may, as well Dunkirk, as Irish, bottoms; and remember that after March it will be most difficult to transport men from Ireland to England.

the rebels being masters of the seas.   So expecting a diligent and particular account in answer to this letter, I rest

Your most assured, constant friend,

CHARLES R.

In case, upon particular men's fancies, the Irish peace should not be ended upon the powers I have already given you, I have thought good to give you this further order (which I hope will prove needless), to endeavour to renew the cessation for a year; for which you shall promise the Irish (if you can have it no cheaper) to join with them against the Scots and Inchiquin; for I hope by that time my condition may be such as the Irish may be glad to accept less, or I be able to give more.

C.R.

x. TO THE MARQUESS OF ORMONDE

Oxford, January 18, 1645.

ORMONDE,

I am sorry to find by Colonel Barry the sad condition of your particular fortune; for which I cannot find so good and speedy remedy as the peace of Ireland (it being likewise most necessary to redress my affairs here); wherefore I command you to dispatch it out of hand; for the doing of which, I hope my public dispatch will give you sufficient instruction and power; yet I have thought it necessary (for your more encouragement in this necessary work) to make this addition with my own hand.

As for Poynings Act, I refer you to my other letter : and for matter of religion, though I have not found it fit to take public notice of the paper which Brown gave you, yet I must command you to give him, the Lord Muskerry and Plunket, particular thanks for it, assuring them that without it there could have been no peace; and that sticking to it, their nation in general, and they in particular, shall have comfort in what they have done. And to show that this is more than words, I do hereby promise them (and command you to see it done) that the penal statutes against Romish Catholics shall not be put in execution, the peace being made, and they remaining in their due obedience. And further, that when the Irish give me that assistance, which they

151

have promised, for the suppressing of this rebellion, and I shall be restored to my rights, then I will consent to the repeal of them by a law.   But all those against appeals to Rome and *præmunire* must stand.   All this in cipher you must impart to none but those three already named, and that with injunction of strictest secrecy.

So again recommending to your care the speedy dispatch of the peace of Ireland, and my necessary supply from thence, as I wrote to you in my last private letter, I rest

Your most assured, constant friend,

CHARLES R.

Poyning's Act had been passed in 1495, and it had placed the Irish legislature in complete subordination to England, for it provided that all measures brought before the former must previously have received the approval of the King and the English Privy Council.   Poyning's Act was repealed in 1782.

The negotiations between the King and Parliament broke down, and both sides prepared for the final struggle.

XI. TO THE MARQUESS OF ORMONDE

Oxford, February 27, 1645.

ORMONDE,

The impossibility of preserving my Protestant subjects in Ireland by a continuation of the war, having moved me to give you those powers and directions, which I have formerly done, for the concluding of a peace there; and the same growing daily much more evident, that alone were reason enough for me to enlarge your powers, and make my commands in the point more positive.   But besides these considerations, it being now manifest that the English rebels have (as far as in them lies) given the command of Ireland to the Scots; that their aim is a total subversion of religion and regal power; and that nothing less will content them or purchase peace here, I think myself bound in conscience not to let slip the means of settling that kingdom (if it may be) fully under my obedience, nor to lose that assistance, which I may hope from my Irish subjects for such scruples as (in a less pressing condition) might reasonably be stuck at by me for their satisfaction. I do therefore command you to conclude a peace with the Irish, whatever it cost, so that my Protestant subjects there may be secured, and my regal authority preserved. But for all this, you are to make me the best bargain you can, and not to discover your enlargement of power till you needs must; and though I leave the managing of this great and necessary work entirely to you, yet I cannot but tell you, that if the suspension of Poyning's Act for such Bills as shall be agreed on between you there, and the present taking away of the penal laws against Papists by a law will do it, I shall not think it a hard bargain, so that freely and vigorously they engage themselves in my assistance against my rebels of England and Scotland, for which no conditions can be too hard, not being against conscience and honour. So I rest

Your most assured, constant friend,
CHARLES R.

On June 14th, 1645, the King was decisively defeated at Naseby.

XII. TO THE MARQUESS OF ORMONDE

Bewdley, June 18, 1645.

ORMONDE,

The late misfortune which I have had makes the Irish assistance more necessary than before; and now the speedy performance of it is almost of as great importance as the thing itself; the which I most earnestly recommend to your wonted care and diligence. For if within these two months you could send me a considerable assistance, I am confident that both my last loss would be soon forgotten, and likewise it may (by the grace of God) put such a turn to my affairs, as to make me in a far better condition before winter than I have been at any time since this rebellion began. And (to deal freely with you) otherwise I am likely to be put to great straits. This bearer, FitzWilliams, came recommended to me by my wife: what interest he hath in that country you will be better able to judge than I; they say very great, but certainly he is a man of great courage and perfect affections to my service;

and as such, I confidently recommend him to you; but what charge to give him, or how to employ him, I leave to your judgement to do, as you shall find best for his service, who is

> Your most real, constant friend,
> CHARLES R.

I desire you to send me speedy and frequent advertisements to what port to direct the ships for transporting your men.

The King's chief hope of restoring his position lay in the arrival of Irish troops, and the Earl of Glamorgan was sent to Ireland to organize an army there.

XIII. TO THE EARL OF GLAMORGAN

Hereford, June 23, 1645.

GLAMORGAN,

I am glad to hear that you are gone to Ireland; and assure you that as myself is no ways disheartened by our late misfortune, so neither is this country, for I could not have expected more from them than they have now freely undertaken, though I had come hither absolute victorious, which makes me hope well of the neighbouring shires, so that (by the grace of God) I hope shortly to recover my late loss with advantage, if such succours come to me from that kingdom which I have reason to expect: but the circumstances of time is that of the greatest consequence, being that which is now the chiefliest and earnestliest recommended to you by

> Your most assured, real, constant friend,
> CHARLES R.

XIV. TO THE MARQUESS OF ORMONDE

Cardiff, July 31, 1645.

ORMONDE,

It hath pleased God, by many successive misfortunes, to reduce my affairs, of late, from a very prosperous condition to so low an ebb as to be a perfect trial of all men's integrity to me, and you being a person whom I consider as most entirely and

generously resolved to stand and fall with your King, I do principally rely upon you, for your uttermost assistance in my present
hazards : I have commanded Digby to acquaint you at large,
with all particulars of my condition; what I have to hope, trust
to, or fear; wherein you will find, that if my expectation of
relief out of Ireland be not in some good measure and speedily
answered, I am likely to be reduced to great extremities. I hope
some of those expresses I sent you since my misfortune by the
battle of Naseby are come to you, and am therefore confident
that you are in a good forwardness, for the sending over to me
a considerable supply of men, artillery, and ammunition : all
that I have to add, is, that the necessity of your speedy performing
them, is made much more pressing by new disasters; so that
I absolutely command you (what hazard soever that kingdom
may run by it) personally to bring me all the forces, of what
sort soever you can draw from thence, and leave the government
there (during your absence) in the fittest hands, that you shall
judge, to discharge it; for I may want you here to command those
forces which will be brought from thence, and such as from hence
shall be joined to them : but you must not understand this as a
permission, for you, to grant to the Irish (in case they will not,
otherwise, have a peace) anything more, in matter of religion,
than what I have allowed you already, except only, in some convenient parishes, where the much greater number are Papists, I
give you power to permit them to have some places, which they
may use as chapels, for their devotions, if there be no other
impediment for obtaining a peace; but I will rather choose to
suffer all extremities, than ever to abandon my religion and particularly either to English or Irish rebels, to which effect I have
commanded Digby to urge to their agents, that were employed
hither, giving you power to cause deliver or suppress the letter,
as you shall judge best, for my service : to conclude, if the Irish
shall so unworthily [*sic*] take advantage of my weak condition,
as to press me to that, which I cannot grant, with a safe conscience, and without it, to reject a peace, I command you, if you
can, to procure a further cessation; if not, to make what divisions
you can, among them; and rather leave to the chance of war,
between them and those forces, which you have not power to

draw to my assistance, than to give my consent to any such allowance of Popery, as must evidently bring destruction to that profession, which, by the grace of God, I shall ever maintain, through
all extremities.   I know, Ormonde, that I impose a very hard
task upon you, but if God prosper me, you will be a happy and
glorious subject; if otherwise, you will perish nobly and generously,
with and for him, who is,

Your constant, real, faithful friend,

CHARLES R.

*In September the King suffered a further serious reverse, for
on the eleventh of that month Rupert surrendered Bristol to
Fairfax on condition of a safe departure for the garrison.*

XV. TO SIR EDWARD NICHOLAS

Hereford, September 14, 1645.

NICHOLAS,

When you shall have considered the strange and most in-
excusable delivery up of the castle and fort of Bristol, and com-
pared it with those many preceding advertisements which have
been given me, I make no doubt but you and all my Council
there will conclude that I could do no less than what you find
here enclosed, in my care of the preservation of my son, of all
you my faithful servants there, and of that important place, my
city of Oxford.

In the first place, you will find a copy of my letter to my
nephew; secondly, a revocation of his commission of general;
thirdly, a warrant to Lieutenant-Colonel Hamilton to exercise
the charge of lieutenant-governor of Oxford in Sir Thomas
Glenham's absence; fourthly, a warrant to the said Lieutenant-
Colonel Hamilton to apprehend the person of Will Legge, present
governor of Oxford; and, lastly, a warrant to be directed to what
person shall be thought fittest for the apprehending my nephew
Rupert, in case of such extremity as shall be hereafter specified,
and not otherwise.

As for the circumstances and the timing of the execution of
all these particulars, as far forth as they may admit of some hours'

delay more or less, I must refer it to my Lord Treasurer's care and yours to advise of, upon the place, how it may be done with most security and accordingly to direct the manner of proceeding. But yet I shall tell you my opinion as far forth as I can judge at this distance, which is, that you should begin with securing the person of Will Legge, before anything be declared concerning my nephew. But that once done, then the sooner you declare to the Lords both the revoking of my nephew's commission, and my making Sir Thomas Glenham governor of Oxford, the better. As for the delivery of my letter to my nephew, if he be at Oxford, I take the proper time for that to be as soon as possibly may be after the securing of Will Legge. But if my nephew be not there, I would then have you hasten my letter unto him; and, in the meantime, put the rest in execution. The warrant for my nephew's commitment is only that you may have the power to do it, if, instead of submitting to and obeying my commands in going beyond sea, you shall find that he practise the raising of mutiny, or any other disturbance in that place, or any other, in which case, the said warrant for his commitment is to be delivered unto whom you and my Lord Treasurer shall think fittest to be directed unto, and by that person to be put in execution.

Lastly, I enjoin you the care to let all the Lords know, that whatever is done in this kind is out of my tender regard of their safety and preservation; and they shall speedily receive for their satisfaction a particular account of the reasons of this necessary proceeding. I rest

Your most assured friend,
CHARLES R.

Tell my son that I shall less grieve to hear that he is knocked on the head than that he should do so mean an action as is the rendering of Bristol castle and fort upon the terms it was.

C.R.

The above indicates sufficiently clearly the contents of the King's letter to Rupert, but the opening lines of the latter may well be quoted to illustrate its severity:

Though the loss of Bristol be a great blow to me, yet your surrendering it as you did is of so much affliction to me, that it makes me forget not only the consideration of that place, but is likewise the greatest trial of my constancy that has yet befallen me.   For, what is to be done after one, that is so near to me as you are both in blood and friendship, submits himself to so mean an action (I give it the easiest term)?   I have so much to say, that I will say no more of it, lest rashness of judgement be laid to my charge; only I must remember you of your letter of the 12th of August, whereby you assured me that (if no mutiny happened) you would keep Bristol for four months; did you keep it for four days?   Was there anything like mutiny?   More questions might be asked; but now, I confess, to little purpose.

XVI. To Prince Maurice

Newton, September 20, 1645.

Nephew,

What through want of time, or unwillingness to speak to you of so unpleasing a subject, I have not yet (which now I must supply) spoken to you freely of your brother Rupert's present condition.   The truth is, that his unhandsome quitting the castle and fort of Bristol hath enforced me to put him off those commands in my army, and have sent him a pass to go beyond seas; now, though I could do no less than this, for which, believe me, I have too much reason upon strict examination, yet I assure you that I am most confident that this great error of his (which, indeed, hath given me more grief than any misfortune since this damnable rebellion) hath no ways proceeded from his change of affection to me or my cause; but merely by having his judgement seduced by rotten-hearted villains making fair pretensions to him; and I am resolved so little to forget his former services, that, whensoever it shall please God to enable me to look upon my friends like a king, he shall thank God for the pains he hath spent in my armies.   So much for him.   Now for yourself.   I know you to be so free from his present misfortune, that it no way staggers me in that good opinion which I have ever had of you; and, so long as you shall not be weary of your employments

under me, I will give you all the encouragement and contentment that lies in my power; however, you shall always find me
Your loving uncle, and most assured friend,

CHARLES R.

*The King's position was now almost hopeless, and only Irish
help could enable him to continue the struggle, for Montrose had
been beaten at Philiphaugh.*

XVII. TO THE MARQUESS OF ORMONDE

Oxford, December 1, 1645.

ORMONDE,

Your long silence (albeit I believe it is not your fault) hath
proved a misfortune to me, thereby wanting those probable
foundations whereby to govern my resolutions. I have therefore made this dispatch (and it is even late enough), that I may
know, with all speed, what I may trust to from Ireland, and to
tell you freely how that kingdom may be of use or prejudice to
me and my directions thereon. Then know my present condition to be such, that assistance from thence can do me no good
unless it come before the beginning of April next; and that
nothing can be of more prejudice to my affairs than that the
peace of Ireland should be concluded without a most certain
assurance of a timely and considerable assistance; as a fruitless
depriving me of the most principal means of persuading the
English rebels to return to their wits. Wherefore, as you are
earnestly to endeavour the present conclusion of the peace, with
positive assurance that before April next I shall have 6,000 well
armed foot from thence (which is that I much wish); so if you
find that people either willing or able to give me this considerable assistance before the beginning of April next, you must upon
no terms conclude the peace without first advertising

Your most assured, faithful, constant friend,

CHARLES R.

You are to observe, that the reason of this particular letter is,
to enlarge you (as much as may be) both in the circumstance of
time and numbers of men; so really I desire the peace of that

country, so that it may conduce, or at least be no hindrance, to that of this, which it will absolutely do (than which I know no greater inconvenience can befall me) except I be assisted from thence by that time, and with those numbers which is herein set down.

Meanwhile, the powers given to Glamorgan had offended Ormonde, and that the former were extensive is clear.

XVIII. To the Pope

MOST HOLY FATHER,

So many and so great proofs of the fidelity and affection of our cousin the Earl of Glamorgan we have received, and such confidence do we deservedly repose in him, that Your Holiness may justly give faith and credence to him in any matter, whereupon he is to treat, in our name, with Your Holiness, either by himself in person or by any other.   Moreover, whatever shall have been positively settled and determined by him, the same we promise to sanction and perform.   In testimony whereof, we have written this very brief letter, confirmed by our own hand and seal; and we have in our wishes and prayers nothing before this, that by your favour we may be restored into that state, in which we may openly avow ourself

Your very humble and obedient servant,

CHARLES R.

At our court at Oxford, October 20th 1645.

Ormonde protested against this diminution of his own authority, and Charles endeavoured to pacify him.

XIX. To the Marquess of Ormonde

January 30, 1646.

ORMONDE,

I cannot but add to my long letter, that upon the word of a Christian, I never intended that Glamorgan should treat anything without your approbation, much less without your knowledge. For besides the injury to you, I was always diffident of his judgement (though I could not think him so extremely weak), as now to my cost I have found him; which you may easily perceive by a postscript in a letter of mine to you, that he should have delivered to you at this his last coming into Ireland; which if you have not had, the reason of it will be worth the knowing, for which I have commanded Digby's service, desiring you to assist him.   And albeit I have too just cause, for the clearing of my honour, to command (as I have done) to prosecute Glamorgan in a legal way; yet I will have you suspend the execution of any sentence against him until you inform me fully of all the proceedings.   For, I believe, it was his misguided zeal, more than any malice, which brought this great misfortune on him and us all.   For your part you have in this, as in all other actions, given me such satisfaction, that I mean other ways, more than by words, to express my estimation of you.   So I rest

Your most assured, constant, faithful friend,

CHARLES R.

No help came from Ireland, for all the English ports were in the hands of the Parliament.   In these circumstances Charles had no other recourse but to treat with his opponents once more.

XX. TO THE SPEAKER OF THE HOUSE OF PEERS

CHARLES R.

His Majesty cannot but extremely wonder, that, after so many expressions on your part of a deep and seeming sense of the miseries of this afflicted kingdom, and of the dangers incident to his person, during the continuance of this unnatural war; your many great and so often repeated protestations, that the raising of these arms hath been only for the necessary defence of God's true religion, His Majesty's honour, safety, and prosperity, the peace, comfort, and security of his people; you should delay a safe conduct to the persons mentioned in His Majesty's message of the fifth of this instant December, which are to be sent unto you with propositions for a well-grounded peace; a thing so far from having been denied at any time by His Majesty whensoever you have desired the same, that he believes it hath been seldom (if ever) practised amongst the most avowed and professed enemies, much less from subjects to their King : but His Majesty is resolved, that no discouragements whatsoever shall make him fail of his part, in doing his utmost endeavours to put an end to these calamities, which, if not in time prevented, must prove the ruin of this unhappy nation; and therefore doth once again desire, that a safe conduct may be forthwith sent for those persons expressed in his former message; and doth here conjure you, as you will answer to Almighty God in that day when He shall make inquisition for all the blood that hath and may yet be spilt in this unnatural war, as you tender the preservation and establishment of the true religion, by all the bonds of duty and allegiance to your King, or compassion to your bleeding and unhappy country, and of charity to yourselves, that you dispose your hearts to a true sense, and employ all your faculties in a most serious endeavour, together with His Majesty, to set a speedy end to these waiting divisions; and then he shall not doubt but that God will yet again give the blessing of peace to this now distracted kingdom.

Given at the Court at Oxford, the 15th day of December, 1645.

XXI. To the Speaker of the House of Peers

CHARLES R.

Notwithstanding the strange and unexpected delays (which can be precedented by no former times) to His Majesty's two former messages, His Majesty will lay aside all expostulations, as rather serving to lose time, than to contribute any remedy to the evils which for the present do afflict this distracted kingdom : therefore, without further preamble, His Majesty thinks it most necessary to send those propositions this way, which he intended to do by the persons mentioned in his former messages : though he well knows the great disadvantage which overtures of this kind have, by the want of being accompanied by well-instructed messengers.

His Majesty conceiving that the former treaties have hitherto proved ineffectual chiefly for want of power in those persons that treated, as likewise because those from whom their power was derived (not possibly having the particular information of every several debate) could not give so clear a judgement as was requisite in so important a business: if therefore His Majesty may have the engagement of the two Houses of Parliament at Westminster, the Commissioners of the Parliament of Scotland, the Mayor, Aldermen, Common Council, and Militia of London, of the chief commanders in Sir Thomas Fairfax's army, as also those in the Scots army, for His Majesty's free and safe coming to, and abode in, London or Westminster (with such of his servants now attending him, and their followers, not exceeding in all the number of three hundred), for the space of forty days; and, after the said time, for his free and safe repair to any of his garrisons of Oxford, Worcester, or Newark, which His Majesty shall nominate at any time before his going from London or Westminster; His Majesty propounds to have a personal treaty with the two Houses of Parliament at Westminster and the Commissioners of the Parliament of Scotland, upon all matters which may conduce to the restoring of peace and happiness to these miserably distracted kingdoms; and to begin with the three heads which were treated on at Uxbridge: and for the better clearing of His Majesty's earnest and sincere intentions of putting an end to these unnatural distractions, knowing that point of security may prove the greatest obstacle to this most blessed work, His Majesty therefore declares, that he is willing to commit the great trust of the Militia of this kingdom, for such time, and with such powers, as are expressed in the paper delivered by His Majesty's Commissioners at Uxbridge, the 6th of February last, to these persons following: *videlicet*, the Lord Privy Seal, the Duke of Richmond, the Marquess of Hertford, the Marquess of Dorchester, the Earl of Dorset Lord Chamberlain, the Earl of Northumberland, the Earl of Essex, Earl of Southampton, Earl of Pembroke, Earl of Salisbury, Earl of Manchester, Earl of Warwick, Earl of Denbigh, Earl of Chichester, Lord Saye, Lord Seymour, Lord Lucas, Lord Lexington, Mr. Denzell Holles, Mr. Pierepont, Mr. Henry Bellasis, Mr. Richard Spencer, Sir Thomas Fairfax, Mr. John Ashburnham, Sir Gervoise Clifton, Sir Henry Vane, Junior, Mr. Robert Wallop, Mr. Thomas Chicheley, Mr. Oliver Cromwell, and Mr. Philip Skippon; supposing that these are persons against whom they can take no just exception : but, if this doth not satisfy, then His Majesty offers to name the one half, and leave the other to the election of the two Houses of Parliament at Westminster, with the powers and limitations before mentioned.

Thus His Majesty calls God and the world to witness of his sincere intentions and real endeavours for the composing and settling of these miserable distractions; which he doubts not but, by the blessing of God, will soon be put to a happy conclusion, if this His Majesty's offer be accepted; otherwise he leaves all the world to judge who are the continuers of this unnatural war : and therefore he once more conjures you, by all the bonds of duty you owe to God and your King, to have so great a compassion on the bleeding and miserable estate of your country, that you join your most serious and hearty endeavours with His Majesty to put a happy and speedy end to these present miseries.

Given at the Court at Oxford, the 26th of December, 1645.

This letter was endorsed ' to be communicated to the two Houses of Parliament at Westminster, and the Commissioners of the Parliament of Scotland.'

XXII. TO THE QUEEN

Oxford, January 4, 1646.

DEAR HEART,

I desired thee to take notice that with the year I begin to new number my letters, hoping to begin a year's course of good luck. I have heard of but seen no letters from thee since Christmas Day; the reason is evident, for our intelligence with the Portugal's agent is obstructed, so that I am not so confident as I was that any of my letters will come safe to thee. But methinks, if Cardinal Mazarin were but half so kind to us as he professes to be, it would be no great difficulty for him to secure our weekly intelligence. And in earnest I desire thee to put him to it, for besides that, if the effects of it succeed, it will be of great consequence to me, I shall very much judge of the reality of his intentions according to his answer in this. If Ashburnham complain to thee of my wilfulness, I am sure it is that way which at least thou wilt excuse, if not justify in me; but, if thou hadst seen a former paper (to which being but an accessory I must not blame his judgement), thou wouldst have commended my choleric rejection of it, the aversion to which it is possible (though I will not confess it until thou sayest so) might have made me too nice in this, of which I will say no more; but consider well that which I sent in the place of it, and then judge.

My great affairs are so much in expectation that for the present I can give thee but little account of them, albeit yet in conjecture (as I believe) that the rebels will not admit of my personal treaty at London, and I hope well of having 2,000 foot and horse, out of my smaller garrisons.   As for the Scots, we yet hear no news of them, neither concerning this treaty, nor of that which I have begun with David Lesley.   And, lastly, that the Duke of York's journey is absolutely broken both in respect of the loss of Hereford, as that the relief of Chester is yet but very doubtful.   But upon this design, having commanded Sir George Radcliffe to wait upon him, I desire thy approbation that he may be sworn gentleman of his bedchamber, for which, though he be very fit, and I assure thee that he is far from being a Puritan, and that it will be much for my son's good to have him settled about him, yet I would not have him sworn without thy consent.   So God bless thee, sweetheart.

CHARLES R.

Even now Montreuil is come hither concerning this treaty. The Queen cannot have a particular account of it till my next.

There had been a suggestion that the Duke of York, who was with his father at Oxford, should go to Ireland, but the loss of Hereford rendered it impracticable.

XXIII. TO THE QUEEN

Oxford, January 11, 1646.

DEAR HEART,

I had no time before Friday last to decipher thine of the 25th of November, which I must answer how late soever (for kindness is never out of date), every line in it being a several way of expressing thy love to me, even there where we differ in judgement, which I know we should not do if thou wert not mistaken in the state of the question; I mean concerning Episcopacy, for I am of thy opinion to a tittle in everything else.   For the difference between me and the rebels concerning the Church is not bare matter of form or ceremony, which are alterable according to occasion, but so real, that if I should give way as is desired, here would be no Church, and by no human probability ever to be recovered; so that, besides the obligation of mine oath, I know nothing to be an higher point of conscience. This being granted, I am sure thy persuasions will be turned into praises of my constancy. And for the truth of my affection, the doubt of which is the only argument against me, I can make it as clear to any not wilful person, as two and three makes five.   But this I am sure of, which none can deny, that my yielding this is a sin of the highest nature, 'if I believe constant as I have said, which really I do.   And, dear heart, thou canst not but be confident that there is no danger which I will not hazard, or pains that I will not undergo, to enjoy the happiness of thy company, there being nothing which really conduceth thereunto which I will not do, which may not make me less worthy of thee.   And to this end I prosecute the Scotch treaty with all the industry and dexterity which God hath given me, not differing in opinion concerning it.   My intended journey to London is likewise for this.   Than which, believe me, no undertaking can be less hazardous (the greatest fear being of my doing some *lache* action, which thy love will hinder thee to apprehend and mine to give the occasion), nor of so great probability of good success.   One of my securities I forgot in my last to mention to thee, which is, that this Parliament without doubt determines with my life, if I give it not some new additional strength, which I protest never to do, but, for the contrary, to follow precisely thy advice therein.

Henrietta Maria had been urging Charles to sacrifice Episcopacy for the sake of a settlement.

XXIV. TO THE SPEAKER OF THE HOUSE OF PEERS

CHARLES REX.

His Majesty thinks not fit now to answer those aspersions which are returned as arguments for his non-admittance to Westminster for a personal treaty, because it would enforce a style not suitable to his end; it being the peace of his miserable kingdoms : yet thus much he cannot but say to those who have sent him this answer, that if they had considered what they have done themselves (in occasioning the shedding of so much innocent blood, by withdrawing themselves from their duty to him; in a time when he had granted so much to his subjects, and in violating the known laws of the kingdom, to draw an exorbitant power to themselves over their fellow subjects (to say no more) to do as they have done), they could not have given such a false character of His Majesty's actions. Wherefore His Majesty must now remember them, that, having some hours before his receiving of their last paper of the 13th of January, sent another message to them of the 15th, wherein, by divers particulars, he enlarges himself, to show the reality for his endeavours for peace, by his desired personal treaty (which he still conceives to be the likeliest way to attain that blessed end); he thinks fit by this message to call for an answer to that, and indeed to all his former; for certainly no rational man can think their last paper can be any answer to his former demands; the scope of it being, that, because there is a war, therefore there should be no treaty for peace, and is impossible to expect that the propositions mentioned should be the ground of a lasting peace; when the persons that send them will not endure to hear their own King speak : but whatever the success hath been of His Majesty's former messages, or how small soever his hopes are of a better, considering the high strain of those who deal with His Majesty; yet he will neither want fatherly bowels to his subjects in general, nor will he forget that God hath appointed him for their King with whom he treats : wherefore he now demands a speedy answer to his last and former messages.

Given at the Court at Oxford this 17th of January, 1646.

xxv. To the Speaker of the House of Peers

CHARLES R.

The procuring peace to these kingdoms by treaty is so much desired by His Majesty, that no unjust aspersions whatsoever, or any other discouragements, shall make him desist from doing his endeavours therein; and therefore have thought fitting so far only to make reply to that paper or answer which he hath received of the 13th of this instant January, as may take away those objections which are made against His Majesty's coming to Westminster; expecting still an answer to his messages of the 15th and 17th, which he hopes by this time have begotten better thoughts and resolutions in the members of both Houses.

And first, therefore, whereas in the said last paper it is objected (as an impediment to His Majesty's personal treaty) that much innocent blood hath been shed in this war by His Majesty's commissions, etc.; he will not now dispute, it being apparent to all the world by whom all this blood hath been spilt; but rather presseth that there should be no more; and to that end only he hath desired this personal treaty, as judging it the most immediate means to abolish so many horrid confusions in all his kingdoms. And it is no argument to say, ' There shall be no such personal treaty because there have been wars '; it being a strong inducement to have such a treaty, to put an end to the war.

Secondly, that there should be no such personal treaty because some of his Irish subjects have repaired to his assistance, it seems an argument altogether as strange as the other; as always urging that there should be no physic administered because the party is sick : and in this particular it hath been often observed unto them, that those whom they call Irish (who have so expressed their loyalty to their sovereign) were indeed for the most part such English Protestants as had been formerly sent into Ireland by the two Houses, and unable to stay there any longer, by the neglect of those that sent them thither, who should there have better provided for them : and for any foreign forces, it is too apparent that their armies have swarmed with them, when His Majesty hath had very few or none.

And whereas, for a third impediment, it is alleged, that the

Prince is in the head of an army in the West; and that there are divers garrisons still kept in His Majesty's obedience, and that there are forces in Scotland; it must be as much confessed as that there is yet no peace; and therefore it is desired that, by such a personal treaty, all these impediments may be removed. And it is not here amiss to put them in mind, how long since His Majesty did press a disbanding of all forces on both sides, the refusing whereof hath been the cause of this objection. And whereas exception is taken, that there is a time limited in the proposition for His Majesty's personal treaty, thereupon inferring that he should again return to hostility; His Majesty protesteth, that he seeks this treaty to avoid future hostility, and procuring a lasting peace; and if he can meet with like inclinations to peace in those he desires to treat with, he will bring such affections and resolutions in himself as shall end all these unhappy bloody differences. As for those engagements which His Majesty hath desired for his security whosoever will call to mind the particular occasions that enforced His Majesty to leave his cities of London and Westminster will judge his demand therein very reasonable, and necessary for his safety: but he no way conceives how the Lord Mayor, Aldermen, Common Council, and Militia of London, are either subject or subordinate to that authority as is alleged, as knowing neither law nor practice for it; and if the two armies be, he believes it is more than can be paralleled by any former times in this kingdom: nor can His Majesty understand how his seeking of personal security can be any breach of privilege, it being likelier to be infringed by hindering His Majesty from coming freely to his two Houses.

As for the objection, that His Majesty omitted to mention the settling religion and securing the peace of his native kingdom, His Majesty declares that he conceives it was involved in his former, and hath been particularly mentioned in his latter message of the 15th present; but, for their better satisfaction, he again expresses that it was, and ever shall be, both his meaning and endeavours in this treaty desired.

And it seems to him very clear, that there is no way for a final ending of such distractions as now afflict this kingdom, but either by treaty or conquest; the latter of which His Majesty hopes none will have the impudence or impiety to wish for; and for the former, if his personal assistance in it be not the most likely way, let any reasonable man judge, when by that means not only all unnecessary delays will be removed, but even the greatest difficulties made easy : and therefore he doth now again earnestly insist upon that proposition, expecting to receive a better answer upon mature consideration.

And can it be imagined that any propositions will be so effectual, being formed before a personal treaty, as such as are framed and propounded upon a full debate on both sides?

Wherefore His Majesty, who is most concerned in the good of his people, and is most desirous to restore peace and happiness to his three kingdoms, doth again instantly desire and answer to his said former messages, to which he hath hitherto received none.

Given at our Court at Oxford, the 24th of January, 1646.

XXVI. To the Speaker of the House of Peers

Charles R.

His Majesty having received information from the Lord Lieutenant and Council in Ireland, that the Earl of Glamorgan hath, without his or their directions or privity, entered into a treaty with some commissioners of the Catholic party there, and also drawn up, and agreed unto, certain articles with the said commissioners, highly derogatory to His Majesty's honour and Royal dignity, and most prejudicial unto the Protestant religion and Church there in Ireland; whereupon the said Earl of Glamorgan is arrested, upon suspicion of high treason, and imprisoned, by the Lord Lieutenant and Council, at the instance, and by the impeachment of the Lord Digby, who (by reason of his place and former employment in those affairs) doth best know how contrary that proceeding of the Earl hath been to His Majesty's intentions and directions, and what great prejudice it might bring to his affairs, if these proceedings of the Earl of Glamorgan's should be any ways understood to have been done by the directions, liking, or approbation, of His Majesty.

His Majesty, having in his former messages for a personal treaty offered to give contentment to his two Houses in the business of Ireland, hath now thought fitting, the better to show his clear intentions, and to give satisfaction to his said Houses of Parliament and the rest of his subjects in all his kingdoms, to send this declaration to the said Houses, containing the whole truth of the business; which is:

That the Earl of Glamorgan, having made offer unto him to raise forces in the kingdom of Ireland, and to conduct them into England for His Majesty's service, had a commission to that purpose, and to that purpose only.

That he had no commission at all to treat of anything else, without the privity and directions of the Lord Lieutenant; much less to capitulate anything concerning religion, or any property belonging either to Church or laity.

That it clearly appears by the Lord Lieutenant's proceedings with the said Earl, that he had no notice at all of what the said Earl had treated, and pretended to have capitulated, with the Irish, until by accident it came to his knowledge.

And His Majesty doth protest, that, until such time as he had advertisement that the person of the said Earl of Glamorgan was arrested, or restrained, as is above said, he never heard, nor had any kind of notice that the said Earl had entered into any kind of treaty or capitulation with those Irish commissioners; much less that he had concluded or signed those articles, so destructive both to Church and State, and so repugnant to His Majesty's professions and known resolutions.

And for the further vindication of His Majesty's honour and integrity, he doth declare, that he is so far from considering anything contained in those papers or writings framed by the said Earl, and those commissioners with whom he treated, as he doth absolutely disavow him therein; and hath given commandment to the Lord Lieutenant and the Council there, to proceed against the said Earl, as one who, either out of falseness, presumption, or folly, hath so hazarded the blemishing of His Majesty's reputation with his good subjects, and so impertinently framed those acts of his own head, without the consent, privity, or directions of His Majesty, or the Lord Lieutenant, or any of His

Majesty's Council there : but time it is that, for the necessary preservation of His Majesty's Protestant subjects in Ireland (whose case was daily represented unto him to be so desperate), His Majesty had given commission to the Lord Lieutenant, to treat and conclude such a peace there, as might be for the safety of that crown, and the preservation of the Protestant religion, and no way derogatory to his own honour and public professions.

But to the end that His Majesty's real intentions in this business of Ireland may be the more clearly understood, and to give more ample satisfaction to both Houses of Parliament, and the Commissioners of the Parliament of Scotland, especially concerning His Majesty's not being engaged in any peace or agreement there; he doth desire, if the two Houses shall resolve to admit of His Majesty's repair to London for a personal treaty, as was formerly proposed, that speedy notice be given thereof to His Majesty; and a pass, or safe conduct with a blank, sent for a messenger, to be immediately dispatched into Ireland, to prevent any accident that may happen to hinder His Majesty's resolutions of leaving the managing of the business of Ireland wholly to the Houses, and to make peace there but with their consent; which, in case it shall please God to bless his endeavours in the treaty with success, His Majesty doth hereby engage himself to do.

And for a further explanation of His Majesty's intentions in his former messages, he doth now declare that if his personal repair to London as aforesaid shall be admitted, and a peace thereon shall ensue, he will then leave the nomination of the persons to be entrusted with the Militia wholly to his two Houses, with such powers and limitations as are expressed in the paper delivered by His Majesty's Commissioners at Uxbridge, the 6th of February, 1645, for the term of seven years, as hath been desired, to begin immediately after the conclusion of the peace, the disbanding of all forces on both sides, and the dismantling of the garrisons erected since these present troubles; so as, at the expiration of the time before-mentioned, the power of the said Militia shall entirely revert and remain as before.

And for the better security, His Majesty (the peace succeeding) will be content, that *pro hac vice* the two Houses shall nominate the admiral, officers of State, and judges, to hold their places during life, or *quam diu se bene gesserint,* which shall be best liked; to be accountable to none but to the King and the two Houses of Parliament.

As for the matter of religion, His Majesty doth further declare, that, by the liberty offered in his message of the 15th present, for the ease of their consciences who will not communicate in the service already established by Act of Parliament in this realm, he intends that all other Protestants (behaving themselves peaceably in and towards the civil government) shall have the free exercise of their religion according to their own way.

And, for the total removing of all fears and jealousies, His Majesty is willing to agree that, upon the conclusion of peace, there shall be a general Act of Oblivion, and of free pardon, passed by Act of Parliaments, in both his kingdoms respectively.

And, lest it should be imagined that, in the making these propositions, His Majesty's kingdom of Scotland, and his subjects there, have been forgotten or neglected, His Majesty declares, that what is here mentioned touching the Militia, and the naming of officers of State and judges, shall likewise extend to his kingdom of Scotland.

And now, His Majesty having so fully and clearly expressed his intentions and desires of making a happy and well-grounded peace; if any person shall decline that happiness, by opposing of so apparent a way of attaining it, he will sufficiently demonstrate to all the world, his intention and design can be no other than the total subversion and change of the ancient and happy government of this kingdom, under which the English nation hath so long flourished.

Given at the Court at Oxford, the 29th of January, 1646.

The Queen was still urging Charles to save himself by the sacrifice of the Church.

XXVII. To the Queen

Oxford, February 19, 1646.

Dear Heart,

Albeit that my personal danger must of necessity precede thine, yet thy safety seems to be hazarded by my resolution concerning Church government. I am doubly grieved to differ with thee in opinion, though I am confident that my judgement, not love, is censured by thee for it. But I hope, whatsoever thou mayst wish, thou wilt not blame me at all, if thou rightly understand the state of the question. For I assure thee, I put little or no difference between setting up the Presbyterian government, or submitting to the Church of Rome. Therefore make the case thine own. With what patience wouldst thou give ear to him who should persuade thee, for worldly respects, to leave the communion of the Roman Church for any other? Indeed, sweetheart, this is my case; for, suppose my concession in this should prove but temporary, it may palliate though not excuse my sin. But it is strange to me how that can be imagined, not remembering any example that concessions in this kind have been recalled, which in this case is more unlikely (if not impossible) than any other, because the means of recovering it is destroyed in the first minute of yielding, it being not only a condition for my assistance, but likewise all the ecclesiastical power so put in their hands, who are irreconcilable enemies to that government which I contend for, as I shall never be able to master. I must confess (to my shame and grief) that heretofore I have for public respects (yet I believe, if thy personal safety had not been at stake, I might have hazarded the rest) yielded unto those things which were no less against my conscience than this, for which I have been so deservedly punished, that a relapse now would be insufferable, and I am most confident that God hath so favoured my hearty (though weak) repentance, that He will be glorified, either by relieving me out of these distresses (which I may humbly hope for, though not presume upon), or in my gallant sufferings for so good a cause, which to eschew by any mean submission cannot but draw God's further justice upon me, both in this and the next world. But let not this sad discourse trouble thee (for, as thou art free from my faults, so doubtless God hath blessings in store for thee), it being only a necessary freedom to show thee, that no slight cause can make me deny to do what thou desirest, who am eternally thine,

CHARLES R.

For God's sake, as thou lovest me, see what may be done for the landing of the 5,000 men, at the place and by the time as I wrote to thee the 1st of February, and with them as much money as possibly thou canst.   I assure thee that the well-doing of this is likely to save both my crown and liberty.

As will have already been gathered, Charles was in negotiation with the Scots as well as with the Parliament, and he now decided, as he could no longer maintain himself at Oxford, to trust himself to the former.

XXVIII. TO THE PRINCE OF WALES

Oxford, March 22, 1646.

CHARLES,

Hoping that this will find you safe with your mother, I think fit to write this short but necessary letter to you.   Then know, that your being where you are, safe from the power of the rebels, is, under God, either my greatest security, or my certain ruin. For, your constancy to religion, obedience to me, and to the rules of honour, will make these insolent men begin to hearken to reason, when they shall see their injustice not like to be crowned with quiet.   But, if you depart from those grounds, for which I have all this time fought, then your leaving this kingdom will be (with too much probability) called sufficient proofs for many of the slanders heretofore laid upon me.

Wherefore, once again I command you, upon my blessing, to be constant to your religion, neither hearkening to Roman superstitions nor the seditious and schismatical doctrines of the Presbyterians and Independents.   For I know that a persecuted Church is not thereby less pure, though less fortunate.   For all other things, I command you to be totally directed by your mother; and, as subordinate to her, by the remainder of that council which I put to you at your parting from hence.   And so, God bless you.

CHARLES R.

175

XXIX. To Lord Digby

Oxford, March 26, 1646.

Since my last to you by Colonel Butler, misfortunes have so multiplied upon me, that I have been forced to send this (to say no more) but strange message to London. Yet, whatever becomes of me, I must never forget my friends, wherever they are.

I am endeavouring to get to London, so that the conditions may be such as a gentleman may own, and that the rebels may acknowledge me as King, being not without hope that I shall be able so to draw either the Presbyterians or Independents to side with me, for extirpating the one or the other, that I shall be really King again.

Howsoever, I desire you to assure all my friends that, if I cannot live as a King, I shall die like a gentleman, without doing that which may make honest men blush for me.

On the morning of April 27th the King left Oxford in disguise and went as far as Hillingdon in the direction of London. There he made up his mind to trust himself to the Scots, with whom Montreuil had been negotiating on his behalf, rather than to the Parliament, and early on May 5th he reached their camp at Southwell. He was never to be a free man again.

CHAPTER VI
THE LAST YEARS
1646-1649

1646-1649

In surrendering to the Scots the King had placed himself in the hands of one of the three parties among his enemies; the other two were the Parliament and the Army, which was supposed to be the servant of the Parliament, but which was already well on the way to becoming the latter's master. The first act of the Scots was to withdraw to Newcastle, where they rightly felt Charles would be more at their mercy.

1. To Sir Edward Nicholas

Newcastle, May 15, 1646.

NICHOLAS,

Since my last, I had neither sufficient time nor matter to write to you; but now I have enough of either, yet I shall, to ease both our pains, contract my thoughts merely to what is (for the present) necessary for you at Oxford. For directions then, know that you are not to expect relief, so that I give you leave to treat for good conditions. Let those of Exeter be your example; the additions must be the taking care particularly of the University, and to try if you can get the Duke of York to be sent hither to me, as also all my servants who will be willing to come (of which number I am sure you are one), but fear you will not get leave, and those goods which I have there.

These directions I would have you keep very secret, that you may make better conditions; for the number and choice I leave to the Lord's discretions, the governor being one; but you must give out that relief will come. Jack Ashburnham is this day gone for France.

I have no more to say; so I rest

Your most assured friend,

CHARLES R.

11. To Sir T. Glenham

CHARLES R.

Trusty and well-beloved, we greet you well. Being desirous to stop the further effusion of the blood of our subjects, and yet respecting the faithful services of all in that our city of Oxford which hath faithfully served us, and hazarded their lives for us : we have thought good to command you to quit that city, and disband the forces under your charge there, you receiving honourable conditions for you and them.

Given at Newcastle, the 18th of May, 1646.

III. To the Prince of Wales

Newcastle, June 2, 1646.

CHARLES,

This is rather to tell you where I am, and that I am well, than to direct you anything, having written fully to your mother what I would have you do, whom I command you to obey in everything (except in religion, concerning which I am confident she will not trouble you) and see that you go no whither without her or my particular directions. Let me hear often from you. So God bless you.

Your loving father,

CHARLES R.

If Jack Ashburnham come where you are, command him to wait upon you, as he was wont, until I shall send for him, if your mother and you be together; if not, he must wait on her.

IV. To the Marquess of Antrim

Newcastle, June 19, 1646.

ANTRIM,

Upon a rumour of your being landed in Scotland, I wrote to you upon Monday last. But now, having more perfect intelligence thereof, I have thought fit to send you this honest, trusty bearer, Sir James Lesley, to show you what direction I have given to Montrose, commanding you to follow the same : which is, to lay down arms; assuring you that your obedience in this is absolutely necessary for my service. For I shall esteem it as much as I have done your readiness to take them up, which I shall always remember to your advantage. Nor have I been unmindful to secure those honest, gallant men, who have ventured themselves for me, not meaning that any should be ruined for their obedience to me, as this bearer will at large declare unto you; as also, how these my commands are best for you (all things considered) and those who are with you, as well as me, whom you shall always find to be

Your most assured, constant, real friend,

CHARLES R.

The Scots had thus used their power to secure the disband-ment of the Royalist forces in their own country, while Oxford had surrendered to the Parliament, without, however, the King's wish that the Duke of York should be allowed to join him at Newcastle being gratified.

Nevertheless, the extremity to which Charles was now reduced in no way weakened his determination not to consent to the abolition of Episcopacy, and the Scots soon realized that he would not serve their turn in the way they had at first hoped.

v. To the Lord Mayor of London

CHARLES R.

Right trusty and well-beloved, we greet you well. Having expressed our resolutions to the two Houses of Parliament of England, and the Committee of Estates of our Parliament of Scotland, to give all just satisfaction to the joint desires of both kingdoms; we have now likewise thought fit to assure the two chief cities of both our kingdoms, that nothing is more grievous to us than the troubles and distractions of our people; and that nothing on earth is more desired by us, than that, in religion and peace, with all the comfortable fruits of both, they may hence-forth live under us in all godliness and honesty : and this pro-fession we make for no other end, but that you may know immediately from ourselves our integrity, and full resolution to comply with our Parliaments in everything for settling truth and peace, and our desire to have all things speedily concluded which shall be found requisite for that end; that our return to that our ancient city may be to the satisfaction of our Parliament, the good liking of you and all our good people, and to our own greater joy and comfort. We bid you heartily farewell.

From Newcastle, the 19th of May, 1646.

vi. To the Queen

Newcastle, June 17, 1646.

DEAR HEART,

I think it fit, for change, to give thee a particular account of the several humours of the Scots. I divide them into four factions : Montroses, the neutrals, the Hamiltons, and the Campbells. The second hath no declared head, but Callander may be said to be the chief of them; as for the other, it is ignorance to ask who were theirs. The three first seem to correspond, the two last are avowed enemies, the second keeps fair quarter with all, and none of them trusts one another.

At the committees in Scotland the Hamiltons are strongest, but here the Campbells. Most of the nobility are for the Hamiltons, because they correspond with the first; but most of the ministers, gentry, and towns, are for the Campbells, so that in voting these are strong enough for the other three, the first being totally excluded, and many of the second. Now, for the particular persons. They all seem to court me, and I behave myself as evenly to all as I can. The Lord Chancellor of Scotland hath more satisfied me than I expected. If he truly act for Montrose's party, as he hath promised (he being now where he may do it), I shall give some belief to his professions. Argyll is very civil and cunning, but his journey to London will show whether he be altered or not (if he be, it must be for the better), being gone with much professions of doing much for my service. Lanerick and Lindsay (I mean the Scot) brag much to me, for having done great services to several of Montrose's friends, of which they have indeed given me some good proofs. Callander is discreet and cautious, but he hath given me very good advice, which is to trust no one farther than I see their actions.

Lothian and Balmermoch (who are Campbellins) I will say nothing of, but leave their description to Montreuil. Dunfermline, who is neutral, makes me believe that I govern him, and I verily think he tells me all he knows.

My opinion upon this whole business is, that these divisions will either serve to make them all join with me, or else God hath prepared this way to punish them for their many rebellions and perfidies. I hope God hath sent me hither for the last punishment that He will inflict upon me for my sins, for assuredly no honest man can prosper in these people's company.

So, longing to hear from thee, and that Prince Charles is safe with thee, I rest eternally thine,

CHARLES R.

At this point Parliament sent up certain propositions, known as those of Newcastle, to the King.

May it please Your Majesty,

We, the Lords and Commons assembled in the Parliament of England, in the name and on the behalf of the kingdom of England and Ireland, and the Commissioners of the Parliament of England, in the name and on the behalf of the kingdom of Scotland, do humbly present unto Your Majesty the humble desires and propositions for a safe and well-grounded peace, agreed upon by the Parliaments of both kingdoms respectively, unto which we do pray Your Majesty's assent; and that they, and all such Bills as shall be tendered to Your Majesty in pursuance of them, or any of them, may be established and enacted for statutes and Acts of Parliament, by Your Majesty's Royal assent, in the Parliament of both kingdoms respectively.

1. Whereas both Houses of the Parliament of England have been necessitated to undertake a war in their just and lawful defence, and afterwards both kingdoms of England and Scotland joined in solemn League and Covenant were engaged to prosecute the same;

That by Act of Parliament in each kingdom respectively, all oaths, declarations and proclamations heretofore had, or hereafter to be had, against both or either of the Houses of Parliament of England, the Parliaments of the kingdom of Scotland, and the late Convention of Estates in Scotland, or the Committees flowing from the Parliament or Convention in Scotland, or their ordinances and proceedings, or against any for adhering unto them, or for doing or executing any office, place or charge, by any authority derived from them; and all the judgements, indictments, outlawries, attainders and inquisitions in any the said causes; and all grants thereupon had or made, or to be made or had, be declared null, suppressed and forbidden : and that this be publicly intimated in all parish churches within His Majesty's dominions, and all other places needful.

2. That His Majesty, according to the laudable example of his Royal father of happy memory, may be pleased to swear and sign the late solemn League and Covenant; and that an Act of Parliament be passed in both kingdoms respectively, for enjoining the taking thereof by all the subjects of the three kingdoms; and the Ordinances concerning the manner of taking the same in both kingdoms be confirmed by Acts of Parliament respectively, with such penalties as, by mutual advice of both kingdoms, shall be agreed upon.

3. That a Bill be passed for the utter abolishing and taking away of all Archbishops, Bishops, their Chancellors and Commissaries, Deans and Sub-Deans, Deans and Chapters, Archdeacons, Canons and Prebendaries, and all Chaunters, Chancellors, Treasurers, Sub-Treasurers, Succentors and Sacrists, and all Vicars Choral and Choristers, old Vicars and new Vicars of any Cathedral or Collegiate Church, and all other under officers, out of the Church of England and dominion of Wales, and out of the Church of Ireland, with such alterations concerning the estates of Prelates, as shall agree with the articles of the late Treaty of the date at Edinburgh, November 29, 1643, and joint Declaration of both kingdoms.

4. That the Ordinances concerning the calling and sitting of the Assembly of Divines be confirmed by Act of Parliament.

5. That reformation of religion, according to the Covenant, be settled by Act of Parliament, in such manner as both Houses have agreed, or shall agree upon, after consultation had with the Assembly of Divines.

6. Forasmuch as both kingdoms are mutually obliged by the same Covenant, to endeavour the nearest conjunction and uniformity in matters of religion, according to the Covenant, as after consultation had with the Divines of both kingdoms assembled, is or shall be jointly agreed upon by both Houses of Parliament of England, and by the Church and kingdom of Scotland, be confirmed by Acts of Parliament of both kingdoms respectively.

7. That for the more effectual disabling Jesuits, Priests, Papists and Popish recusants from disturbing the State and deluding the laws, and for the better discovering and speedy conviction of recusants, an oath be established by Act of Parliament, to be administered to them, wherein they shall abjure and renounce the Pope's supremacy, the doctrine of transubstantiation, purgatory, worshipping of the consecrated host, crucifixes and images, and all other Popish superstitions and errors; and refusing the said oath, being tendered in such manner as shall be appointed by the said Act, to be a sufficient conviction of recusancy.

8. An Act of Parliament for education of the children of Papists by Protestants in the Protestant religion.

9. An Act for the true levying of the penalties against them, which penalties to be levied and disposed in such manner as both Houses shall agree on, wherein to be provided that His Majesty shall have no loss.

10. That an Act be passed in Parliament, whereby the practices of Papists against the State may be prevented, and the laws against them duly executed, and a stricter course taken to prevent the saying or hearing of Mass in the Court or any other part of this kingdom.

11. The like for the kingdom of Scotland, concerning the four last preceding propositions, in such manner as the Estates of the Parliament there shall think fit.

12. That the King do give his Royal assent to an Act for the due observance of the Lord's Day;

And to the Bill for the suppression of innovations in churches and chapels, in and about the worship of God, etc.;

And for the better advancement of the preaching of God's Holy Word in all parts of this kingdom;

And to the Bill against the enjoying of pluralities of benefices by spiritual persons, and non-residency;

And to an Act to be framed and agreed upon by both Houses of Parliament, for the reforming and regulating of both Universities, of the Colleges of Westminster, Winchester and Eton;

And to such Act or Acts for raising of moneys for the payment and satisfaction of the public debts and damages of the kingdom, and other public uses, as shall hereafter be agreed on by both Houses of Parliament: and that if the King doth not give his assent thereunto, then it being done by both Houses of Parliament, the same shall be as valid to all intents and purposes, as if the Royal assent had been given thereunto.

The like for the kingdom of Scotland.

And that His Majesty give assurance of his consenting in the Parliament of Scotland to an Act acknowledging and ratifying the Acts of the Convention of Estates of Scotland, called by the Council and Conservers of the Peace and the Commissioners for the common burdens, and assembled the 22nd of June, 1643, and several times continued since, and of the Parliament of that kingdom since convened.

13. That the Lords and Commons in the Parliament of England assembled, shall during the space of twenty years from the 1st of July, 1646, arm, train, and discipline, or caused to be armed, trained, and disciplined, all the forces of the kingdoms of England and Ireland and dominion of Wales, the Isles of Guernsey and Jersey, and the town of Berwick upon Tweed, already raised both for sea and land service; and shall arm, train and discipline, or cause to be raised, levied, armed, trained and disciplined, any other forces for land and sea service, in the kingdoms dominions, and places aforesaid, as in their judgements they shall from time to time, during the said space of twenty years, think fit and appoint: and that neither the King, his heirs or successors, nor any other but such as shall act by the authority or approbation of the said Lords and Commons, shall during the said space of twenty years exercise any of the powers aforesaid.

And the like for the kingdom of Scotland, if the Estates of the Parliament there shall think fit.

That money be raised and levied for the maintenance and use of the said forces for land service, and of the navy and forces for sea service, in such sort and by such ways and means as the said Lords and Commons shall from time to time, during the said space of twenty years, think fit and appoint, and not otherwise. That all the said forces, both for land and sea service, so raised or levied, or to be raised or levied, and also the admiralty and navy, shall from time to time, during the said space of twenty years, be employed, managed, ordered and disposed by the said Lords and Commons, in such sort and by such ways and means as they shall think fit and appoint, and not otherwise. And the said Lords and Commons, during the said space of twenty years, shall have power:

(i) To suppress all forces raised or to be raised, without authority and consent of the said Lords and Commons, to the disturbance of the public peace of the kingdoms of England and Ireland and dominion of Wales, the Isles of Guernsey and Jersey, and the town of Berwick upon Tweed, or any of them.

(ii) To suppress any foreign forces who shall invade or endeavour to invade the kingdoms of England and Ireland, dominion of Wales, the Isles of Guernsey and Jersey, and the town of Berwick upon Tweed, or any of them.

(iii) To conjoin such forces of the kingdom of England with the forces of the kingdom of Scotland as the said Lords and Commons shall from time to time, during the said space of twenty years, judge fit and necessary; to resist all foreign invasions, and to suppress any forces raised or to be raised against or within either of the said kingdoms, to the disturbance of the public peace of the said kingdoms, or any of them, by any authority under the Great Seal, or any warrant whatsoever, without consent of the said Lords and Commons of the Parliament of England or the Estates of the Parliament of Scotland respectively. And that no forces of either kingdom shall go into or continue in the other kingdom, without the advice and desire of the said Lords and Commons of the Parliament of England, and the Parliament of the kingdom of Scotland, or such as shall be by them appointed for that purpose: and that after the expiration of the said twenty years, neither the King, his heirs or successors, or any person or persons, by colour or pretence of any commission, power, deputation or authority to be derived from the King, his heirs or successors, or any of them shall raise, arm, train, discipline, employ, order, manage, disband or dispose of any of the forces by sea or land, of the kingdoms of England and Ireland, the dominion of Wales, Isles of Guernsey and Jersey, and the town of Berwick upon Tweed: nor exercise any of the said powers or authorities in the precedent articles mentioned and expressed to be during the said space of twenty years, in the said Lords and Commons : nor do any act or thing concerning the execution of the said powers or authorities, or any of them, without the consent of the said Lords and Commons first had and obtained. That after the expiration of the said twenty years, in all cases wherein the Lords and Commons shall declare the safety of the kingdom to be concerned, and shall thereupon pass any Bill or Bills for the raising, arming, disciplining, employing, managing, ordering or disposing of the forces by sea or land, of the kingdoms of England and Ireland, the dominion of Wales, Isles of Guernsey and Jersey, and the town of Berwick upon Tweed, or of any part of the said forces, or concerning the admiralty and Navy, or concerning the levying of moneys for the raising, maintenance or use of the said forces for land service, or of the Navy and forces for sea service, or of any part of them : and if that the Royal assent to such Bill or Bills shall not be given in the House of Peers within such time after the passing thereof by both Houses of Parliament, as the said Houses shall judge fit and convenient, that then such Bill or Bills so passed by the said Lords and Commons as aforesaid, and to which the Royal assent shall not be given as is herein before expressed, shall nevertheless after declaration of the said Lords and Commons made in that behalf, have the force and strength of an Act or Acts of Parliament, and shall be as valid to all intents and purposes as if the Royal assent had been given thereunto.

Provided, that the City of London shall have and enjoy all the taking away of the ordinary legal power of Sheriffs, Justices of Peace, Mayors, Bailiffs, Coroners, Constables, Headboroughs, or other officers of justice, not being military officers, concerning the administration of justice; so as neither the said Sheriffs, Justices of the Peace, Mayors, Bailiffs, Coroners, Constables, Headboroughs, and other officers, nor any of them, do levy, conduct, employ or command any forces whatsoever, by colour or pretence of any commission of array, or extraordinary command from His Majesty, his heirs or successors, without the consent of the said Lords and Commons.

And if any persons shall be gathered and assembled together in warlike manner or otherwise, to the number of thirty persons, and shall not forthwith disband themselves, being required thereto by the said Lords and Commons, or command from them or any of them, especially authorized for that purpose, then such person or persons not so disbanding themselves, shall be guilty and incur the pains of high treason, being first declared guilty of such offence by the said Lords and Commons; any commission under the Great Seal, or other warrant to the contrary notwithstanding: and he or they that shall offend herein, to be incapable of any pardon from His Majesty, his heirs or successors, and their estates shall be disposed as the said Lords and Commons shall think fit, and not otherwise.

Provided, that the City of London shall have and enjoy all their rights, liberties and franchises, customs and usages, in the raising and employing the forces of that City for the defence thereof, in full and ample manner, to all intents and purposes, as they have or might have used or enjoyed the same at any time before the making of the said Act or proposition; to the end that City may be fully assured it is not the intention of the Parliament to take from them any privileges or immunities in raising or disposing of their forces which they have or might have used or enjoyed heretofore.

The like for the kingdom of Scotland, if the Estates of the Parliament there shall think fit.

14. That by Act of Parliament all Peers made since the day that Edward Lord Lyttleton, then Lord Keeper of the Great Seal, deserted the Parliament, and that the said Great Seal was surreptitiously conveyed away from the Parliament, being the 21st day of May, 1642, and who shall be hereafter made, shall not sit or vote in the Parliament of England, without consent of both Houses of Parliament; and that all honour and title conferred on any without consent of both Houses of Parliament since the 20th of May, 1642, being the day that both Houses declared that the King, seduced by evil counsel, intended to raise war against the Parliament, be null and void.

The like for the kingdom of Scotland, those being excepted whose patents were passed the Great Seal before the 14th of June, 1644.

15. That an Act be passed in the Parliaments of both

Houses respectively, for confirmation of the Treaties passed between the two kingdoms; viz., the large Treaty, the late Treaty for the coming of the Scots Army into England, and the settling of the garrison of Berwick, of the 29th of November, 1643, and the Treaty between Ireland of the 6th of August, 1642, for the bringing of 10,000 Scots into the province of Ulster in Ireland; with all other Ordinances and proceedings passed between the two kingdoms, and whereunto they are obliged by the aforesaid Treaties.

And that Algernon Earl of Northumberland, John Earl of Rutland, Philip Earl of Pembroke and Montgomery, Robert Earl of Essex, Theophilus Earl of Lincoln, James Earl of Suffolk, Robert Earl of Warwick, Edward Earl of Manchester, Henry Earl of Stamford, Francis Lord Dacres, Philip Lord Wharton, Francis Lord Willoughby, Dudley Lord North, John Lord Hunsdon, William Lord Gray, Edward Lord Howard of Escrick, Thomas Lord Bruce, Ferdinando Lord Fairfax, Mr. Nathaniel Fiennes, Sir William Armin, Sir Philip Stapleton, Sir Henry Vane, senior, Mr. William Pierpoint, Sir Edward Ayscough, Sir William Strickland, Sir Arthur Haslerig, Sir John Fenwick, Sir William Brereton, Sir Thomas Widdrington, Mr. John Toll, Mr. Gilbert Millington, Sir William Constable, Sir John Wray, Sir Henry Vane, junior, Mr. Henry Darley, Oliver St. John, Esq., His Majesty's Solicitor-General, Sir Denzil Hollis, Mr. Alexander Rigby, Mr. Cornelius Holland, Mr. Samuel Vassal, Mr. Peregrine Pelham, John Glyn, Esq., Recorder of London, Mr. Henry Martin, Mr. Alderman Hoyle, Mr. John Blackiston, Mr. Serjeant Wilde, Mr. Richard Barrois, Sir Anthony Irby, Mr. Ashhurst, Mr. Billingham, and Mr. Tolson, Members of both Houses of the Parliament of England, shall be the Commissioners for the kingdom of England, for conservation of the peace between the two kingdoms; to act according to the powers in that behalf expressed in the articles of the large Treaty, and not otherwise.

That His Majesty give his assent to what the two kingdoms shall agree upon, in prosecution of the articles of the large Treaty, which are not yet finished.

16. That an Act be passed in the Parliaments of both

kingdoms respectively, for establishing the joint Declaration of both kingdoms bearing date the 30th of January, 1643, in England, and 1644 in Scotland; with the qualifications ensuing :

1st Qualification. That the persons who shall expect no pardon be only these following : Rupert and Maurice, Counts Palatine of the Rhine, James Earl of Derby, John Earl of Bristol, William Earl of Newcastle, Francis Lord Cottington, George Lord Digby, Matthew Wren, Bishop of Ely, Sir Robert Heath, Knt., Dr. Bramhall, Bishop of Derry, Sir William Widdrington, Colonel George Goring, Henry Jermyn, Esq., Sir Ralph Hopton, Sir John Byron, Sir Francis Doddington, Sir Francis Strangeways, Mr. Endymion Porter, Sir George Radcliffe, Sir Marmaduke Langdale, Henry Vaughan, Esq., now called Sir Henry Vaughan, Sir Francis Windebank, Sir Richard Granville, Mr. Edward Hyde, now called Sir Edward Hyde, Sir John Marley, Sir Nicholas Cole, Sir Thomas Riddell, junior, Sir John Culpepper, Mr. Richard Lloyd, now called Sir Richard Lloyd, Mr. David Jenkins, Sir George Strode, George Carteret, Esq., now called Sir George Carteret, Sir Charles Dallison, Knt., Richard Lane, Esq., now called Sir Richard Lane, Sir Edward Nicholas, John Ashburnham, Esq., Sir Edward Herbert, Knt., Attorney-General, Earl of Traquair, Lord Harris, Lord Reay, George Gordon, sometime Marquis of Huntly, James Graham, sometime Earl of Montrose, Robert Maxwell, late Earl of Nithsdale, Robert Dalzell, sometime Earl of Carnwath, James Gordon, sometime Viscount of Aboyne, Ludovic Lindsay, sometime Earl of Crawford, James Ogilvy, sometime Earl of Airlie, James Ogilvy, sometime Lord Ogilvy, Patrick Ruthven, sometime Earl of Forth, James King, sometime Lord Eythin, Alaster Macdonald, Irvine the younger of Drum, Gordon the younger of Gight, Leslie of Auchintoul, Colonel John Cochrane, Graham of Gorthie, Mr. John Maxwell, sometime pretended Bishop of Ross, and all such others as being processed by the Estates for treason, shall be condemned before Act of Oblivion be passed.

2nd Qualification. All Papists and Popish recusants who have been, now are, or shall be actually in arms, or voluntarily assisting against the Parliament or Estates of either kingdom;

and by name the Marquess of Winton, Earl of Worcester, Edward Lord Herbert of Raglan, son to the Earl of Worcester, Lord Brudenell, Caryl Molyneux, Esq., Lord Arundel of Wardour, Sir Francis Howard, Sir John Wintour, Sir Charles Smith, Sir John Preston, Sir Basil Brooke, Lord Audley, Earl of Castlehaven, in the kingdom of Ireland, William Sheldon, of Beely, Esq., Sir Henry Bedingfield.

3rd Qualification. All persons who have had any hand in the plotting, designing or assisting the rebellion of Ireland, except such persons who have only assisted the said rebellion, have rendered themselves, or come in to the Parliament of England.

4th Qualification. That Humphrey Bennet, Esq., Sir Edward Ford, Sir John Penruddock, Sir George Vaughan, Sir John Weld, Sir Robert Lee, Sir John Pate, John Acland, Edmund Windham, Esq., Sir John Fitzherbert, Sir Edward Lawrence, Sir Ralph Dutton, Henry Lingen, Esq., Sir William Russell of Worcestershire, Thomas Lee of Adlington, Esq., Sir John Girlington, Sir Paul Neale, Sir William Thorold, Sir Edward Hussey, Sir Thomas Liddell, senior, Sir Philip Musgrave, Sir John Digby of Nottinghamshire, Sir Henry Fletcher, Sir Richard Minshull, Lawrence Halstead, John Denham, Esq., Sir Edmund Fortescue, Peter St. Hill, Esq., Sir Thomas Tyldesley, Sir Henry Griffith, Michael Wharton, Esq., Sir Henry Spiller, Mr. George Benion, now called Sir George Benion, Sir Edward Walgrave, Sir Robert Ouseley, Sir John Mandy, Lord Cholmley, Sir Thomas Acton, Sir Lewis Dives, Sir Peter Osborne, Samuel Thornton, Esq., Sir John Lucas, John Blaney, Esq., Sir Thomas Chedle, Sir Nicholas Kemish, Hugh Lloyd, Esq., Sir Nicholas Crispe, Sir Peter Ricaut.

And all such of the Scottish nation as have concurred in the votes at Oxford against the kingdom of Scotland and their proceedings, or have sworn or subscribed the Declaration against the Convention and Covenant; and all such as have assisted the rebellion in the North, or the invasion in the South of the said kingdom of Scotland, or the late invasion made there by the Irish, and their adherents, be removed from His Majesty's counsels, and be restrained from coming within the verge of the Court; and that they may not without the advice and consent of both Houses of the Parliament of England, or the Estates in the Parliament of Scotland respectively, bear any office, or have any employment concerning the State or Commonwealth : and in case any of them should offend therein, to be guilty of high treason, and incapable of any pardon from His Majesty, and their estates to be disposed of as both Houses of the Parliament of England, or the Estates of the Parliament in Scotland respectively shall think fit : and that one full third part upon full value of the estates of the persons aforesaid, made incapable of employment as aforesaid, be employed for the payment of the public debts and damages, according to the Declaration.

1st Branch. That the late members, or any who pretended themselves late members of either House of Parliament, who have not only deserted the Parliament, but have also sat in the unlawful assembly at Oxford, called or pretended by some to be a Parliament, and voted both kingdoms traitors, and have not voluntarily rendered themselves before the last of October, 1644, be removed from His Majesty's counsels, and be restrained from coming within the verge of the Court; and that they may not, without advice and consent of both kingdoms, bear any office or have any employment concerning the State of Commonwealth. And in case any of them shall offend therein, to be guilty of high treason, and be incapable of any pardon by His Majesty; and their estates to be disposed as both Houses of Parliament in England, or the Estates of the Parliament of Scotland respectively shall think fit.

2nd Branch. That the late members, or any who pretended themselves members of either House of Parliament, who have sat in the unlawful assembly at Oxford, called or pretended by some to be a Parliament, and have not voluntarily rendered themselves before the last of October, 1644, be removed from His Majesty's counsels, and restrained from coming within the verge of the Court; and that they may not, without the advice and consent of both Houses of Parliament, bear any office or have any employment concerning the State or Commonwealth. And in case any of them shall offend therein, to be guilty of high treason, and incapable of any pardon from His Majesty,

o

and their estates to be disposed as both Houses of Parliament in England shall think fit.

3rd Branch. That the late members, or any who pretended themselves members of either House of Parliament, who have deserted the Parliament, and adhered to the enemies thereof, and have not rendered themselves before the last of October, 1644, be removed from His Majesty's counsels, and be restrained from coming within the verge of the Court; and that they may not, without the advice and consent of both Houses of Parliament, bear any office or have any employment concerning the State or Commonwealth. And in case any of them shall offend therein, to be guilty of high treason, and incapable of any pardon from His Majesty, and their estates to be disposed as both Houses of Parliament in England shall think fit.

5th Qualification. That all judges and officers towards the law, common or civil, who have deserted the Parliament and adhered to the enemies thereof, be incapable of any place of judicature, or office towards the law, common or civil : and that all serjeants, councillors, and attorneys, doctors, advocates, and proctors of the law, common or civil, either in public or private, shall not be capable of any preferment or employment in the Commonwealth, without the advice and consent of both Houses of Parliament : and that no Bishop or Clergyman, no Master or Fellow of any College or Hall in either of the Universities, or elsewhere, or any Master of school or hospital, or any ecclesiastical person, who hath deserted the Parliament and adhered to the enemies thereof, shall hold or enjoy, or be capable of any preferment or employment in Church or Commonwealth. But all their said several preferments, places and promotions, shall be utterly void, as if they were naturally dead : nor shall they otherwise use their function of the ministry, without advice and consent of both Houses of Parliament : provided, that no lapse shall incur by this vacancy until six months past after notice thereof.

6th Qualification. That all persons who have been actually in arms against the Parliament, or have counselled or voluntarily assisted the enemies thereof, are disabled to be Sheriffs, Justices of the Peace, Mayors, or other Head Officers of any City or

Corporation, Commissioners of *Oyer* and *Terminer*, or to sit and serve as members or assistants in either of the Houses of Parliament, or to have any military employments in this kingdom without the consent of both Houses of Parliament.

7th Qualification.   The persons of all others to be free of all personal censure, notwithstanding any act or thing done in or concerning this war, they taking the Covenant.

8th Qualification.   The estates of those persons excepted in the first three precedent qualifications, and the estates of Edward Lord Lyttleton and of William Laud, late Archbishop of Canterbury, to pay public debts and damages.

9th Qualification.   1st Branch : that two full parts in three to be divided of all the estates of the members of either House of Parliament, who have not only deserted the Parliament, but have also voted both kingdoms traitors, and have not rendered themselves before the 1st of December, 1645, shall be taken and employed for the payment of the public debts and damages of the kingdom.

2nd Branch : that two full parts in three to be divided of the estates of such late members of either House of Parliament as sat in the unlawful assembly at Oxford, and shall not have rendered themselves before the 1st of December, 1645, shall be taken and employed for the payment of the public debts and damages of the kingdom.

3rd Branch : that one full moiety of the estates of such persons, late members of either of the Houses of Parliament, who have deserted the Parliament, and adhered to the enemies thereof, and shall not have rendered themselves before the 1st of December, 1645, shall be taken and employed for the payment of public debts and damages of the kingdom.

10th Qualification.   That a full third part of the value of the estates of all judges and officers towards the law, common or civil, and of all serjeants, councillors and attorneys, doctors, advocates and proctors of the law, common or civil; and of all Bishops, Clergymen, Masters and Fellows of any College or Hall in either of the Universities, or elsewhere; and of all Masters of hospitals, and of ecclesiastical persons, who have deserted the Parliament and adhered to the enemies thereof, and have not rendered themselves before the 1st of December, 1645, shall be taken and employed for the payment of public debts and damages of the kingdom.

That a full sixth part of the value of the estates of the persons excepted in the sixth qualifications concerning such as have been actually in arms against the Parliament, or have counselled or voluntarily assisted the enemies thereof, and are disabled according to the said qualification, to be taken and employed for the payment of the public debts and damages of the kingdom.

11th Qualification. That the persons and estates of all common soldiers and others of the kingdom of England, who in lands or goods be not worth £200 sterling, and the persons and estates of all common soldiers and others of the kingdom of Scotland, who in his lands or goods be not worth £100 sterling, be at liberty and discharged.

1st Branch. This proposition to stand as to the English, and as to the Scots likewise, if the Parliament of Scotland or their Commissioners shall think fit.

2nd Branch. That the 1st of May last is now the day limited for the persons to come in, that are comprised within the former qualification.

That an Act be passed, whereby the debts of the kingdom and the persons of delinquents, and the value of their estates may be known: and which Act shall appoint in what manner the confiscations and proportions before mentioned may be levied and applied to the discharge of the said engagements.

The like for the kingdom of Scotland, if the Estates of the Parliament, or such as shall have power from them, shall think fit.

17. That an Act of Parliament be passed to declare and make void the cessation of Ireland, and all Treaties and conclusions of peace, or any articles thereupon with the rebels, without consent of both Houses of Parliament; and to settle the prosecution of the wars of Ireland, as both Houses of the Parliament of England have agreed, or shall agree upon, after consultation had with the Assembly of Divines here.

That the Deputy or Chief Governor, or other Governors of Ireland, and the Presidents of the several provinces of that kingdom, be nominated by both the Houses of the Parliament of England; or in the intervals of Parliament as both Houses of the Parliament of England shall nominate and appoint for that purpose: and that the Chancellor or Lord Keeper, Lord Treasurer, Commissioners of the Great Seal or Treasury, Lord Warden of the Cinque Ports, Chancellor of the Exchequer and Duchy, Secretaries of State, Master of the Rolls, Judges of both Benches, and Barons of the Exchequer, of the kingdoms of England and Ireland, and the Vice-Treasurer and Treasurer at War, of the kingdom of Ireland, be nominated by both Houses of the Parliament of England, to continue *quam diu se bene gesserint*; and in the intervals of Parliament by the afore-mentioned Committee, to be approved or disallowed by both Houses at their next sitting.

The like for the kingdom of Scotland, concerning the nomination of the Lords of the Privy Council, Lords of Session and Exchequer, Offices of State and Justice-General, in such manner as the Estates of Parliament there shall think fit.

18. That the Militia of the City of London, and liberties thereof, may be in the ordering and government of the Lord Mayor, Aldermen, and Commons in Council assembled, or such as they shall from time to time appoint (whereof the Lord Mayor and Sheriffs for the time being to be three), to be employed and directed from time to time, in such manner as shall be agreed on and appointed by both Houses of Parliament.

That no citizen of the City of London, nor any of the forces of the said City, should be drawn forth or compelled to go out of the said City, or liberties thereof, for military service, without their own free consent.

That an Act be passed for granting and confirming of the charters, customs, liberties and franchises of the City of London, notwithstanding any *nonuser, misuser,* or *abuser.*

That the Tower of London may be in the government of the City of London, and the chief officer and governor thereof, from time to time, be nominated and removable by the Common Council: and for prevention of inconveniences which may happen by the long intermission of Common Councils, it is desired that there may be an Act that all by-laws and ordinances already made, or hereafter to be made by the Lord Mayor, Aldermen, and Commons in Common Council assembled, touching the calling, continuing, directing and regulating the said Common Councils, be as effectual in law to all intents and purposes, as if the same were particularly enacted by the authority of Parliament. And that the Lord Mayor, Aldermen, and Commons in Common Council may add to or repeal the said Ordinances from time to time, as they shall see cause.

That such other propositions as shall be made for the City, for their further safety, welfare and government, and shall be approved of by both Houses of Parliament, may be granted and confirmed by Act of Parliament.

19. That all grants, commissions, presentations, writs, processes, proceedings, and other things passed under the Great Seal of England, in the custody of the Lords and others Commissioners appointed by both Houses of Parliament for the custody thereof, and by Act of Parliament with the Royal assent, shall be declared and enacted to be of like force and effect to all intents and purposes, as the same or like grants, commissions, presentations, writs, processes, proceedings, and other things under the Great Seal of England in any time heretofore were or have been : and that for time to come, the said Great Seal, now remaining in custody of the said Commissioners, continue and be used for the Great Seal of England : and that all grants, commissions and presentations, writs, processes, proceedings and other things whatsoever, passed under or by authority of any other Great Seal since the 22nd day of May, *anno Dom.* 1642, or hereafter to be passed, be invalid, and of no effect to all intents and purposes; except such writs, process and commissions, as being passed under any other Great Seal in the custody of the Commissioners aforesaid, on or after the said 22nd of May, and before the 28th day of November, *anno Dom.* 1643, were afterwards proceeded upon, returned into, or put in use in any of the King's Courts at Westminster; and except the grant to Mr. Justice Bacon to be one of the Justices of the King's Bench; and except all acts and proceedings by virtue of any such commissions of gaol-delivery, assize, and *Nisi Prius* or *Oyer* and *Terminer*, passed under any Great Seal than the Seal

aforesaid, in the custody of the said Commissioners, before the 1st of October, 1642.

And that all grants of offices, lands, tenements or hereditaments, made or passed under the Great Seal of Ireland, unto any person or persons, bodies politic or corporate, since the cessation made in Ireland the 15th day of September, 1643, shall be null and void : and that all honours and titles conferred upon any person or persons in the said kingdom of Ireland, since the said cessation, shall be null and void.

The King's attitude towards these proposals can be gauged from the following letter.

VII.TO THE LORDS JERMYN AND CULPEPPER, AND MR. JOHN ASHBURNHAM

Newcastle, Wednesday, July 22, 1646.

SIRS,

Since you three have joined yourselves in a letter to me, I will not sever you in my answer. Then know, what severally, what jointly, I received upon Saturday last, six letters from you (and four from the Queen), whereof I shall only answer to that of the 19th July, which will serve for all, as to public business.

It is no small comfort for me to find that I have some friends yet, that neither have forsaken me, nor are doubtful of me; for of late I have found many demases, and I cannot but say, that if opportunity could have ruined my constancy, I had not at this time deserved your confidence. Indeed, it is almost incredible (it had been altogether to me, if I had not seen it) with what impudence I have been assaulted to yield unto these London propositions, no man dissenting. In a word, what Ashburnham saw concerning the Covenant was but slight insinuations to what I have found since (incivilities only excepted, which, to say the truth, are left off); for now I am faced down, that this is all for my service; and, if I will be ruled by them, I cannot miss to be a great and glorious King, it being upon debate the result of all my faithful servants in London. I only mention this, to show you that it is likely I shall still deserve your confidence.

But now let me warn you all (I include my wife and son) truly to deserve that praise of constancy which you command in me. For I am deceived if you be not sooner put to it than I have been. Wherefore I conjure you, by your unspotted faithfulness, by all that you love, by all that is good, that no threatenings, no apprehensions of danger to my person, make you stir one jot from any foundation in relation to that authority which the Prince of Wales is born to. I have already cast up what I am like to suffer, which I shall meet (by the grace of God) with that constancy that befits me. Only I desire that consolation, that assurance from you, as I may justly hope that my cause shall not end with my misfortunes, by assuring me that misplaced pity to me do not prejudice my son's right. And, mistake me not, for I am in this so far from abandoning myself, that I believe this resolution is the best way for my preservation; however, that no man's person ought to be put in balance with this cause.

Now, as for your advice to me, you speak my very soul in everything but one; that is, the Church. Remember your own rule, not to expect to redeem that which is given away by Act of Parliament. Shall I then give away the Church? And excuse me to tell you that I believe you do not understand what this is that you are content (I confess not upon very easy terms) I should give away. I will begin to show you, first, what it is in point of policy; and first, negatively. It is not the change of Church government which is chiefly aimed at (though that were too much); but it is by that pretext to take away the dependency of the Church from the Crown, which, let me tell you, I hold to be of equal consequence to that of the Militia; for people are governed by the pulpit more than the sword in times of peace. Nor will the Scots be content with the alteration of government, except the Covenant be likewise established, the which does not only make good all their former rebellions, but likewise lays a firm and fruitful foundation for such pastimes in all times to come. Now, for the theological part: I assure you the change would be no less and worse than if Popery were brought in; for we should have neither lawful priests nor sacraments duly administered, nor God publicly served, but according to the foolish fancy of every idle person; but we should have the doctrine against kings fiercer set up than amongst the Jesuits.

In a word, set your hearts at rest; I will less yield to this than the Militia, my conscience being irreconcilably engaged against it. Wherefore, I conjure you as Christians to assist me particularly in this also. Yet I say not the Scots are to be shaken off; but to be sought with all possible industry, *usque ad aras*; nor do I mislike your fancy concerning the Prince of Wales treating with the Independents, wherein I give you full liberty (according to your own cautions) to try your fortunes, though I believe it will not hit.

viii. To the Queen

Newcastle, July 23, 1646.

DEAR HEART,

Saturday last did recompense the former week's failing, for then I received the dispatch of both, which gave me the more pains; but that was fully recompensed by reading thy letters, being thereby confirmed (but I assure thee not altered) concerning my opinion of the London propositions, and be confident that no importunity nor threatening shall stagger my constancy.

This day the London lords will be here, but I will use all possible industry to defer their audience, to expect the French ambassador, and those particular advices which were promised me by the letters that Jermyn, Culpepper, and Ashburnham wrote to me by the Queen's command.

As for the things which thine of the 12th of July accuse me of, I only say this; I believe the Queen will find, upon good examination, that I have not erred, unless it were concerning Ormonde, for which I have since made amends. I have sent such commands to Prince Charles as the Queen desires; and for any other particulars, my former letters have answered them all, and tell Jermyn, from me, that I will make him know the eminent service he hath done me concerning Prince Charles his coming to thee, as soon as it shall please God to enable me to reward honest men. Likewise thank heartily, in my name, Culpepper, for his part in that business; but, above all, thou must make my acknowledgements to the Queen of England (for none else can do it), it being her love that maintains my life, her kindness that upholds my courage, which makes me eternally hers,

CHARLES R.

A few days later the King sent his answer to the Parliament.

IX. TO THE SPEAKER OF THE HOUSE OF PEERS

CHARLES R.

The propositions tendered to His Majesty by the Commissioners from the Lords and Commons assembled in the Parliament of England at Westminster, and the Commissioners of the Parliament of Scotland (to which the Houses of Parliament have taken twice so many months for deliberation, as they have assigned days for His Majesty's answer), do import so great alterations in government both in the Church and kingdom, as it is very difficult to return a particular and positive answer, before a full debate, wherein these propositions, and the necessary explanations, true sense and reasons thereof, be rightly weighed and understood; and that His Majesty (upon a full view of the whole propositions) may know what is left, as well as what is taken away and changed: in all which he finds (upon discourse with the said Commissioners) that they are so bound up from any capacity either to give reasons for the demands they bring, or to give ear to such desires as His Majesty is to propound, as it is impossible for him to give such a present judgement of, and answer to these propositions, whereby he can answer to God that a safe and well-grounded peace will ensue (which is evident to all the world can never be, unless the just power of the Crown, as well as the freedom and propriety of the subject, with the just liberty and privileges of Parliament, be likewise settled): to which end His Majesty desires and proposeth to come to London, or any of his houses thereabouts, upon the public faith and security of the two Houses of his Parliament, and the Scots Commissioners, that he shall be there with freedom, honour and safety; where by his personal presence he may not only raise a mutual confidence between him and his people, but also have these doubts cleared, and these difficulties explained unto him, which he now conceives to be destructive to his just regal power, if he should give a full consent to these propositions as they now stand : as likewise, that he may make known to them such his reasonable demands, as he is most assured will be very much conducible to that peace which all good men desire and pray for, by the settling of religion, the just privileges of Parliament, with the freedom and propriety of the subject : and His Majesty assures them, that as he can never condescend unto what is absolutely destructive to that just power which, by the laws of God and the land, he is born unto; so he will cheerfully grant and give his assent unto all such Bills (at the desires of his two Houses), or reasonable demands for Scotland, which shall be really for the good and peace of his people, not having regard to his own particular (much less of anybody's else) in respect of the happiness of these kingdoms. Wherefore His Majesty conjures them as Christians, as subjects, and as men who desire to leave a good name behind them, that they will so receive and make use of this answer, that all issues of blood may be stopped, and these unhappy distractions peaceably settled.

At Newcastle, the 1st of August, 1646.

CHARLES R.

Upon assurance of a happy agreement, His Majesty will immediately send for the Prince his son, absolutely answering for his perfect obedience.

x. To the Lords Jermyn and Culpepper, and Mr. John Ashburnham

Newcastle, Wednesday, August 19, 1646.

Yours of the 17th I received upon Monday last, which gave me much contentment, finding that the answer that I have given to the proposition doth concur fully with your judgement. And now you must not take ill, that I preach constancy to you as much as you have done to me. For, as you had reason to do so, because of the company I am in, I believe to have no less, considering how your judgements have been abused by a fallacious treaty concerning Church government, which the Scots have thought to make use of as a shoehorn to draw on all their ends. For which there is not so infallible a way under Heaven as the establishing of Presbyterian government with the extirpation of Episcopacy (they scorn the notion to settle the one, except the other be totally abolished); for thereby the doctrine of rebellion is made canonical, their former acts approved, and mine condemned. Besides how can I keep that innocency which you (with so much reason) oft and earnestly persuade me to preserve, if I should abandon the Church? Believe it, religion is the only firm foundation of all power; that cast loose, or depraved, no government can be stable. For where was there ever obedience where religion did not teach it? But which is most of all, how can we expect God's blessing, if we relinquish his Church? And I am most confident that religion will much sooner regain the Militia than the Militia will religion.

Thus in my harsh, brief way (not having time to make large discourses) I do my endeavours to make your judgement concur with mine in this particular; as they do in all the rest. For albeit, I believe that my letters upon this point may have silenced you by way of obedience, yet I am not satisfied unless your reasons be likewise convinced.

Now, as to the proceedings here, I have yet no certainty to send you; but there are two things much discoursed, both naught, first, that the London rebels will seek to satisfy the Scots, which thought no hard work whereby to make them return their army, and quit their garrisons, before they will delare anything concerning my person. Secondly, their great desire is to make the Duke of York King. Albeit, these hitherto are but discourse, yet are they not to be condemned. And you will be deceived if you do not expect the Scots have not resolved to destroy the essence of monarchy (that is to say, reduce my power in England to what they have made it in Scotland), from which nothing can divert them but a visible, strong declared party for me, and either the Prince of Wales or I at the head of a good army. And do not think that any other eloquence will make the English or Scots rebels hearken to any reason for the business of Ireland alone (which yourselves confess that I must stick to) will hinder all accommodation, until (as I have said) other sort of arguments be used.

Wherefore my opinion is, that you presently begin to press France and all the rest of my friends, both to declare for my restoration, and set some visible course on foot to order it. I will say no more at this time, but only that you will not forget to answer the query in my last letter concerning myself.

So farewell.

Charles was taking the only line open to him in the circumstances, namely to play for time. Meanwhile, the Scots and the Parliament were reaching an agreement by which the former were to deliver the King to the latter on payment for their services in the late war. This alarmed the Independents, who, as we have seen above, began to flirt with the Royalists.

XI. To the Prince of Wales

Newcastle, August 26, 1646.

CHARLES,

I had not sent you this honest, trusty servant of mine, Doctor Steward, but that the iniquity of these times hath hindered his attendance upon me, the which, since (for the present) I could not help, I thought the best service he could do me was to wait on you. Wherefore I command you not only to admit him in the quality of Dean of your chapel, as he is to me, but likewise that you will take his advice, and give very much reverence to his opinion in everything which concerns conscience or Church affairs. Upon which occasion I cannot but give you some short directions in relation to the distractions of these unhappy times.

As I know that you are not now to learn that chiefest particular duty of a King is to maintain the true religion (without which he can never expect to have God's blessing), so I assure you that this duty can never be right performed without the Church is rightly governed, not only in relation to conscience, but likewise for the necessary subsistence of the Crown. For, take it as an infallible maxim from me, that, as the Church can never flourish without the protection of the Crown, so the dependency of the Church upon the Crown is the chiefest support of regal authority.   This is that which is so well under-stood by the English and Scots rebels, that no concessions will content them without the change of Church government, by which that necessary and ancient relation which the Church hath had to the Crown is taken away.   Wherefore, my first direction to you is, to be constant in the maintenance of the Episcopacy, not only for the reasons above said, but likewise to hinder the growth of Presbyterian doctrine, which cannot but bring anarchy into any country, wherever it shall come for any time.

Next to religion, the power of the sword is the truest judge and greatest support of sovereignty which is unknown to none (as it may be that of religion is to some).   Wherefore, concerning this, I will only say that whosoever will persuade you to part with it, does but in a civil way desire you to be no King; reward and punishment (which are the inseparable effects of regal power) necessarily depending upon it, and without which a King can neither be loved nor feared of his subjects.

I will end this letter with a negative direction, which is, never to abandon the protection of your friends upon any pretence whatsoever.

XII. To the Lords Jermyn and Culpepper, and Mr. John Ashburnham

Newcastle, September 21, 1646.

I have now deciphered (which when I wrote last I had not) and considered of the draft you sent me for an answer to the London propositions, which I find (to my inexpressible grief and astonishment) to be not only directly against my conscience, but absolutely destructive to your ends, which is the maintenance of monarchy.   For you have taken such care for the perpetual establishing of Presbyterian government, that you have not for-gotten the Universities; and you have (as I believe purposely) omitted other things better worthy the remembering, as the naming of officers.   It is true you pretend to give an honourable mention of Episcopal government, but so meanly, and in a way so sure not to do that effect which it faintly offers, that it is a shame to see it.   And then for Ireland (though I concur with you fully in the intention), it is a poor juggling answer, and such a one that the silliest understanding must at first sight easily look through. Indeed, for the rest, I confess it smells much of the old strain; and I perceive you imagine that the dexterity of the latter part will cure the inconvenient concessions in the former, which is a great mistake. For albeit all were agreed unto as is set down, it will be in the power of pulpits (without transgressing the law) to dethrone me at their pleasure, at least to keep me in subjection. But, suppose they thank me for my concessions, and demur upon the rest, what then? You will say all is but conditional, so that I am obliged to do nothing. I grant this were a good answer, if I had a power to dispute, and that the conditions were not against my conscience. But as it is, besides the hazarding of my soul for nothing, what I have yielded unto will be held for good; and I may expect the rest, when all the Lower House turn saints, or mankind leave factions.

Now you may wonder why I have taken all these pains, for you will find that I shall not be put to a particular answer to the propositions; but this point of religion hath so great and necessary an influence throughout all my affairs, that I find it most necessary to rectify your judgements herein; for, albeit my condition be sufficiently sad, yet it is made so strangely worse by your misunderstanding the point of Church government, whereby I am made the scourge of my kingdom and family, that rather than I will undergo that burden, I will (laying all other considerations aside) hazard to go to France, to clear my reputation to the Queen, and all the world, that I stick not upon scruples, but undoubted realities, both in relation to conscience and policy. Indeed, this is a right way to make me a Papist; for if I follow your present advices concerning religion, I foresee such a necessity for it, that the time will come you will persuade me with more earnestness to submit to the Pope, than now you do for my concession to Presbyterian government; for, questionless, it is less ill, in many respects, to submit to one than many Popes.

I think Dr. Steward will be with you before this letter; wherefore, and I do again jointly and severally recommend him unto you, commanding you to hear and advise with him in this point of religion.

Charles now put forward a compromise of his own, but his opponents would have none of it.

XIII. To the Bishop of London

Newcastle, September 30, 1646.

My Lord,

My knowledge of your work and learning, and particularly in resolving cases of conscience, makes me at this time (I confess) put you to a hard and bold task, nor would I do it, but that I am confident you know not what fear is in a good cause. Yet I hope you believe I shall be loath to press you to a needless danger, assuring you that I will yield to none of your seculars in my care of your preservation. I need not tell you the many persuasions and threatenings that have been used to me, for making me change Episcopal into Presbyterian government; which, absolutely to do, is so directly against my conscience, that (by the grace of God) no misery shall ever make me.

But I hold myself obliged, by all honest means, to eschew the mischief of this too visible storm; and I think some kind of compliance to the iniquity of the times may be fit, as my case is, which at another time were unlawful. These are the grounds which have made me think of this enclosed proposition, the which as, one way, it looks handsome to me; so, in another, I am fearful lest I cannot make it with a safe conscience, of which I command you to give me your opinion upon your allegiance, conjuring you that you will deal plainly and freely with me, as you will answer it at the dreadful day of judgement.

I conceive the question to be, whether I may with a safe conscience give way to this proposed temporary compliance, with a resolution to recover and maintain that doctrine and discipline wherein I have been bred.

The duty of my oath is herein to be chiefly considered, I flattering myself that in this way I better comply with it, than being constant to a flat denial, considering how unable I am by force to obtain that which, this way, there wants not a probability to recover, if accepted, otherwise there is no harm done. For my regal authority once settled, I make no question of recovering Episcopal government, and God is my witness, my chief end in regaining my power is to do the Church service.

So expecting your reasons to strengthen your opinion, whatsoever it be, I rest

Your most assured, and faithful, constant friend,

CHARLES R.

I desire your opinion in the particulars, as well as in the general of my proposition; for it is very possible you may like the scope of it, and yet mend much in the penning of it. I give you leave to take the assistance of the Bishop of Salisbury and Doctor Sheldon, or either of them, and let me have your answer with all convenient speed. None knows of this but Will Murray, who promises exact secrecy. If your opinions and reasons shall confirm me in making of this proposition, then you, some way, may be seen in it; otherwise, I promise you that your opinion shall be concealed.

The King's proposals, enclosed in this letter, were as follow:

Whatsoever was the necessity for reformation in religion, at the beginning of this Parliament, no man will now make the least question of it. And I believe it is little less evident, that the present distractions are so great, and of such a nature, as it is much out of the power of any human fiat to settle them; there being no way, in my opinion, to restore that happy tranquillity which the Church of England hath lately and miserably lost, but by a solemn, free, and serious debate of a well-chosen number of divines of each opinion; for certainly persecution never was nor will be found a good way for conversion. These considerations have made me form a proposition, which I believe no man but myself hath thought on : it is, that concerning matters of religion, I will be content that all things remain for three years *in statu quo nunc,* so as I and my household be not hindered from using that form of God's service which we have always done. And that in the meantime a committee be chosen of both Houses—the fewer the better—to consult and debate with sixty well-chosen divines; that is to say, twenty of my naming, as many of the Presbyterians, and as many of the Independents, how the

P

Church shall be settled and governed at the end of three years, or sooner, if parties, or differences, may be sooner agreed.   I do not mean that these committees shall have any other power than of hearing, debating, and reporting; for I always understand that the determination be left to me, with the two Houses. Now, if this be accepted, I expect that this should rather facilitate than retard the settling of civil matters : giving you power to make use of these, as you shall judge best for that reasonable end, which all good men desire.

xiv. To the Lords Jermyn and Culpepper, and Mr. John Ashburnham

Newcastle, October 27, 1646.

If what I have offered by Will Murray's journey to London do not make the Scots declare for me, in case my offers be rejected at London (as I believe they will) the devil owes them a shame; and you may see, if you be not blind, that they will rather hazard their own ruin than help me, except I do that which will be sure to make me and my successors titular Kings. And I believe they are flattering themselves that their union with England will secure them, though I and the monarchy be ruined, hardens their obstinacy against me.   And this makes me offer an opinion to you, which at first I suppose you will think a paradox. It is, that my remaining in these kingdoms, though I be not a direct prisoner, is the only means, in my mind, to secure the Scots, and settle a new government here, without a breach between the two nations.   For so long as I remain as I am, though in Scotland, I (being but a cipher as to power) shall be no impediment to the change of government.   And yet the English will not dare to break with the Scots, lest they, setting me up to claim my right, should raise a great party for me in England; whereas, if I were in a secure freedom anywhere else, I believe the two nations must needs fall out, and so give me an opportunity, either to join with the weaker party, or frame one of my own; for then men will begin to perceive that, without my establishing, there can be no peace.   Now, how strange soever this fancy of mine may seem at first to you, I earnestly desire of you to consider of it well; for I have discoursed with M. de

Bellievre, who confesses that, if my condition should happen to be as I have stated it, he knows not what to object against me. And, seriously, if I did not suspect that the just distaste I have to the Scots (especially wanting the liberty of my conscience) does make me partial to any opinion which is in order to the quitting of their company, I would take my oath that I never was of righter judgement all my life. Wherefore again, I desire you to consider well of it; and if you find reason in what I say that you will think to prepare things accordingly.

The belief of the King that he might be a tertius gaudens *in the quarrels between the Scots and Parliament rendered him very desirous of being in London.*

XV. To the Speaker of the House of Peers

CHARLES R.

His Majesty's thoughts being always sincerely bent to the peace of his kingdoms, was and will be ever desirous to take all ways which might the most clearly appear the candour of his intentions to his people : and to this end could find no better way than to propose a personal free debate with his two Houses of Parliament upon all the present differences; yet finding, very much against his expectations, that this offer was laid aside, His Majesty bent all his thoughts to make his intentions fully known, by a particular answer to the propositions delivered to him in the name of both kingdoms, 24th July last : but the more he endeavoured it, he more plainly saw that any answer he could make would be subject to misinformations and misconstructions, which upon his own paraphrases and explanations he is most confident will give so good satisfaction, as would doubtless cause a happy and lasting peace. Lest therefore that good intentions may produce ill effects, His Majesty again proposes and desires to come to London, or any of his houses thereabouts, upon the public faith and security of his two Houses of Parliament and the Scots Commissioners, that he shall be there with honour, freedom and safety : where, by his personal presence, he may not only raise a mutual confidence between him and his people, but also have those doubts cleared and those difficulties explained to him, without which he cannot, but with the aforesaid mischievous inconveniences, give a particular answer to the Propositions : and with which he doubts not but so to manifest his real intentions for the settling of religion, the just privileges of Parliament, with the freedom and propriety of the subject, that it shall not be in the power of wicked and malicious men to hinder the establishing of that firm peace which all honest men desire : assuring them that as he will make no other demands but such as he believes confidently to be just, and much conducing to the tranquillity of the people : so he will be most willing to condescend unto them in whatsoever shall be really for their good and happiness : not doubting likewise but you will also have a due regard to maintain the just power of the Crown, according to your many protestations and professions : for certainly except King and people have reciprocal care each of other, neither can be happy.

To conclude, 'tis your King who desires to be heard, the which if refused to a subject by a King, he would be thought a tyrant for it, and for that end which all men profess to desire. Wherefore His Majesty conjures you, as you desire to show yourselves really what you profess, even as you are good Christians and subjects, that you will accept this his offer, which he is confident God will so bless, that it will be the readiest means by which these kingdoms may again become a comfort to their friends, and a terror to their enemies.

Newcastle, December 20, 1646.

Early in February, 1647, the Scots, having received £200,000, handed the King over to commissioners appointed by Parliament, who took him to Holmby House in Northamptonshire.

XVI. To the Speaker of the House of Peers

Holmby, February 17, 1646.

Since I have never dissembled nor hid my conscience, and that I am not yet satisfied with those alterations in religion to which you desire my consent, I will not lose time in giving reasons (which are obvious to everybody) why it is fit for me to

be attended by some of my chaplains whose opinions as clergymen I esteem and reverence, not only for the exercise of my
conscience, but also ever for clearing my judgement concerning
the present differences in religion; as I have at full declared to
Mr. Marshall and his fellow minister, having showed them that
this is the best and likeliest means of giving me satisfaction
(which without it I cannot have) in these things, whereby the
distractions of this Church may be the better settled.   Wherefore
I desire that at least two of these reverend divines, whose names
I have here set down, may have free liberty to wait upon me,
for the discharging of their duty to me according to their
function.

CHARLES R.

Bishop of London.
Bishop of Salisbury.
Bishop of Peterborough.
Doctor Sheldon, Clerk of my Closet.
Doctor March, Dean of York.
Doctor Sanderson.
Doctor Bayly.
Doctor Haywood.
Doctor Beale.
Doctor Fuller.
Doctor Hammon.
Doctor Tayler.

XVII. To the Speaker of the House of Peers

Holmby, March 6, 1646.

It being now seventeen days since I wrote to you from hence,
and not yet receiving any answer to what I then desired, I cannot
but now again renew the same unto you: and indeed, concerning anything but the necessary duty of a Christian, I would
not thus at this time trouble you with any of my desires.   But
my being attended by some of my chaplains whom I esteem and
reverence, is that which is so necessary for me (even considering my present condition), whether it be in relation to my conscience or a happy settlement of the present distractions in religion,
that I will slight divers kinds of censures, rather than not to

213

obtain what I demand : nor shall I do you the wrong, as in this to doubt the obtaining of my wish, it being totally grounded upon reason; for, desiring you to consider (not thinking it needful to mention) the divers reasons which no Christian can be ignorant of, for point of conscience, I must assure you that I cannot as I ought take into consideration those alterations in religion which have and will be offered unto me, without such help as I desire, because I can never judge rightly of, or be altered in, anything of my opinion, so long as any ordinary way of finding out the truth is denied me : but when this is granted me, I promise you faithfully, not to strive for victory in argument, but to seek and submit to truth (according to that judgement which God hath given me); always holding it my best and greatest conquest, to give contentment to my two Houses of Parliament in all things which I conceive not to be against my conscience or honour; not doubting likewise but that you will be ready to satisfy me in reasonable things, as I hope to find in this particular concerning the attendance of my chaplains upon me.

Charles R.

While Parliament was thus engaging in a series of petty insults to its prisoner, its power was steadily declining before that of the Army. Charles had been expecting the Newcastle propositions in a revised form, but as these did not arrive he addressed Parliament once more.

XVIII. To the Speaker of the House of Peers

Charles R.

As the daily expectation of the coming of the Propositions hath made His Majesty this long time to forbear the giving of his answer unto them, so the appearance of their sending being now no more, for anything he can hear, than it was at his first coming hither, notwithstanding that the Earl of Lauderdale hath been at London these ten days (whose not coming was said to be the only stop), hath caused His Majesty thus to anticipate their coming unto him; and yet, considering his condition, that his servants are denied access to him, all but very few, and those by appointment, not his own election, and that it is a declared crime

for any but the Commissioners, or such who are particularly
permitted by them, to converse with His Majesty; or that any
letters should be given to or received from him; may he not truly
say that he is not in case fit to make confessions or give
answers, since he is not master of those ordinary actions which
are the undoubted rights of every free-born man, how mean
soever his birth be. And certainly he would still be silent on
this subject until his condition were much mended (did he not
prefer such a right understanding between him and his Parliament of both kingdoms, which may make a firm and lasting peace
in all his dominions, before any particular of his own or any
earthly blessing), and therefore His Majesty hath diligently
employed his utmost endeavours (for divers months past) so to
inform his understanding and satisfy his conscience, that he
might be able to give such answers to the Propositions as would
be most agreeable to his Parliaments; but he ingenuously proposes that, notwithstanding all the pains that he hath taken
thereon, the nature of some of them appears such unto him, that
(without disclaiming that reason which God hath given him to
judge by for the good of him and his people, and without putting
the greatest violence upon his own conscience) he cannot give his
consent to all of them; yet His Majesty (that it may appear to all
the world how desirous he is to give full satisfaction) hath
thought fit hereby to express his readiness to grant what he may,
and his willingness to receive from them, and that personally, if
his two Houses at Westminster shall approve thereof, such
further information in the rest, as may but convince his judgement and satisfy those doubts which are not yet clear to him;
desiring them also to consider that, if His Majesty intended to
wind himself out of these troubles by indirect means, were it
not most easy for him now readily to consent to whatsoever hath
or shall be proposed unto him, and afterwards choose his time to
break all, alleging that forced concessions are not to be kept :
surely he might, and not yet incur a hard censure from any indifferent men. But maxims of this kind are not the guides of His
Majesty's actions; for he freely and clearly avows that he holds
it unlawful for any man, and most base in a King, to recede from
his promises for having been obtained by force or under restraint.

Wherefore His Majesty, not only rejecting those arts which he esteems unworthy of him, but even passing by that which he might well insist upon as a point of honour, in respect of his present condition, thus answers the first Proposition :

That, upon His Majesty's coming to London, he will heartily join in all that shall concern the honour of his two kingdoms or the Assembly of States of Scotland, or of the Commissioners or Deputies of either kingdoms, particularly in those things which are desired in that Proposition; upon confidence that all of them respectively with the same tenderness will look upon those things which concern His Majesty's honour.

In answer to all the Propositions concerning religion, His Majesty proposeth that he will confirm the Presbyterian government, the Assembly of Divines at Westminster, and the Directory, for three years (being the time set down by the two Houses), so that His Majesty and his household be not hindered from using that form of God's service which they have formerly; and also that a free consultation and debate be had with the Divines at Westminster (twenty of His Majesty's nomination being added unto them), whereby it may be determined by His Majesty and the two Houses, how the Church shall be governed after the said three years, or sooner if differences may be agreed.

Touching the Covenant, His Majesty is not therein yet satisfied, and desires to respite his particular answer thereunto until his coming to London : because, it being a matter of conscience, he cannot give a resolution therein till he may be assisted with the advice of some of his own chaplains (which hath hitherto been denied him), and such other divines as shall be most proper to inform him therein; and then he will make clearly appear both his zeal to the Protestant profession and the union of these two kingdoms, which he conceives to be the main drift of the Covenant.

To the seventh and eighth Propositions, His Majesty will consent.

To the ninth, His Majesty doubts not but to give good satisfaction, when he shall have been particularly informed how the said penalties shall be levied and disposed of.

To the tenth, His Majesty's answer is, that he hath been

always ready to prevent the practices of Papists; and therefore is
content to pass an Act of Parliament for that purpose, and also
that the laws against them be duly executed.

His Majesty will give his consent to the Act for the due
observation of the Lord's Day, for the suppression of innovations, and those concerning the preaching of God's Word, and
touching non-residence and pluralities.

And His Majesty will be willing to pass such Act or Acts as
shall be requisite to raise moneys for the payment and satisfying
of all public debts: expecting also that his will be therein concluded.

As to the Proposition touching the Militia: though His
Majesty cannot consent unto it *in terminis* as it is proposed
(because thereby, he conceives, he wholly parts with the power
of the sword entrusted to him by God and the laws of the land
for the protection and government of his people, thereby at once
divesting himself, and disinheriting his posterity of that right and
prerogative of the Crown which is absolutely necessary to the
kingly office, and so weakening monarchy in this kingdom that
little more than the name and shadow of it will remain), yet, if
it be only security for the preservation of the peace of this
kingdom after these unhappy troubles, and the due performance
of all the agreements which are now to be concluded, which is
desired (which His Majesty always understood to be the case,
and hopes that herein he is not mistaken), His Majesty will give
abundant satisfaction; to which end he is willing to consent, by
Act of Parliament, that the whole power of the Militia, both by
sea and land, for the space of ten years, be in such persons as
the two Houses of Parliament shall nominate (giving them
power, during the said term, to change the said persons, and to
substitute others in their places at pleasure), and afterwards to
return to the proper channel again, as it was in the times of
Queen Elizabeth and King James of blessed memory. And now
His Majesty conjures his two Houses of Parliament, as they are
Englishmen and lovers of peace, by the duty they owe to His
Majesty their King, and by the bowels of compassion they have
to their fellow-subjects, that they will accept of this His Majesty's
offer, whereby the joyful news of peace may be restored to this

languishing kingdom. His Majesty will grant the like to the kingdom of Scotland, if it be desired; and he will agree to all things that are propounded touching the conserving of peace between the two kingdoms.

Touching Ireland, other things being agreed, His Majesty will give satisfaction therein.

As to the mutual declarations proposed to be established in both kingdoms by Act of Parliament, and the qualifications, modifications and branches, which follow in the Propositions, His Majesty only professes that he doth not sufficiently understand, nor is able to reconcile many things contained in them; but this he well knows, that a general act of oblivion is the best bond of peace, and that after intestine trouble, the wisdom of this and other kingdoms hath usually and happily, in all ages, granted general pardons, whereby the numerous discontentments of many persons and families otherwise exposed to ruin might not become fuel to new disorders, or seed of future troubles. His Majesty therefore desires that his two Houses of Parliament would seriously descend into these considerations, and likewise tenderly look upon his condition herein, and the perpetual dishonour that must cleave to him, if he should thus abandon so many persons of condition and fortune that have engaged themselves with and for him out of a sense of duty; and propounds, as a very acceptable testimony of their affection to him, that a general act of oblivion and full pardon be forthwith passed by Act of Parliament.

Touching the new Great Seal, His Majesty is very willing to confirm both it and all acts done by virtue thereof until this present time; so that it be not thereby pressed to make void those acts of his done by virtue of his Great Seal, which in honour and justice he is obliged to maintain; and that the future government thereof may be in His Majesty, according to the due course of law.

Concerning the officers mentioned in the 17th Article, His Majesty, when he shall come to Westminster, will gratify his Parliament all that possibly he may, without destroying the relations which are necessary to the Crown.

His Majesty will willingly consent to the Act for the confirmation of the privileges and customs of the City of London, and all that is mentioned in the Propositions for their particular advantage.

And now that His Majesty hath thus far endeavoured to comply with the desires of his two Houses of Parliament, to the end that this agreement may be firm and lasting, without the least force or question of restraint to blemish the same, His Majesty earnestly desires presently to be admitted to his Parliament at Westminster, with that honour which is due to their Sovereign, there solemnly to confirm the same, and legally to pass the Acts before mentioned; and to give and receive as well satisfaction in all the remaining particulars, as likewise such other pledges of mutual love, trust and confidence, as shall most concern the good and prosperity of him and his people, upon which happy agreement His Majesty will dispatch his directions to the Prince his son, to return immediately to him, and will undertake for his ready obedience thereunto.

Whether this letter would have had any effect is doubtful, for on June 3rd Cromwell and his officers, in reply to the order of Parliament for the disbandment of the Army, sent Cornet Joyce to Holmby with a detachment of cavalry. Joyce decided to remove the King from Holmby, and when asked for his commission to do so pointed to his troopers. 'It is as fair a commission,' observed Charles, ' and as well written as I have seen a commission written in my life.'

The Army now made its own suggestions for a general pacification, and they were as follows:

The Heads of the Proposals agreed upon by his Excellency Sir Thomas Fairfax and the Council of the Army, to be tendered to the Commissioners of Parliament residing with the Army, and with them to be treated on by the Commissioners of the Army : containing the particulars of their desires in pursuance of their former declarations and papers, in order to the clearing and securing of the rights and liberties of the kingdom, and the settling a just and lasting peace. To which are added some further particular desires (for the removing and redressing of

divers pressing grievances), being also comprised in or necessary pursuance of their former representations and papers
appointed to be treated upon.

I. That (things hereafter proposed, being provided for by
this Parliament) a certain period may (by Act of Parliament) be
set for the ending of this Parliament (such period to be put
within a year at most), and in the same Act provision to be
made for the succession and constitution of Parliaments in
future, as followeth:

1. That Parliaments may biennially be called and meet at a
certain day, with such provision for the certainty thereof, as in
the late Act was made for triennial Parliaments; and what
further or other provision shall be found needful by the
Parliament to reduce it to more certainty; and upon the passing
of this, the said Act for triennial Parliaments to be repealed.

2. Each biennial Parliament to sit 120 days certain (unless
adjourned or dissolved sooner by their own consent), afterwards
to be adjournable or dissolvable by the King, and no Parliament
to sit past 240 days from their first meeting, or some other
limited number of days now to be agreed on; upon the expiration whereof each Parliament to dissolve of course, if not otherwise dissolved sooner.

3. The King, upon advice of the Council of State, in the
intervals between biennial Parliaments, to call a Parliament
extraordinary, provided it meet above 70 days before the next
biennial day, and be dissolved at least 60 days before the same;
so as the course of biennial elections may never be interrupted.

4. That this Parliament and each succeeding biennial
Parliament, at or before adjournment or dissolution thereof, may
appoint Committees to continue during the interval for such
purposes as are in any of these Proposals referred to such
Committees.

5. That the elections of the Commons for succeeding Parliaments may be distributed to all counties, or other parts or
divisions of the kingdom, according to some rule of equality or
proportion, so as all counties may have a number of Parliament
members allowed to their choice, proportionable to the respective rates they bear in the common charges and burdens of the

kingdom, according to some other rule of equality or proportion, to render the House of Commons (as near as may be) an
equal representative of the whole; and in order thereunto, that
a present consideration be had to take off the elections of burgesses for poor decayed or inconsiderable towns, and to give some
present addition to the number of Parliament members for great
counties that have now less than their due proportion, to bring
all (at present), as near as may be, to such a rule of proportion
as aforesaid.

6. That effectual provision be made for future freedom of
elections, and certainty of due returns.

7. That the House of Commons alone have the power from
time to time to set down further orders and rules for the ends
expressed in the two last preceding articles, so as to reduce the
elections of members for that House to more and more perfection
of equality in the distribution, freedom in the election, order
in the proceeding thereto, and certainty in the returns, with
orders and rules (in that case) to be in laws.

8. That there be a liberty for entering dissents in the House
of Commons, with provision that no member be censurable for
ought said or voted in the House further than to exclusion
from that trust; and that only by the judgement of the House
itself.

9. That the judicial power, or power of final judgement in
the Lords and Commons (and their power of exposition and
application of law, without further appeal), may be cleared; and
that no officer of justice, minister of state, or other person
adjudged by them, may be capable of protection or pardon from
the King without their advice or consent.

10. That the right and liberty of the Commons of England
may be cleared and vindicated as to a due exemption from any
judgement, trial or other proceeding against them by the House
of Peers, without the concurring judgement of the House of
Commons: as also from any other judgement, sentence or proceeding against them, other than by their equals, or according to
the law of the land.

11. The same Act to provide that grand jurymen may be
chosen by and for several parts or divisions of each county

respectively, in some equal way (and not to remain as now, at the discretion of an Under-Sheriff to be put on or off), and that such grand jurymen for their respective counties, may at each Assize present the name of persons to be made Justices of the Peace from time to time, as the county hath need for any to be added to the Commission, and at the Summer Assize to present the names of three persons, out of whom the King may pick one to be Sheriff for the next year.

II. For the future security of Parliament and the Militia in general, in order thereunto, that it be provided by Act of Parliament :

1. That the power of the Militia by sea and land, during the space of ten years next ensuing, shall be ordered and disposed by the Lords and Commons assembled, and to be assembled in the Parliament or Parliaments of England, by such persons as they shall nominate and appoint for that purpose from time to time during the said space.

2. That the said power shall not be ordered, disposed or exercised by the King's Majesty that now is, or by any person or persons by any authority derived from him, during the said space, or at any time hereafter by His said Majesty, without the advice and consent of the said Lords and Commons, or of such Committees or Council in the intervals of Parliament as they shall appoint.

3. That during the same space of ten years the said Lords and Commons may by Bill or Ordinance raise and dispose of what moneys and for what forces they shall from time to time find necessary; as also for payment of the public debts and damages, and for all other public uses of the kingdom.

4. And to the end the temporary security intended by the three particulars last precedent may be the better assured, it may therefore be provided :

That no subjects that have been in hostility against the Parliament in the late war, shall be capable of bearing any office of power or public trust in the Commonwealth during the space of five years, without the consent of Parliament or of the Council of State; or to sit as members or assistants of either House of Parliament, until the second biennial Parliament be passed.

222

III. For the present form of disposing the Militia in order to the peace and safety of this kingdom and the service of Ireland:

1. That there be Commissioners for the Admiralty, with the Vice-Admiral and Rear-Admiral, now to be agreed on, with power for the forming, regulating, appointing of officers and providing for the Navy, and for ordering the same to, and in the ordinary service of the Kingdom; and that there be a sufficient provision and establishment for pay and maintenance thereof.

2. That there be a General for command of the land forces that are to be in pay both in England, Ireland and Wales, both for field and garrison.

3. That there be Commissions in the several counties for the standing Militia of the respective counties (consisting of trained bands and auxiliaries not in pay), with power for the proportioning, forming, regulating, training and disciplining of them.

4. That there be a Council of State, with power to superintend and direct the several and particular powers of the Militia last mentioned, for the peace and safety of this kingdom, and of Ireland.

5. That the same Council may have power as the King's Privy Council, for and in all foreign negotiations; provided that the making of war or peace with any other kingdom or state shall not be without the advice and consent of Parliament.

6. That the said power of the Council of State be put into the hands of trusty and able persons now to be agreed on, and the same persons to continue in that power (*si bene se gesserint*) for the certain term not exceeding seven years.

7. That there be a sufficient establishment now provided for the salary forces both in England and Ireland, the establishment to continue until two months after the meeting of the first biennial Parliament.

IV. That an Act be passed for disposing the great offices for ten years by the Lords and Commons in Parliament; or by such Committees as they shall appoint for that purpose in the intervals (with submission to the approbation of the next Parliament), and after ten years they to nominate three, and the King out of that number to appoint one for the succession upon any vacancy.

V. That an Act be passed for restraining of any Peers made since the 21st day of May, 1642, or to be hereafter made, from having any power to sit or vote in Parliament without consent of both Houses.

VI. That an Act be passed for recalling and making void all declarations and other proceedings against the Parliament, or against any that have acted by or under their authority in the late war, or in relation to it; and that the Ordinances for indemnity may be confirmed.

VII. That an Act be passed for making void all grants, etc., under the Great Seal, that was conveyed away from the Parliament, since the time that it was so conveyed away (except as in the Parliament's propositions), and for making those valid that have been or shall be passed under the Great Seal, made by the authority of both Houses of Parliament.

VIII. That an Act be passed for confirmation of the Treaties between the two kingdoms of England and Scotland, and for appointing conservators of the peace between them.

IX. That the Ordinance for taking away the Court of Wards and Liveries be confirmed by Act of Parliament; provided His Majesty's revenue be not damnified therein, nor those that last held offices in the same left without reparation some other way.

X. An Act to declare void the cessation of Ireland, etc., and to leave the prosecution of that war to the Lords and Commons in the Parliament of England.

XI. An Act to be passed to take away all coercive power, authority, and jurisdiction of Bishops and all other Ecclesiastical Officers whatsoever, extending to any civil penalties upon any : and to repeal all laws whereby the civil magistracy hath been, or is bound, upon any ecclesiastical censure to proceed (*ex officio*) unto any civil penalties against any persons so censured.

XII. That there be a repeal of all Acts or clauses in any Act enjoining the use of the Book of Common Prayer, and imposing any penalties for neglect thereof; as also of all Acts or clauses of any Act, imposing any penalty for not coming to church, or for meetings elsewhere for prayer or other religious duties, exercises or ordinances, and some other provision to be made for discovering of Papists and Popish recusants, and for disabling them, and of all Jesuits or priests from disturbing the State.

XIII. That the taking of the Covenant be not enforced upon any, nor any penalties imposed on the refusers, whereby men might be restrained to take it against their judgements or consciences; but all Orders and Ordinances tending to that purpose to be repealed.

XIV. That (the things here before proposed being provided, for settling and securing the rights, liberties, peace and safety of the kingdom) His Majesty's person, his Queen, and Royal issue, may be restored to a condition of safety, honour and freedom in this nation, without diminution to their personal rights, or further limitation to the exercise of the regal power than according to the particulars foregoing.

XV. For the matter of composition :

1. That a less number out of the persons excepted in the two first qualifications (not exceeding five for the English) being nominated particularly by the Parliament, who (together with the persons in the Irish Rebellion, included in the third qualification) may be reserved to the further judgement of the Parliament as they shall find cause, all other excepted persons may be remitted from the exception, and admitted to the composition.

2. That the rates of all future compositions may be lessened and limited, not to exceed the several proportions hereafter expressed respectively. That is to say :

(1) For all persons formerly excepted, not above a third part.

(2) For the late members of Parliament under the first branch of the fourth qualification in the Propositions, a fourth part.

(3) For other members of Parliament in the second and third branches of the same qualification, a sixth part.

(4) For the persons nominated in the said fourth qualification, and those included in the tenth qualification, an eighth part.

R

(5) For all others included in the sixth qualification, a tenth part : and that real debts either upon record, or proved by witnesses, be considered and abated in the valuation of their estates in all the cases aforesaid.

3. That those who shall hereafter come to compound, may not have the Covenant put upon them as a condition without which they may not compound, but in case they shall not willingly take it, they may pass their compositions without it.

4. That the persons and estates of all English not worth £200 in land or goods, be at liberty and discharged : and that the King's menial servants that never took up arms, but only attended his person according to their offices, may be freed from composition, or to pay (at most) but the proportion of one year's revenue, or a twentieth part.

5. That in order to the making and perfecting of compositions at the rates aforesaid, the rents, revenues, and other duties and profits of all sequestered estates whatsoever (except the estates of such persons who shall be continued under exception as before), be from henceforth suspended and detained in the hands of the respective tenants, occupants and others from whom they are due, for the space of six months following.

6. That the faith of the Army, or other forces of the Parliament given in articles upon surrenders to any of the King's party, may be fully made good; and where any breach thereof shall appear to have been made, full reparation and satisfaction may be given to the parties injured, and the persons offending (being found out) may be compelled thereto.

XVI. That there may be a general Act of Oblivion to extend unto all (except the persons to be continued in exception as before), to absolve from all trespasses, misdemeanours, etc., done in prosecution of the war; and from all trouble or prejudice for or concerning the same (after their compositions past), and to restore them to all privileges, etc., belonging to other subjects, provided as in the fourth particular under the second general head aforegoing concerning security.

And whereas there have been of late strong endeavours and practices of a factious and desperate party to embroil this kingdom in a new war, and for that purpose to induce the King, the Queen, and the Prince to declare for the said party, and also to excite and stir up all those of the King's late party to appear and engage for the same, which attempts and designs, many of the King's party (out of their desires to avoid further misery to the kingdom) have contributed their endeavours to prevent (as for divers of them we have had particular assurance): we do therefore desire, that such of the King's party who shall appear to have expressed, and shall hereafter express, that way their good affections to the peace and welfare of the kingdom, and to hinder the embroiling of the same in a new war, may be freed and exempted from compositions, or to pay but one year's revenue or a twentieth part.

These particulars aforegoing are the heads of such Proposals as we have agreed on to tender in order to the settling of the peace of this kingdom, leaving the terms of peace for the kingdom of Scotland to stand as in the late Propositions of both kingdoms, until that kingdom shall agree to any alteration.

Next to the Proposals aforesaid for the present settling of a peace, we shall desire that no other time may be lost by the Parliament for dispatch of other things tending to the welfare, ease and just satisfaction of the kingdom, and in special manner :

I. That the just and necessary liberty of the people to represent their grievances and desires by way of petition, may be cleared and vindicated, according to the fifth head in the late representation or Declaration of the Army sent from St. Albans.

II. That (in pursuance of the same head in the said Declaration) the common grievances of this people may be speedily considered of, and effectually redressed, and in particular :

1. That the excise may be taken off from such commodities, whereon the poor people of the land do ordinarily live, and a certain time to be limited for taking off the whole.

2. That the oppressions and encroachments of forest laws may be prevented for the future.

3. All monopolies (old or new) and restraints to freedom of trade to be taken off.

4. That a course may be taken, and Commissioners appointed to remedy and rectify the inequality of rates lying upon several

counties, and several parts of each county in respect of others, and to settle the proportion of land rates to more equality throughout the kingdom; in order to which we shall offer some further particulars, which we hope may be useful.

5. The present unequal troublesome and contentious way of ministers' maintenance by tithes to be considered of, and some remedy applied.

6. That the rules and course of law, and the officers of it, may be so reduced and reformed, as that all suits and questions of right may be more clear and certain in the issues, and not so tedious nor chargeable in the proceedings as now; in order to which we shall offer some further particulars hereafter.

7. That prisoners for debt or other creditors (who have estates to discharge them) may not by embracing imprisonment, or any other ways, have advantage to defraud their creditors, but that the estates of all men may be some way made liable to their debts (as well as tradesmen are by commissions of bankrupt), whether they be imprisoned for it or not; and that such prisoners for debt, who have not wherewith to pay, or at least do yield up what they have to their creditors, may be freed from imprisonment or some way provided for, so as neither they nor their families may perish by imprisonment.

8. Some provision to be made, that none may be compelled by penalty or otherwise to answer unto questions tending to the accusing of themselves or their nearest relations in criminal causes; and no man's life to be taken away under two witnesses.

9. That consideration may be had of all statutes, and the laws or customs of Corporations, imposing any oaths either to repeal, or else to qualify and provide against the same, so far as they may extend or be construed to the molestation or ensnaring of religious and peaceable people, merely for nonconformity in religion.

III. That according to the sixth head in the Declaration of the Army, the large power given to Committees or Deputy-Lieutenants during the late times of war and distraction, may be speedily taken into consideration to be recalled and made void, and that such powers of that nature as shall appear necessary to be continued, may be put into a regulated way, and left to as little arbitrariness as the statute and necessity of the things (wherein they are conversant) will bear.

IV. That (according to the seventh head in the said Declaration) an effectual course may be taken that the kingdom may be righted, and satisfied in point of accounts for the vast sums that have been levied.

V. That provision may be made for payment of arrears to the Army, and the rest of the soldiers of the kingdom who have concurred with the Army in the late desires and proceedings thereof; and in the next place for payment of the public debts and damages of the kingdom; and that to be performed, first to such persons whose debt or damages (upon the public account) are great, and their estates small, so as they are thereby reduced to a difficulty of subsistence: in order to all which, and to the fourth particular last proceeding, we shall speedily offer some further particulars (in the nature of rules), which we hope will be of good use towards public satisfaction.

August 1, 1647.

Signed by the appointment of his Excellency Sir Thomas Fairfax and the Council of War.

Charles, however, hoped that the divisions among his enemies would enable him to obtain better terms in the near future, and on September 9th he sent a somewhat evasive reply.

XIX. To the Speaker of the House of Peers

CHARLES REX.

His Majesty cannot choose but be passionately sensible (as he believes all his good subjects are) of the late great distractions, and still languishing and unsettled state of this kingdom; and he calls God to witness, and is willing to give testimony to all the world, of his readiness to contribute his utmost endeavours for restoring it to a happy and flourishing condition.

His Majesty having perused the Propositions now brought to him, finds them the same in effect which were offered to him at

Newcastle : to some of which, as he could not then consent without violation of his conscience and honour, so neither can he agree to others now, conceiving them in many respects more disagreeable to the present condition of affairs than when they were formerly presented to him, as being destructive to the main principal interests of the Army, and of all those whose affections concur with them : and His Majesty having seen the Proposals of the Army to the Commissioners from his two Houses residing with them, and with them to be treated on in order to the clearing and securing the rights and liberties of the kingdom, and the settling a just and lasting peace, to which Proposals, as he conceives his two Houses not to be strangers, so he believes they will think with him, that they much more conduce to the satisfaction of all interests, and may be a fitter foundation for a lasting peace, than the Propositions which at this time are tendered to him.

He therefore propounds (as the best way in his judgement in order to peace) that his two Houses would instantly take into consideration those Proposals, upon which there may be a personal treaty with His Majesty, and upon such other Propositions as His Majesty shall make, hoping that the said Proposals may be so moderated in the said treaty as to render them the more capable of His Majesty's full concessions, wherein he resolves to give full satisfaction unto his people for whatsoever shall concern the settling of the Protestant profession, with liberty to tender consciences, and the securing of the laws, liberties and properties of all his subjects, and the just privileges of Parliament for the future; and likewise by his present deportment in this treaty, he will make the world clearly judge of his intentions in the matter of future government : in which treaty His Majesty will be pleased (if it be thought fit) that Commissioners from the Army (whose the Proposals are) may likewise be admitted.

His Majesty therefore conjures his two Houses of Parliament by the duty they owe to God and His Majesty their King, and by the bowels of compassion they have to their fellow subjects, both for relief of their present sufferings, and to prevent future miseries, that they will forthwith accept His Majesty's offer,

whereby the joyful news of peace may be restored to this distressed kingdom.

And for what concerns the kingdom of Scotland mentioned
in the Propositions, His Majesty will very willingly treat upon
those particulars with Scotch Commissioners, and doubts not but
to give a reasonable satisfaction to that His Majesty's kingdom.

*After his departure from Holmby House the King was moved
from one place to another, and this gave him the opportunity of
occasionally seeing his children. The Duke of York had been
captured at the surrender of Oxford in the previous year.*

xx. To the Duke of York

Casam, July 4, 1647.

JAMES,

I am in hope that you may be permitted, with your brother
and sister, to come to some place betwixt this and London,
where I may see you.

To this end, therefore, I command you to ask leave of the
two Houses to make a journey (if it may be) for a night or two.

But rather than not see you, I will be content that you come
to some convenient place to dine, and go back again at night.

And foreseeing the fear of your being brought within the
power of the Army as I am, may be objected, to hinder this my
desire.

I have full assurance from Sir Thomas Fairfax, and the
chief officers that there will be no interruption or impediment
made by them for your return now and when you please. So
God bless you.

Your loving father,
CHARLES R.

Send me word as soon as you can of the time and place
where I shall have the contentment of seeing you, your brother
and sister.

XXI. To Princess Elizabeth

Hampton Court, October 27, 1647.

DEAR DAUGHTER,

This is to assure you that it is not through forgetfulness nor any want of kindness, that I have not, all this time, sent for you; but for such reasons as is fitter for you to imagine (which you may easily do) than me to write. But now I hope to see you upon Friday or Saturday next, as your brother James can more particularly tell you, to whom referring you, I rest

Your loving father,

CHARLES R.

As the year 1647 drew to its close it looked as if the King's hopes might well be realized. All over England and Wales the Royalists were ready to strike another blow, while the Scots were so alarmed at the growing power of the Army and the Independents that they were prepared to recede to no inconsiderable extent from the position they had taken up when Charles was in their power at Newcastle. In these circumstances, the King felt he would be freer if he were no longer under the supervision of the Army, and on November 11th he effected his escape from Hampton Court to Carisbrooke, in the Isle of Wight. From there he conducted further fruitless negotiations with the Parliament, and in December came to terms with the Scots.

XXII

CHARLES R.

His Majesty giving belief to the professions of those who have entered into the League and Covenant, and that their intentions are real for preservation of His Majesty's person and authority according to their allegiance, and no ways to diminish his just power and greatness, His Majesty, so soon as he can with freedom, honour and safety be present in a free Parliament, is content to confirm the said League and Covenant by Act of Parliament in both kingdoms, for security of all who have taken or shall take the said Covenant, provided that none who is unwilling shall be constrained to take it. His Majesty will likewise confirm by Act of Parliament in England, Presbyterian

Government, by directory for worship, and Assembly of Divines
at Westminster for three years, so that His Majesty and his
household be not hindered from using that form of Divine
Service he hath formerly practised; and that a free debate and
consultation be had with the Divines at Westminster, twenty
of His Majesty's nomination being added unto them, and with
such as shall be sent from the Church of Scotland, whereby it
may be determined by His Majesty and the two Houses how the
Church government, after the said three years, shall be fully
established as is most agreeable to the Word of God : that an
effectual course shall be taken by Act of Parliament, and all
other ways needful or expedient, for suppressing the opinions
and practices of anti-Trinitarians, Anabaptists, Antinomians,
Arminians, Familists, Brownists, Separatists, Independents,
Libertines, and Seekers, and generally for suppressing all
blasphemy, heresy, schism, and all such scandalous doctrines and
practices as are contrary to the light of nature, or to the known
principles of Christianity, whether concerning faith, worship or
conversation, or to the power of Godliness, or which may be
destructive to order and government, or to the peace of the
Church and kingdom; that in the next session of Parliament after
that the kingdom of Scotland shall declare for His Majesty in
pursuance of this Agreement, he shall in person or by commission confirm the League and Covenant according to the first
Article.   Concerning the Acts passed in the last triennial Parliament of his kingdom of Scotland, and the Committees appointed
by the same, His Majesty is content then also to give assurance
by Act of Parliament that neither he nor his successors shall
quarrel, call in question, or command the contrary of any of
them, nor question any for giving obedience to the same; and
whereas after the return of the Scottish Army to Scotland, the
Houses of Parliament of England did resolve and appoint the
Army under command of Sir Thomas Fairfax to disband, and
they having entered into an engagement to the contrary, His
Majesty was carried away from Holmby against his will by a
party of the said Army, and detained in their power until he
was forced to fly from amongst them to the Isle of Wight; and
since that time His Majesty and the Commissioners of the

kingdom of Scotland have earnestly pressed that His Majesty might come to London in safety, honour and freedom for a personal treaty with the two Houses and the Commissioners of the Parliament of Scotland, which hath not been granted : and whereas the said Army hath in a violent manner forced away divers members of both Houses from the discharge of their trust, and possessed themselves of the City of London and all the strengths and garrisons of the kingdom, and, through the power and influence of the said Army and their adherents, Propositions and Bills have been sent to His Majesty without the advice and consent of the kingdom of Scotland, contrary to the Treaty between the kingdoms, which are destructive to religion, His Majesty's just rights, the privileges of Parliament, and liberty of the subject, from which Propositions and Bills the said Scots Commissioners have dissented in the name of the kingdom of Scotland; and, forasmuch as His Majesty is willing to give satisfaction concerning the settling of religion and other matter in difference, as is expressed in this Agreement, the kingdom of Scotland doth oblige and engage themselves first in a peaceable way and manner to endeavour that His Majesty may come to London in safety, honour and freedom for a personal treaty with the Houses of Parliament and the Commissioners of Scotland upon such Propositions as shall be mutually agreed on between the kingdoms, and such Propositions as His Majesty shall think fit to make; and that for this end all armies may be disbanded, and in case this shall not be granted, that Declarations shall be emitted by the kingdom of Scotland in pursuance of this Agreement, against the unjust proceedings of the two Houses of Parliament towards His Majesty and the kingdom of Scotland, wherein they shall assert the right which belongs to the Crown in the power of the Militia, the Great Seal, bestowing of honours and offices of trust, choice of Privy Councillors, the right of the King's negative voice in Parliament; and that the Queen's Majesty, the Prince, and the rest of the Royal issue, ought to remain where His Majesty shall think fit, in either of the kingdoms, with safety, honour, and freedom; and upon the issuing of the said Declarations, that an army shall be sent from Scotland into England, for preservation and establishment of

religion, for defence of His Majesty's person and authority, and
restoring him to his government, to the just rights of the Crown
and his full revenues, for defence of the privileges of Parliament
and liberties of the subject, for making a firm union between the
kingdoms, under His Majesty and his posterity, and settling a
lasting peace; in pursuance whereof the kingdom of Scotland will
endeavour that there may be a free and full Parliament in
England, and that His Majesty may be with them in honour,
safety and freedom, and that a speedy period be set to this present
Parliament, and that the said army shall be upon the march
before the said peaceable message and Declaration be delivered to
the House; and it is further agreed that all such in the kingdom
of Scotland in pursuance of this Agreement, shall be protected
by His Majesty in their persons and estates; and that all such His
Majesty's subjects of England and Ireland as shall join with him
in pursuance of this Agreement may come to the Scotch and join
with them, or else put themselves into other bodies in England
and Wales for prosecution of the same ends as the King's Majesty
shall judge most convenient, and under such Commanders or
Generals of the English nation as His Majesty shall think fit, and
that all such shall be protected by the kingdom of Scotland and
their army in their persons and estates, and where any injury or
wrong is done to them therein, that they shall be careful to see
them fully repaired so far as is in their power to do, and likewise, where any injury or wrong is done to those that join with
the kingdom of Scotland, His Majesty shall be careful for their
full reparation; that His Majesty or any by his authority or
knowledge shall not make nor admit of any cessation, pacification, nor agreement for peace whatsoever, nor of any Treaty,
Propositions, Bills, or any other ways for that end, with the
Houses of Parliament or any army or party in England and
Ireland, without the advice and consent of the kingdom of
Scotland; nor any having their authority shall either make or
admit of any of these any manner of way with any whatsoever
without His Majesty's advice and consent; that, upon the
settling of a peace, there be an Act of Oblivion to be agreed on
by His Majesty and both his Parliaments of both kingdoms; that
His Majesty, the Prince, or both shall come into Scotland upon

the invitation of that kingdom and their declaration that they shall be in safety, freedom and honour, when possibly they can come with safety and conveniency; and that His Majesty shall contribute his utmost endeavours both at home and abroad for assisting the kingdom of Scotland in carrying on this war by sea and land, and for their supply of moneys, army, ammunition, and all other things requisite, as also for guarding the coasts of Scotland with ships, and protecting all Scottish merchants in the free exercise of trade and commerce with other nations; and His Majesty is very willing and doth authorize the Scots Army to possess themselves of Berwick, Carlisle, Newcastle-upon-Tyne, Tynemouth, and Hartlepool, for to be places of retreat and magazine, and, when the peace of the kingdom is settled, the kingdom of Scotland shall remove their forces, and deliver back again the said towns and castles; that, according to the large Treaty, payment may be made of the remainder of the brotherly assistance which yet rests unpaid; and likewise of the £200,000 due upon the late Treaty made with the Houses of Parliament for the return of the Scots army, as also that payment shall be made to the kingdom of Scotland for the charge and expense of their army in this future war, together with due recompense for the losses which they shall sustain therein : that due satisfaction, according to the Treaty on that behalf between the kingdoms, shall be made to the Scottish army in Ireland, out of the land of that kingdom or otherwise; that His Majesty, according to the intention of his father, shall endeavour a complete union of the kingdoms, so as they may be one under His Majesty and his posterity; and, if that cannot be speedily effected, that all liberties, privileges, concerning commerce, traffic, and manufactories peculiar to the subjects of either nation, shall be common to the subjects of both kingdoms without distinction; and that there be a communication of mutual capacity of all other privileges of the subject in the two kingdoms; that a competent number of ships shall be yearly assigned and appointed out of His Majesty's Navy, which shall attend the coast of Scotland for a guard and freedom of trade to his subjects of that nation; that His Majesty doth declare that his successors as well as himself are obliged to the performances of the Articles and conditions

236

of this Agreement; that His Majesty shall not be obliged to the performance of the aforesaid Articles until the kingdom of Scotland shall declare for him in pursuance of this Agreement, and that the whole Articles and conditions aforesaid shall be finished, perfected and performed before the return of the Scots army; and that when they return into Scotland at the same time, *simul et semel*, all arms be disbanded in England.

Carisbrooke, December 26.

CHARLES REX.

We do declare and oblige ourselves *in verbo principis*, that the kingdom of Scotland engaging to perform the written Articles, we shall perform our part therein as is above expressed in the said Articles.

At Carisbrooke Castle, December 26.

We, whose names are underwritten, do hereby engage ourselves upon our honour, faith and conscience, and all that is dearest to honest men, to endeavour to the utmost of our powers that the kingdom of Scotland shall engage to perform the within written conditions in so far as relates to them, His Majesty engaging to perform his part of the aforesaid Articles; and we are most confident that the kingdom of Scotland will do the same; and we are most willing, upon the perfecting of the said Agreement, to hazard our lives and fortunes in pursuance thereof. By the clause of confirming Presbyterian government by Act of Parliament, His Majesty hath declared to us that he is neither obliged to desire the settling of Presbyterian government, nor to present a Bill for that effect; and we likewise understand that no person whatsoever suffer in his estate or corporal punishment for not submitting to Presbyterian government, His Majesty understanding that this shall not extend to those that are mentioned in the clause against toleration.

This was declared in the presence of Lord Loudoun, Lord Lauderdale, Lord Lanerick, and the King took them as witnesses and not assentors, December 27.

LOUDOUN, LAUDERDALE, LANERICK.

XXIII

CHARLES REX.

His Majesty, out of the natural affection he bears to his ancient and native kingdom, and to demonstrate how sensible he is of their affection expressed to him in the time of his extremity, and how heartily desirous he is to put marks of his grace and favour upon his subjects of that nation which may remain to all posterity, doth declare that he is resolved :

That Scottish men equally with English be employed by His Majesty and his successors, in foreign negotiations and treaties in all time coming;

That a considerable and competent number of Scotsmen be upon His Majesty's Council, and his successors' in England, and so reciprocally the same number of Englishmen upon His Majesty's Council in Scotland. That Scottish men according to the number and proportion (of a third part in number and quality be employed) in places of trust and offices about His Majesty's person, the Queen's Majesty, the Prince and the rest of the Royal issue, and their families in all time coming.

That His Majesty and the Prince, or at least one of them, shall reside in Scotland frequently as their occasions can permit —whereby their subjects of that kingdom may be known unto them.

Parliament's reply to this move was to vote that no more negotiations should take place with the King, and the issue between the latter and his opponents was once more to be decided by the sword. The Royalists rose, and the Scots came South, but neither was a match for the military genius of Cromwell.

By August, 1648, the Army was undisputed master of the situation, and Charles was at its mercy. For a few brief weeks, however, there were fresh negotiations at Newport with the Parliament, which was as much threatened by the predominance of the Army as was the King himself. The latter's state of mind is to be seen in his letters to his children.

xxiv. To Princess Elizabeth

Newport, December 14, 1648.

DEAR DAUGHTER,

It is not want of affection that makes me write so seldom to you, but want of matter, such as I could wish; and indeed am I loath to write to those I love when I am out of humour (as I have been these days by past), lest my letters should trouble those I desire to please. But having this opportunity, I would not lose it; though at this time I have nothing to say, but God bless you! So I rest

Your loving father,

CHARLES R.

Give your brother my blessing with a kiss, and commend me kindly to my Lady Northumberland, by the same token.

xxv. To the Prince of Wales

Newport, November 29, 1648.

SON,

By what hath been said, you may see how long we have laboured in search of peace. Do not you be discouraged to tread those ways, to restore yourself to your right; but prefer the way of peace. Show the greatness of your mind, rather to conquer your enemies by pardoning than punishing. If you saw how unmanly and unchristianly this implacable disposition is in our evil willers, you would avoid that spirit. Censure us not, for having parted with too much of our own right; the price was great; the commodity was security to us, peace to our people. And we are confident another Parliament would remember how useful a King's power is to a people's liberty.

Of how much have we divested ourself, that we and they might meet again in a due Parliamentary way to agree the bounds for Prince and people! And in this, give belief to our experience, never to affect more greatness or prerogative than what is really and intrinsically for the good of our subjects (not satisfaction of favourites). And, if you thus use it, you will never want means to be a father to all, and a bountiful Prince to any you would be extraordinarily gracious to. You may perceive all men trust their treasure, where it returns them interest: and if Princes, like the sea, receive and repay all the fresh streams and rivers trust them with, they will not grudge, but pride themselves, to make them up an ocean.

These considerations may make you a great Prince, as your father is now a low one; and your state may be so much the more established, as mine hath been shaken. For subjects have learnt (we dare say) that victories over their Princes are but triumphs over themselves; and so, will be more unwilling to hearken to changes hereafter.

The English nation are a sober people; however at present under some infatuation. We know not but this may be the last time we may speak to you or the world publicly. We are sensible into what hands we are fallen; and yet we bless God we have those inward refreshments, that the malice of our enemies cannot disturb. We have learnt to own ourself by retiring into ourself, and therefore can the better digest what befalls us; not doubting but God can restrain our enemies' malice, and turn their fierceness unto his praise.

To conclude, if God give you success, use it humbly and far from revenge. If He restore you to your right upon hard conditions, whatever you promise, keep. Those men which have forced laws which they were bound to observe, will find their triumphs full of troubles. Do not think anything in this world worth obtaining by foul and unjust means. You are the son of our love; and, as we direct you to what we have recommended to you, so we assure you, we do not more affectionately pray for you (to whom we are a natural parent) than we do, that the ancient glory and renown of this nation be not buried in irreligion and fanatic humour : and that all our subjects (to whom we are a political parent) may have such sober thoughts as to seek their peace in the orthodox profession of the Christian religion, as it was established since the Reformation in this kingdom, and not in new revelation; and that the ancient laws, with the interpretation according to the known practices, may once again be a hedge about them; that you may in due time govern, and they be governed, as in the fear of the Lord.

C.R.

The Commissioners are gone; the corn is now in the ground; we expect the harvest.   If the fruit be peace, we hope the God of peace will, in time, reduce all to truth and order again : which that He may do, is the prayer of   C.R.

The leaders of the Army, of whom Cromwell was the fore-most, now put an end to the negotiations which were still dragging on at Newport, and on December 1st the King was taken to Hurst Castle for eighteen days, while ' Pride's Purge' ensured a House of Commons that would vote his death.   Charles was brought to London, and on January 20th, 1649, appeared before those appointed to try him.
The charge against the King was as follows:

That the said Charles Stuart, being admitted King of England, and therein trusted with a limited power to govern by and according to the laws of the land, and not otherwise; and by his trust, oath, and office, being obliged to use the power committed to him for the good and benefit of the people, and for the preservation of their rights and liberties; yet, nevertheless, out of a wicked design to erect and uphold in himself an unlimited and tyrannical power to rule according to his will, and to over-throw the rights and liberties of the people, yea, to take away and make void the foundations thereof, and of all redress and remedy of misgovernment, which by the fundamental constitutions of this kingdom were reserved on the people's behalf in the right and power of frequent and successive Parliaments, or national meet-ings in Council; he, the said Charles Stuart, for accomplishment of such his designs, and for the protecting of himself and his adherents in his and their wicked practices, to the same ends hath traitorously and maliciously levied war against the present Parliament, and the people therein represented, particularly upon or about the 30th day of June, in the year of our Lord 1642, at Beverley, in the County of York; and upon or about the 24th day of August in the same year, at the County of the Town of Nottingham, where and when he set up his standard of war; and also on or about the 23rd day of October in the same year, at Edgehill or Keynton-field, in the County of Warwick; and upon or about the 30th day of November in the same year, at Brentford, in the County of Middlesex; and upon or about the 30th day of August, in the year of our Lord, 1643, at the Caversham Bridge, near Reading, in the County of Berks; and upon or about the 30th day of October in the year last mentioned, at or upon the City of Gloucester; and upon or about the 30th day of November in the year last mentioned, at Newbury, in the County of Berks; and upon or about the 31st day of July, in the year of our Lord 1644, at Cropredy Bridge, in the County of Oxon; and upon or about the 30th day of September in the year last mentioned, at Bodmin and other places near adjacent, in the County of Cornwall; and upon or about the 30th day of November in the year last mentioned, at Newbury aforesaid; and upon or about the 8th day of June, in the year of our Lord 1645, at the Town of Leicester; and also upon the 14th day of the same month in the same year, at Naseby-field, in the County of Northampton. At which several times and places, or most of them, and at many other places in this land, at several other times within the years aforementioned, and in the year of our Lord 1646, he, the said Charles Stuart, hath caused and procured many thousands of the free people of this nation to be slain; and by divisions, parties, and insurrections within this land, by invasions from foreign parts, endeavoured and procured by him, and by many other evil ways and means, he, the said Charles Stuart, hath not only maintained and carried on the said war both by land and sea, during the years beforementioned, but also hath renewed, or caused to be renewed, the said war against the Parliament and good people of this nation in this present year 1648, in the Counties of Kent, Essex, Surrey, Sussex, Middlesex, and many other Counties and places in England and Wales, and also by sea. And particularly he, the said Charles Stuart, hath for that purpose given commission to his son the Prince, and others, whereby, besides multitudes of other persons, many such as were by the Parliament entrusted and employed for the safety of the nation (being by him or his agents corrupted to the betraying of their trust, and revolting from the Parliament), have had entertainment and commission for the continuing and renewing of war and hostility against the said Parliament and people as aforesaid. By which cruel and unnatural wars, by him, the said Charles Stuart, levied, continued, and renewed as aforesaid, much innocent blood of the free people of this nation hath been spilt, many families have been undone, the public treasure wasted and exhausted, trade obstructed and miserably decayed, vast expense and damage to the nation incurred, and many parts of this land spoiled, some of them even to desolation. And for further prosecution of his said evil designs, he, the said Charles Stuart, doth still continue his commissions to the said Prince, and other rebels and revolters, both English and foreigners, and to the Earl of Ormond, and the Irish rebels and revolters associated with him; from whom further invasions upon this land are threatened, upon the procurement, and on the behalf of the said Charles Stuart.

All which wicked designs, wars, and evil practices of him, the said Charles Stuart, have been, and are carried on for the advancement and upholding of a personal interest of will, power, and pretended prerogative to himself and his family, against the public interest, common right, liberty, justice, and peace of the people of this nation, by and from whom he was entrusted as aforesaid.

By all which it appeareth that the said Charles Stuart hath been, and is the occasioner, author, and continuer of the said unnatural cruel and bloody wars; and therein guilty of all the treasons, murders, rapines, burnings, spoils, desolations, damages and mischiefs to this nation, acted and committed in the said wars, or occasioned thereby.

What took place at the trial is best described in the words of the official report.

XXVI

Lord President (i.e. Bradshaw). Charles Stuart, King of England, the Commons of England assembled in Parliament being deeply sensible of the calamities that have been brought upon this nation, which is fixed upon you as the principal author of it, have resolved to make inquisition for blood; and according to that debt and duty they owe to justice, to God, the kingdom, and themselves, and according to the fundamental power that rests in themselves, they have resolved to bring you to Trial and Judgement: and for that purpose have constituted this High Court of Justice, before which you are brought.

This said, Mr. Cook, Solicitor for the Commonwealth, standing within a bar on the right hand of the prisoner, offered to speak: but the King having a staff in his hand, held it up, and laid it upon the said Mr. Cook's shoulder two or three times, bidding him hold. Nevertheless, the Lord President ordering him to go on, he said:

Mr. Cook. My Lord, I am commanded to charge Charles Stuart, King of England, in the name of the Commons of England, with treason and high misdemeanours: I desire the said charge may be read.

The charge being read, the Lord President replied:

Lord President. Sir, you have now heard your charge, containing such matter as appears in it; you find, that in the close of it, it is prayed to the Court, in the behalf of the Commons of England, that you answer to your charge. The Court expects your answer.

King. I would know by what power I am called hither; I was not long ago in the Isle of Wight; how I came there, is a longer story than I think it fit at this present time for me to speak of; but there I entered into a Treaty with both Houses of Parliament, with as much public faith as it is possible to be had of any people in the world. I treated there with a number of honourable lords and gentlemen, and treated honestly and uprightly; I cannot say but they did very nobly with me, we were upon the conclusion of the Treaty. Now I would know by what authority, I mean lawful; there are many unlawful authorities in the world, thieves and robbers by the highways; but I would know by what authority I was brought from thence, and carried from place to place, and I know not what: and when I know what lawful authority, I shall answer. Remember, I am your King, your lawful King, and what sins you bring upon your heads, and the judgement of God upon this land; think well upon it, I say, think well upon it, before you go further from one sin to a greater: therefore let me know by what lawful authority I am seated here, and I shall not be unwilling to answer. In the meantime, I shall not betray my trust; I have a trust committed to me by God, by old and lawful descent; I will not betray it, to answer to a new unlawful authority, therefore resolve me that, and you shall hear more of me.

Lord President. If you had been pleased and have observed what was hinted to you by the Court at your first coming hither, you would have known by what authority; which authority requires you, in the name of the people of England, of which you are elected King, to answer them.

King. No, Sir, I deny that.

Lord President. If you acknowledge not the authority of the Court, they must proceed.

King. I do tell them so; England was never an elective kingdom, but an hereditary kingdom for near these thousand years; therefore let me know by what authority I am called hither : I do stand more for the liberty of my people than any here that come to be my pretended judges; and therefore let me know by what lawful authority I am seated here, and I will answer it; otherwise I will not answer it.

Lord President. Sir, how really you have managed your trust, is known : your way of answer is to interrogate the Court which beseems not you in this condition. You have been told of it twice or thrice.

King. Here is a gentleman, Lieutenant-Colonel Cobbet; ask him if he did not bring me from the Isle of Wight by force. I do not come here as submitting to the Court : I will stand as much for the privilege of the House of Commons, rightly understood, as any man whatsoever. I see no House of Lords here that may constitute a Parliament; and the King too should have been. Is this the bringing of the King to his Parliament? Is this the bringing an end to the Treaty in the public faith of the world? Let me see a legal authority warranted by the constitutions of the kingdom, and I will answer.

Lord President. Sir, you have propounded a question, and have been answered. Seeing you will not answer, the Court will consider how to proceed : in the meantime, those that brought you hither, are to take charge of you back again.   This Court desires to know, whether this be all the answer you will give, or no.

King.   Sir, I desire that you would give me, and all the world, satisfaction in this.   Let me tell you, it is not a slight thing you are about.   I am sworn to keep the peace, by that duty I owe to God and my country, and I will do it to the last breath of my body; and therefore you shall do well to satisfy first God, and then the country, by what authority you do it : if you do it by an usurped authority you cannot answer.   There is a God in Heaven, that will call you, and all that give you power, to account.   Satisfy me in that, and I will answer; otherwise I betray my trust, and the liberties of the people : and therefore think of that, and then I shall be willing.   For I do avow, that it is as great a sin to withstand lawful authority, as it is to submit to a tyrannical, or any other ways unlawful authority; and therefore satisfy me that, and you shall receive my answer.

Lord President.   The Court expects you should give them a final answer; their purpose is to adjourn to Monday next; if you do not satisfy yourself, though we do tell you our authority, and it is upon God's authority and the kingdom; and that peace you speak of will be kept in the doing of justice, and that is our present work.

King.   For answer, let me tell you, you have shown no lawful authority to satisfy any reasonable man.

Lord President.   That is, in your apprehension; we are satisfied that are your judges.

King.   It is not my apprehension, nor yours neither, that ought to decide it.

Lord President.   The Court hath heard you, and you are to be disposed of as they have commanded.

The Court adjourns to the Painted Chamber, on Monday at ten of the clock in the forenoon, and thence hither.

It is to be observed that as the charge was reading against the King, the head of his staff fell off, which he wondered at; and seeing none to take it up, he stoops for it himself.

As the King went away, facing the Court, he said, ' I do not fear that ' (meaning the sword). The people in the Hall, as he went down the stairs, cried out, some ' God save the King,' and most for ' Justice '.

At the High Court of Justice in Westminster Hall,
Monday, January 22, 1649.

O Yes! made; silence commanded; the Court called, and answered to their names. Silence commanded upon pain of imprisonment, and the Captain of the Guard to apprehend all such as make disturbance. Upon the King's coming in a shout was made. Command given by the Court to the Captain of the Guard, to fetch and take into his custody those who make any disturbance.

Mr. Solicitor. May it please your lordship, my Lord President; I did at the last Court in the behalf of the Commons of England, exhibit and give in to this court a charge of high treason, and other high crimes, against the prisoner at the bar; whereof I do accuse him in the name of the people of England : and the charge was read unto him, and his answer required. My Lord, he was not then pleased to give an answer, but instead of answering, did there dispute the authority of this High Court. My humble motion to this High Court in behalf of the kingdom of England is, that the prisoner may be directed to make a positive answer, either by way of confession or negation; which if he shall refuse to do, that the matter of the charge may be taken *pro confesso,* and the Court may proceed according to justice.

Lord President. Sir, you may remember at the last Court you were told the occasion of your being brought hither, and you heard a charge read against you, containing a charge of high treason and other high crimes against this realm of England : you heard likewise, that it was prayed in the behalf of the people, that you should give an answer to that charge, that thereupon such proceedings might be had, as should be agreeable to justice. You were then pleased to make some scruples concerning the authority of this Court, and knew not by what authority you were brought hither: you did divers times propound your questions, and were as often answered, that it was by authority of the Commons of England assembled in Parliament, that did think fit to call you to account for those high and capital misdemeanours wherewith you were then charged. Since that the Court hath taken into consideration what you then said; they are fully satisfied with it too; and they do require it, that you do give a positive and particular answer to this charge that is exhibited against you: they do expect you should either confess or deny it; if you deny, it is offered in the behalf of the kingdom to be made good against you: their authority they do avow to the whole world, that the whole kingdom are to rest satisfied in, and you are to rest satisfied with it. And therefore you are to lose no more time, but to give a positive answer thereunto.

King. When I was here last, it is very true, I made that question; truly if it were only my own particular case, I would have satisfied myself with the protestation I made the last time I was here against the legality of this Court, and that a king cannot be tried by any superior jurisdiction on earth; but it is not my case alone, it is the freedom and the liberty of the people of England; and do you pretend what you will, I stand more for their liberties. For if power without law may make laws, may alter the fundamental laws of the kingdom, I do not know what subject he is in England, that can be sure of his life, or anything that he calls his own: therefore when that I came here, I did expect particular persons to know by what law, what authority you did proceed against me here. And therefore I am a little to seek what to say to you in this particular, because the affirmative is to be proved, the negative often is very hard to do: but since I cannot persuade you to do it, I shall tell you my reasons as short as I can. My reasons why in conscience and the duty I owe to God first, and my people next, for the preservation of their lives, liberties, and estates, I conceive I cannot answer this, till I be satisfied of the legality of it. All proceedings against any man whatsoever——

Lord President. Sir, I must interrupt you, which I would not do, but that what you do is not agreeable to the proceedings of any court of justice : you are about to enter into argument, dispute concerning the authority of this Court, before whom you appear as a prisoner, and are charged as a high delinquent : if you take upon you to dispute the authority of the Court, we may not do it, nor will any court give way unto it : you are to submit unto it, you are to give a punctual and direct answer, whether you will answer your charge or no, and what your answer is.

King. Sir, by your favour, I do not know the forms of law; I do know law and reason, though I am no lawyer professed; but I know as much law as any gentleman in England; and there-fore (under favour) I do plead for the liberties of the people of England more than you do : and therefore if I should impose a belief upon any man, without reasons given for it, it were unreasonable; but I must tell you, that that reason that I have, as thus informed, I cannot yield unto it.

Lord President. Sir, I must interrupt you, you may not be permitted : you speak of law and reason; it is fit there should be law and reason, and there is both against you. Sir, the vote of the Commons of England assembled in Parliament, it is the reason of the kingdom, and they are these that have given to that law, according to which you should have ruled and reigned. Sir, you are not to dispute our authority, you are told it again by the Court. Sir, it will be taken notice of, that you stand in contempt of the Court, and your contempt will be recorded accordingly.

King. I do not know how a King can be a delinquent, but by any law that ever I heard of, all men (delinquents, or what you will), let me tell you, they may put in demurrers against any proceeding as legal : and I do demand that, and demand to be heard with my reasons; if you deny that, you deny reason.

Lord President. Sir, you have offered something unto you, the sense of the Court. Sir, neither you nor any man are permitted to dispute that point; you are concluded, you may not demur to the jurisdiction of the Court : if you do, I must let you know, that they over-rule your demurrer; they sit here by the authority of the Commons of England, and all your predecessors and you are responsible and you are responsible to them.

King.   I deny that; show me one precedent.

Lord President.   Sir, you ought not to interrupt while the Court is speaking to you.   This point is not to be debated by you, neither will the Court permit you to do it : if you offer it by way of demurrer to the jurisdiction of the Court, they have considered of their jurisdiction, they do affirm 'their own jurisdiction.

King.   I say, Sir, by your favour, that the Commons of England was never a Court of Judicature; I would know how they came to be so.

Lord President.   Sir, you are not to be permitted to go on in that speech and these discourses.

Then the clerk of the Court read as followeth :

' Charles Stuart, King of England, you have been accused on behalf of the people of England of high treason, and other high crimes; the Court have determined that you ought to answer the same.'

King.   I will answer the same as soon as I know by what authority you do this.

Lord President.   If this be all that you will say, then, Gentlemen, you that brought the prisoner hither, take charge of him back again.

King.   I do require that I may give in my reasons why I do not answer, and give me time for that.

Lord President.   Sir, it is not for prisoners to require.

King.   Prisoners!   Sir, I am not an ordinary prisoner.

Lord President.   The Court hath considered of their jurisdiction, and they have already affirmed their jurisdiction; if you will not answer, we shall give order to record your default.

King.   You never heard my reasons yet.

Lord President.   Sir, your reasons are not to be heard against the highest jurisdiction.

King. Show me that jurisdiction where reason is not to be heard.

Lord President. Sir, we show it you here, the Commons of England, and the next time you are brought, you will know more of the pleasure of the Court, and, it may be, their final determination.

King. Show me where ever the House of Commons was a Court of Judicature of that kind.

Lord President. Serjeant, take away the prisoner.

King. Well, Sir, remember that the King is not suffered to give in his reasons for the liberty and freedom of all his subjects.

Lord President. Sir, you are not to have liberty to use this language. How great a friend you have been to the laws and liberties of the people, let all England and the world judge.

King. Sir, under favour, it was the liberty, freedom, and laws of the subject that ever I took—defended myself with arms; I never took up arms against the people, but for the laws.

Lord President. The command of the Court must be obeyed; no answer will be given to the charge.

King. Well, Sir!

At the High Court of Justice in Westminster Hall, Tuesday, January 23, 1649.

Mr. Cook, Solicitor General. May it please your Lordship my Lord President; this is now the third time, that by the great grace and favour of this High Court, the prisoner hath been brought to the bar before any issue found in the cause. My Lord, I did at the first Court exhibit a charge against him, containing the highest treasons that ever was wrought upon the theatre of England; that a King of England, trusted to keep the law, that had taken an oath so to do, that had tribute paid him for that end, should be guilty of a wicked design to subvert and destroy our laws, and introduce an arbitrary and tyrannical government, in defiance of the Parliament and their authority, set up his standard for war against his Parliament and people : and I did

humbly pray, in the behalf of the people of England, that he
might speedily be required to make an answer to the charge.
But, my Lord, instead of making any answer, he did then
dispute the authority of this High Court. Your Lordship was
pleased to give him a further day to consider, and to put in
his answer; which day being yesterday, I did humbly move, that
he might be required to give a direct and positive answer, either
by denying or confession of it; but, my Lord, he was then
pleased for to demur to the jurisdiction of the Court; which the
Court did then over-rule, and commanded him to give a direct
and positive answer. My Lord, besides this great delay of justice,
I shall now humbly move your Lordship for speedy judgement
against him. My Lord, I might press your Lordship upon the
whole, that according to the known rules of the law of the land,
that if a prisoner shall stand as contumacious in contempt, and
shall not put in an issuable plea, guilty or not guilty of the
charge given against him, whereby he may come to a fair trial,
that, as by an implicit confession, it may be taken *pro confesso,* as
it hath been done to those who have deserved more favour than
the prisoner at the bar has done. But, besides, my Lord, I shall
humbly press your Lordship upon the whole fact. The House
of Commons, the supreme authority and jurisdiction of the
kingdom, they have declared, that it is notorious, that the matter
of the charge is true, as it is in truth, my Lord, as clear as
crystal, and as the sun that shines at noon-day : which if your
Lordship and the Court be not satisfied in, I have notwithstanding, on the people of England's behalf, several witnesses to
produce. And therefore I do humbly pray, and yet I must
confess it is not so much I, as the innocent blood that hath been
shed, the cry whereof is very great for justice and judgement;
and therefore I do humbly pray, that speedy judgement be pronounced against the prisoner at the bar.

Lord President. Sir, you have heard what is moved by the
counsel on the behalf of the kingdom against you. Sir, you
may well remember, and if you do not, the Court cannot forget,
what dilatory dealings the Court hath found at your hands. You
were pleased to propound some questions, you have had our
resolutions upon them. You were told, over and over again,

that the Court did affirm their own jurisdiction; that it was not for you, nor any other man, to dispute the jurisdiction of the supreme and highest authority of England, from which there is no appeal, and touching which there must be no dispute : yet you did persist in such carriage, as you gave no manner of obedience, nor did you acknowledge any authority in them, nor the High Court that constituted this Court of Justice. Sir, I must let you know from the Court, that they are very sensible of these delays of yours, and that they ought not, being thus authorized by the supreme Court of England, to be thus trifled withal; and that they might in justice, if they pleased, and according to the rules of justice, take advantage of these delays, and proceed to pronounce judgement against you : yet nevertheless they are pleased to give direction, and on their behalfs I do require you, that you make a positive answer unto this charge that is against you, Sir, in plain terms, for justice knows no respect of persons; you are to give your positive and final answer in plain English, whether you be guilty or not guilty of these treasons laid to your charge.

The King, after a pause, said :

King. When I was here yesterday, I did desire to speak for the liberties of the people of England; I was interrupted; I desire to know yet whether I may speak freely or not.

Lord President. Sir, you have had the resolution of the Court upon the like question the last day, and you were told, that having such a charge of so high a nature against you, and your work was, that you ought to acknowledge the jurisdiction of the Court, and to answer to your charge. Sir, if you answer to your charge, which the Court gives you leave now to do, though they might have taken the advantage of your contempt; yet if you be able to answer to your charge, when you have once answered, you shall be heard at large, make the best defence you can. But, Sir, I must let you know from the Court, as their commands, that you are not permitted to issue out any other discourses, till such time as you have given a positive answer concerning the matter that is charged upon you.

King. For the charge, I value it not a rush; it is the liberty of the people of England that I stand for.   For me to acknowledge a new court, that I never heard of before, I that am your King, that should be an example to all the people of England, for to uphold justice, to maintain the old laws; indeed I do not know how to do it.   You spoke very well the first day that I came here (on Saturday) of the obligations that I had laid upon me by God, to the maintenance of the liberties of my people; the same obligation you spake of, I do acknowledge to God that I owe to Him, and to my people, to defend as much as in me lies the ancient laws of the kingdom: therefore, until that I may know that this is not against the fundamental laws of the kingdom, by your favour I can put in no particular charge.   If you will give me time, I will show you my reasons why I cannot do it, and this——

Here, being interrupted, he said:

By your favour, you ought not to interrupt me: how I came here, I know not; there's no law for it to make your King your prisoner.   I was in a Treaty upon the public faith of the kingdom, that was the known—two Houses of Parliament that was the representatives of the kingdom; and when I had almost made an end of the Treaty, then I was hurried away, and brought hither: and therefore——

Here the Lord President said, Sir, you must know the pleasure of the Court.

King.   By your favour, Sir.

Lord President.   Nay, Sir, by your favour, you may not be permitted to fall into those discourses; you appear as a delinquent, you have not acknowledged the authority of the Court, the Court craves it not of you; but once more they command you to give your positive answer.   Clerk, do your duty.

King.   Duty, Sir!

The Clerk reads:

' Charles Stuart, King of England, you are accused in behalf of the Commons of England of divers crimes and treasons, which charge hath been read unto you; the Court now requires you to give your positive and final answer, by way of confession or denial of the charge.'

King. Sir, I say again to you, so that I might give satisfaction to the people of England of the clearness of my proceeding, not by way of answer, not in this way, but to satisfy them that I have done nothing against that trust that has been committed to me, I would do it; but to acknowledge a new Court, against their privileges, to alter the fundamental laws of the kingdom—Sir, you must excuse me.

Lord President. Sir, this is the third time that you have publicly disowned this Court, and put an affront upon it. How far you have preserved the privileges of the people, your actions have spoke it; but truly, Sir, men's intentions ought to be known by their actions; you have written your meaning in bloody characters throughout the whole kingdom. But, Sir, you understand the pleasure of the Court—Clerk, record the default —and, Gentlemen, you that took charge of the prisoner, take him back again.

King. I will only say this one word more to you : if it were only my own particular, I would not say any more, nor interrupt you.

Lord President. Sir, you have heard the pleasure of the Court, and you are (notwithstanding you will not understand it) to find that you are before a court of justice.

The Proceedings of the High Court of Justice sitting in Westminster Hall, on Saturday the 27th of January, 1649

King. I shall desire a word to be heard a little, and I hope I shall give no occasion of interruption.

Lord President. You may answer in your time, hear the Court first.

King. If it please you, Sir, I desire to be heard, and I shall not give any occasion of interruption, and it is only in a word : a sudden judgement.

Lord President. Sir, you shall be heard in due time, but you are to hear the Court first.

King. Sir, I desire—it will be in order to what I believe the

Court will say; and therefore, Sir, a hasty judgement is not so soon recalled.

Lord President. Sir, you shall be heard before the judgement be given, and in the meantime you may forbear.

King. Well, Sir, shall I be heard before the judgement be given?

Lord President. Gentlemen, it is well known to all, or most of you here present, that the prisoner at the bar hath been several times convened and brought before the Court to make answer to a charge of treason, and other high crimes exhibited against him in the name of the people of England (Here a malignant lady (Lady Fairfax) interrupted the Court, saying ' Not half the people '; but she was soon silenced); to which charge being required to answer he hath been so far from obeying the commands of the Court by submitting to their justice, as he began to take upon him to offer reasoning and debate unto the authority of the Court, and of the highest court that constituted them to try and judge him : but being over-ruled in that, and required to make his answer, he was still pleased to continue contumacious, and to refuse to submit or answer. Hereupon the Court, that they may not be wanting to themselves, to the trust reposed in them, nor that any man's wilfulness prevent justice, they have thought fit to take the matter into their consideration; they have considered of the charge, they have considered of the contumacy, and of that confession, which in law doth arise upon that contumacy : they have likewise considered of the notoriety of the fact charged upon this prisoner, and upon the whole matter they are resolved, and have agreed upon a sentence to be now pronounced against this prisoner : but in respect he doth desire to be heard, before the sentence be read and pronounced, the Court hath resolved that they will hear him. Yet, Sir, thus much I must tell you beforehand, which you have been minded of at other courts, that if that you have to say be to offer any debate concerning jurisdiction, you are not to be heard in it; you have offered it formerly, and you have indeed struck at the root, that is, the power and supreme authority of the Commons of England, which this Court will not admit a debate of; and which indeed is an irrational thing in them to do, being a Court that acts upon authority derived from them, that they should presume to judge upon their superior, from whom there is no appeal. But, Sir, if you have anything to say in defence of yourself concerning the matter charged, the Court hath given me command to let you know they will hear you.

King. Since that I see that you will not hear anything of debate concerning that which I confess I thought most material for the peace of the kingdom, and for the liberty of the subject, I shall wave it; I shall speak nothing to it, but only I must tell you, that this many a day all things have been taken away from me, but that, that I call more dear to me than my life, which is my conscience and my honour : and if I had respect to my life more than the peace of the kingdom, the liberty of the subject, certainly I should have made a particular defence for myself; for by that at leastwise I might have delayed an ugly sentence, which I believe will pass upon me. Therefore certainly, Sir, as a man that hath some understanding, some knowledge of the world, if that my true zeal to my country had not overborne the care that I have of my own preservation, I should have gone another way to work than that I have done. Now, Sir, I conceive that a hasty sentence once passed, may sooner be repented than recalled; and truly, the selfsame desire that I have for the peace of the kingdom, and the liberty of the subject, more than my own particular, does make me now at last desire, that having something for to say that concerns both, I desire before sentence be given, that I may be heard in the Painted Chamber before the Lords and Commons. This delay cannot be prejudicial to you, whatsoever I say, if that I say no reason, those that hear me must be judges : I cannot be judge of that, which I have : if it be reason, and really for the welfare of the kingdom, and the liberty of the subject, I am sure on't, very well it is worth the hearing; therefore I do conjure you, as you love that which you pretend, I hope it is real, the liberty of the subject, the peace of the kingdom, that you will grant me the hearing, before any sentence be passed. I only desire this, that you will take this into your consideration, it may be you have not heard of it beforehand; if you will, I'll retire, and you may think of it; but if I cannot get this liberty, I do here protest, that so far shows of liberty and peace are pure shows, and not otherwise, since you will not hear your King.

The Clerk read the sentence, which was drawn up in parchment :

'Whereas the Commons of England in Parliament had appointed them a High Court of Justice, for the trying of Charles Stuart, King of England, before whom he had been three times convened; and at the first time a charge of high treason, and other crimes and misdemeanours was read in the behalf of the kingdom of England,' etc. (Here the Clerk read the charge.) 'Which charge being read unto him, as aforesaid, he the said Charles Stuart was required to give his answer : but he refused so to do; and so expressed the several passages of his trial in refusing to answer. For all which treasons and crimes this Court doth adjudge, that the said Charles Stuart, as a tyrant, traitor, murderer, and a public enemy, shall be put to death, by the severing his head from his body.'

After the sentence was read the Lord President said, This sentence now read and published is the act, sentence, judgement, and resolution of the whole Court.

Here the Court stood up, as assenting to what the President said.

King.   Will you hear me a word, Sir?

Lord President.   Sir, you are not to be heard after the sentence.

King.   No, Sir!

Lord President.   No, Sir; by your favour, Sir. Guard, withdraw your prisoner.

King.   I may speak after the sentence—by your favour, Sir, I may speak after the sentence ever.

By your favour (Hold!) the sentence, Sir——

I say, Sir, I do——

I am not suffered for to speak : expect what justice other people will have.

The speech which the King had intended to deliver on January 22nd was as follows:

XXVII

Having already made my protestations, not only against the illegality of this pretended Court, but also, that no earthly power can justly call me (who am your King) in question as a delinquent, I would not any more open my mouth upon this occasion, more than to refer myself to what I have spoken, were I in this case alone concerned : but the duty I owe to God in the preservation of the true liberty of my people will not suffer me at this time to be silent : for, how can any free-born subject of England call life or anything he possesseth his own, if power without right daily make new, and abrogate the old fundamental laws of the land which I now take to be the present case? Wherefore when I came hither, I expected that you would have endeavoured to have satisfied me concerning these grounds which hinder me to answer to your pretended impeachment. But since I see that nothing I can say will move you to it (though negatives are not so naturally proved as affirmatives) yet I will show you the reason why I am confident you cannot judge me, nor indeed the meanest man in England : for I will not (like you) without showing a reason, seek to impose a belief upon my subjects.

There is no proceeding just against any man, but what is warranted, either by God's laws or the municipal laws of the country where he lives. Now I am most confident this day's proceeding cannot be warranted by God's laws; for, on the contrary, the authority of obedience unto Kings is clearly warranted, and strictly commanded in both the Old and New Testament, which, if denied, I am ready instantly to prove.

And for the question now in hand, there it is said, that ' where the word of a King is, there is power; and who may say unto him, what doest thou? ' (Eccles. viii. 4). Then for the law of this land, I am no less confident, that no learned lawyer will affirm that an impeachment can lie against the King, they all going in his name : and one of their maxims is, that the King can do no wrong. Besides, the law upon which you ground your proceedings, must either be old or new : if old, show it; if new, tell what authority, warranted by the fundamental laws of the land, hath made it, and when. But how the House of Commons can erect a Court of Judicature, which was never one itself (as is well known to all lawyers) I leave to God and the world to judge. And it were full as strange, that they should pretend to make laws without King or Lords' House, to any that have heard speak of the laws of England.

And admitting, but not granting, that the people of England's commission could grant your pretended power, I see nothing you can show for that; for certainly you never asked the question of the tenth man in the kingdom, and in this way you manifestly wrong even the poorest ploughman, if you demand not his free consent; nor can you pretend any colour for this your pretended commission, without the consent at least of the major part of every man in England of whatsoever quality or condition, which I am sure you never went about to seek, so far are you from having it. Thus you see that I speak not for my own right alone, as I am your King, but also for the true liberty of all my subjects, which consists not in the power of government, but in living under such laws, such a government, as may give themselves the best assurance of their lives, and property of their goods; nor in this must or do I forget the privileges of both Houses of Parliament, which this day's proceedings do not only violate, but likewise occasion the greatest breach of their public faith that (I believe) was ever heard of, with which I am far from charging the two Houses; for all the pretended crimes laid against me bear date long before this Treaty at Newport, in which I having concluded as much as in me lay, and hopefully expecting the Houses' agreement thereunto, I was suddenly surprised and hurried from thence as a prisoner; upon which account I am against my will brought hither, where since I am come, I cannot but to my power defend the ancient laws and liberties of this kingdom, together with my own just right. Then for anything I can see, the higher House is totally excluded; and for the House of Commons, it is too well known that the major part of them are detained or deterred from sitting; so as if I had no other, this were sufficient for me to protest against the lawfulness of your pretended Court. Besides all this, the peace of the kingdom is not the least in my thoughts; and what hope of settlement is there, so long as power reigns without rule or law, changing the whole frame of that government under which this kingdom hath flourished for many hundred years? (nor will I say what will fall out in case this lawless, unjust proceeding against me do go on) and believe it, the Commons of England will not thank you for this change; for they will remember how happy they have been of late years under the reigns of Queen Elizabeth, the King my father, and myself, until the beginning of these unhappy troubles, and will have cause to doubt, that they shall never be so happy under any new: and by this time it will be too sensibly evident, that the arms I took up were only to defend the fundamental laws of this kingdom against those who have supposed my power hath totally changed the ancient government.

Thus, having showed you briefly the reasons why I cannot submit to your pretended authority, without violating the trust which I have from God for the welfare and liberty of my people, I expect from you either clear reasons to convince my judgement, showing me that I am in an error (and then truly I will answer) or that you will withdraw your proceedings.

This I intended to speak in Westminster Hall, on Monday, January 22, but against reason was hindered to show my reasons.

Before his execution, Charles gave a letter to the Bishop of London for the Prince of Wales.

XXVIII. TO THE PRINCE OF WALES

SON,

If these papers, with some others, wherein I have set down the private reflections of my conscience, and my most impartial thoughts, touching the chief passages which have been most remarkable, or disputed in my late troubles, come to your hands, to whom they are chiefly designed, they may be so far useful to you, as to state your judgement aright in what hath passed; whereof a pious use is the best can be made; and they may also give you some directions how to remedy the present distempers, and prevent (if God will) the like for time to come.

It is some kind of deceiving and lessening the injury of my long restraint, when I find my leisure and solitude have produced something worthy of myself, and useful to you; that neither you, nor any other, may hereafter measure my cause by the success, nor my judgement of things by my misfortunes, which I count the greater by far, because they have so far lighted upon you and some others whom I have most cause to love as well as myself, and of whose unmerited sufferings I have a greater sense than of my own.

But this advantage of wisdom you have done above most princes; that you have begun, and now spent some years of discretion in the experience of troubles, and exercise of patience, wherein piety and all virtues, both moral and political, are commonly better planted to a thriving, as trees set in winter, than in warmth and serenity of times, or amidst those delights which usually attend princes' courts in times of peace and plenty, which are prone either to root up all plants of true virtue and honour, or to be contented only with some leaves and wi⁺hering formalities of them without any real fruits, such as tend to the public good, for which princes should always remember they are born, and by Providence designed.

The evidence of which different education the Holy Writ affords us in the contemplation of David and Rehoboam, the one prepared by many afflictions for a flourishing kingdom, the other softened by the unparalleled prosperity of Solomon's court; and so corrupted to the great diminution, both for peace, honour, and kingdom, by those flatteries, which are as inseparable from prosperous princes as flies are from fruit in summer, whom adversity, like cold weather, drives away.

I had rather you should be Charles *le bon*, than *le grand*, good, than great; I hope God hath designed you to be both; having so early put you into that exercise of His grace and gifts bestowed upon you, which may best weed out all vicious inclinations, and dispose you to those princely endowments and employments, which will most gain the love, and intend the welfare of those over whom God shall place you.

With God, I would have you begin and end, who is King of Kings, the sovereign disposer of the kingdoms of the world. who pulleth down one and setteth up another.

The best government and highest sovereignty you can attain to is to be subject to Him, that the sceptre of His word and spirit may rule in your heart.

The true glory of princes consists in advancing God's glory, in the maintenance of true religion and the Church's good; also in the dispensation of civil power, with justice and honour to the public peace.

Piety will make you prosperous, at least it will keep you from becoming miserable; nor is he much a loser that loseth all, yet saveth his own soul at last.

To which centre of true happiness, God (I trust) hath and will graciously direct all these black lines of affliction which He hath been pleased to draw on me, and by which He hath (I hope) drawn me nearer to Himself. You have already tasted of that cup whereof I have liberally drunk; which I look upon as God's physic, having that in healthfulness which it wants in pleasure.

Above all, I would have you, as I hope you are already, well grounded and settled in your religion, the best profession of which I have ever esteemed that of the Church of England, in which you have been educated; yet I would have your own judgement and reason now sealed to that sacred bond which education hath written, that it may be judiciously your own religion, and not other men's custom or tradition which you profess.

In this I charge you to persevere, as coming nearest to God's word for doctrine, and to the primitive examples for government, with some little amendment which I have otherwise expressed, and often offered, though in vain. Your fixation in matters of religion will not be more necessary for your soul's than your kingdom's peace, when God shall bring you to them.

For I have observed, that the devil of rebellion doth commonly turn himself into an angel of reformation; and the old serpent can pretend new lights, when some men's consciences accuse them for sedition and faction, they stop its mouth with the name and noise of religion; when piety pleads for peace and patience, they cry out zeal.

So that, unless in this point you be well settled, you shall never want temptations to destroy you and yours, under pretension of reforming matters of religion; for that seems even to the worst of men, as the best and most auspicious beginning of their worst designs.

Where, besides the novelty which is taken enough with the vulgar, every one hath an affectation, by seeming forward to an outward reformation of religion, to be thought zealous; hoping to cover those irreligious deformities whereto they are conscious, by a severity of censuring other men's opinions and actions.

Take heed of abetting any factions, or applying to any public discriminations in matters of religion, contrary to what is in your judgement and the churches well settled; your partial adhering as head to any one side gains you not so great advantage in some men's hearts (who are prone to be of their King's religion) as it loseth you in others; who think themselves and their profession first despised, then persecuted by you; take such a course as may either with calmness and charity quite remove the seeming differences and offences by impartiality, or so order affairs in point of power that you shall not need to fear or flatter any faction.

For, if ever you stand in need of them, or must stand to their courtesy, you are undone. The serpent will devour the dove; you may never expect less of loyalty, justice, or humanity than from those who engage in religious rebellions; their interest is always made God's, under the colours of piety, ambitious policies march, not only with greatest security, but applause as to the populacy; you may hear from them Jacob's voice, but you shall feel they have Esau's hands.

Nothing seemed less considerable than the Presbyterian faction in England for many years, so compliant they were to public order; nor, indeed, was their party great either in Church or State as to men's judgements; but as soon as discontents drove men into sidings, as ill humours fall to the disaffected part, which causes inflammations, so did all at first who affected any novelties adhere to that side, as the most remarkable and specious note of difference (then) in point of religion.

All the lesser factions at first were officious servants to Presbytery, their great master, till time and military success, discovering to each their peculiar advantages invited them to part stakes; and leaving the joint stock of uniform religion, they pretended each to drive for their party the trade of profits and preferments to the breaking and undoing not only of the Church and State, but even of Presbytery itself, which seemed and hoped at first to have engrossed all.

Let nothing seem little or despicable to you in matters which concern religion and the Church's peace, so as to neglect a speedy reforming and effectually suppressing errors and schisms; what seem at first but as a hand-breadth, by seditious spirits, as by strong winds, are soon made a cover and darken the whole heaven.

When you have done justice to God, your own soul and His Church in the profession and preservation of truth and unity in religion, the next main hinge on which your prosperity will depend and move, is that of civil justice, wherein the settled laws of these kingdoms, to which you are rightly heir, are the most excellent rules you can govern by, which by an admirable temperament give very much to subjects industry, liberty, and happiness; and yet reserve enough to the majesty and prerogative of any king who owns his people as subjects, not as slaves, whose subjection as it preserves their property, peace, and safety, so it will never diminish your rights, nor their ingenious liberties; which consist in the enjoyment of the fruits of their industry and the benefit of those laws to which themselves have consented.

Never charge your head with such a crown as shall, by its heaviness, oppress the whole body, the weakness of whose parts cannot return anything of strength, honour, or safety to the head, but a necessary debilitation and ruin.

Your prerogative is best showed and exercised in remitting rather than exacting the rigour of the laws; there being nothing worse than legal tyranny.

In these two points of preservation of established religion and laws, I may (without vanity) turn the reproach of my sufferings, as to the world's censure, into the honour of a kind of martyr-dom, as to the testimony of my own conscience; the troubles of my kingdoms, having nothing else to object against me but this, that I prefer religion and laws established before those alterations they propounded.

And so indeed I do, and ever shall, till I am convinced by better arguments than what hitherto have been chiefly used towards me—tumults, armies, and prisons.

I cannot yet learn that lesson, nor I hope ever will you, that it is safe for a King to gratify any faction with the perturbation of the laws, in which is wrapt up the public interest and the good of the community.

How God will deal with me, as to the removal of these pressures and indignities, which His justice, by the very unjust hands of some of my subjects, hath been pleased to lay upon me I cannot tell; nor am I much solicitous what wrong I suffer from men, while I retain in my soul what I believe is right before God.

I have offered all for reformation and safety that in reason, honour, and conscience I can, reserving only what I cannot consent unto without an irreparable injury to my own soul, the Church, and my people, and you also as the next and undoubted heir of my kingdoms.

To which, if the Divine Providence, to whom no difficulties are insuperable, shall in His due time, after my decease, bring you as I hope He will, my counsel and charge to you is, that you seriously consider the former real or objected miscarriages which might occasion my troubles, that you may avoid them.

Never repose so much upon any man's single counsel, fidelity, and discretion, in managing affairs of the first magnitude (that is, matters of religion and justice), as to create in yourself or others a diffidence of your own judgement, which is likely to be always more constant and impartial to the interests of your crown and kingdom than any man's.

Next beware of exasperating any factions by the crossness and asperity of some men's passions, humours, or private opinions employed by you, grounded only upon the differences in lesser matters, which are but the skirts and suburbs of religion.

Wherein a charitable connivance and Christian toleration

often dissipates their strength, whom rougher opposition fortifies, and puts the despised and oppressed party into such combinations as may most enable them to get a full revenge on those that count their persecutors, who are commonly assisted by that vulgar commiseration which attends all that are said to suffer under the notion of religion.

Provided the differences amount not to an insolent opposition of laws and government, or religion established as to the essentials of them; such motions and mimings are intolerable.

Always keep up solid piety, and those fundamental truths which mend both hearts and lives of men with impartial favour and justice.

Take heed that outward circumstances and formalities of religion devour not at all, or the best encouragements of learning, industry, and piety; but with an equal eye and impartial hand distribute favours and rewards to all men, as you find them for their real goodness both in abilities and fidelity worthy and capable of them.

This will be sure to gain you the hearts of the best and the most, too; who, though they be not good themselves, yet are glad to see the severer ways of virtue at any time sweetened by temporal rewards.

I have, you see, conflicted with different and opposite factions (for so I must needs call and count all those that act not in any conformity to the laws established in Church and State) : no sooner have they by force subdued what they counted their common enemy (that is all those that adhered to the laws and to me), and are secured from that fear, but they are divided to so high a rivalry as sets them more at defiance against each other than against their antagonist.

Time will dissipate all factions, when once the rough hours of private men's covetous and ambitious designs shall discover themselves; which were at first wrapt up and hidden under the soft and smooth pretensions of religion, reformation, and liberty : as the wolf is not cruel, so he will be more justly hated, when he shall appear no better than a wolf under sheep's clothing.

But as for the seduced train of the vulgar, who, in their

267

simplicity, follow those disguises, my charge and counsel to you is, that as you need no palliations for any designs (as other men), so you study really to exceed (in true and constant demonstrations of goodness, piety, and virtue towards the people) even all those men, that make the greatest noise and ostentation of religion; so you shall neither fear any detection (as they do, who have but the face and mask of goodness), nor shall you frustrate the just expectations of your people, who cannot in reason promise themselves so much good from any subject's novelties as from the virtuous constancy of their King.

When these mountains of congealed factions shall, by the sunshine of God's mercy and the splendour of your virtues, be thawed and dissipated, and the abused vulgar shall have learned that none are greater oppressors of their estates, liberties, and consciences than those men, that entitle themselves the patrons and vindicators of them, only to usurp power over them; let, then, no passion betray you to any study of revenge upon those whose own sin and folly will sufficiently punish them in due time. But as soon as the forked arrow of factious emulations is drawn out, use all princely arts and clemency to heal the wounds that the smart of the cure may not equal the anguish of the hurt.

I have offered acts of indemnity and oblivion, to so great a latitude, as may include all, that can but suspect themselves to be any way obnoxious to the laws, and which might serve to exclude all future jealousies and insecurities.

I would have you always propense to the same way, whenever it shall be desired and accepted, let it be granted, not only as an act of state policy and necessity, but of Christian charity and choice.

It is all I have now left me, a power to forgive those that have deprived me of all; and I thank God I have a heart to do it, and joy as much in this grace, which God hath given me, as in all my former enjoyments; for this is a greater argument of God's love to me than any prosperity can be. Be confident (as I am) that the most of all sides, who have done amiss, have done so, not out of malice, but misinformation, or misapprehension of things.

None will be more loyal and faithful to me and you, than those subjects who, sensible of their errors and our injuries, will feel, in their own souls, most vehement motives to repentance, and earnest desire to make some reparations for their former defects.

As your quality sets you beyond any duel with any subject, so the nobleness of your mind must raise you above the meditating any revenge, or executing your anger upon the many.

The more conscious you shall be to your own merits upon your people, the more prone you will be to expect all love and loyalty from them, and to inflict no punishment upon them for former miscarriages; and you will have more inward complacency in pardoning one, than in punishing a thousand.

This I write to you, not despairing of God's mercy, and my subjects' affections towards you, both which I hope you will study to deserve; yet we cannot merit of God but by His own mercy.

If God shall see fit to restore me, and you after me, to those enjoyments which the laws have assigned to us, and no subjects, without an high degree of guilt and sin can divest us of; then may I have better opportunity when I shall be so happy to see you in peace, to let you more fully understand the things that belong to God's glory, your own honour, and the kingdom's peace.

But if you never see my face again, and God will have me buried in such a barbarous imprisonment and obscurity (which the perfecting some men's designs requires) wherein few hearts that love me are permitted to exchange a word or a look with me, I do require and entreat you as your father and your King, that you never suffer your heart to receive the least check against or disaffection from the true religion established in the Church of England.

I tell you I have tried it, and, after much search and many disputes, hath concluded it to be the best in the world, not only in the community, as Christian, but also in the special notion, as reformed, keeping the middle way between the pomp of superstitious tyranny, and the meanness of fantastic anarchy.

Not but that (the draught being excellent as to the main,

both for doctrine and government, in the Church of England) some lines, as in very good figures, may haply need some sweetening, or polishing, which might here have easily been done by a safe and gentle hand, if some men's precipitancy had not violently demanded such rude alterations, as would have quite destroyed all the beauty and proportions of the world.

The scandal of the late troubles which some may object and urge to you against the Protestant religion established in England, is easily answered to them, or your own thoughts in this, that scarce any one who hath been a beginner, or an active persecutor of this late war against the Church, the laws, and me, either was or is a true lover, embracer, or practiser of the Protestant religion established in England, which neither gives such rules, nor ever before set such examples.

'Tis true, some heretofore had the boldness to present threatening petitions to their princes and Parliaments, which others of the same faction (but of worse spirits) have now put in execution; but let not counterfeit and disorderly zeal abate your value and esteem of true piety; both of them are to be known by their fruits; the sweetness of the vine and the fig-tree is not to be despised, though the brambles and thorns should pretend to bear figs and grapes, thereby to rule over the trees.

Nor would I have you to entertain any aversion or dislike of Parliaments, which, in their right constitution with freedom and honour, will never hinder or diminish your greatness, but will rather be an interchanging of love, loyalty, and confidence, between a prince and his people.

Nor would the events of this black Parliament have been other than such (however much biased by factions in the elections) if it had been preserved from the insolencies of popular dictates, and tumultuary impressions; the sad effects of which will no doubt make all Parliaments after this more cautious to preserve that freedom and honour which belongs to such assemblies (when once they have fully shaken off this yoke of vulgar encroachment), since the public interest consists in the mutual and common good both of prince and people.

Nothing can be more happy for all than, in fair, grave, and honourable ways, to contribute their counsels in common, enacting all things by public consent, without tyranny or tumults. We must not starve ourselves, because some have surfeited of whole-some food.

And if neither I nor you be ever restored to our right, but God, in His severest justice, will punish my subjects with con-tinuance in their sin, and suffer them to be deluded with the prosperity of their wickedness, I hope God will give me and you that grace which will teach and enable us to want, as well as to wear a crown, which is not worth taking up, or enjoying upon sordid, dishonourable, and irreligious terms.

Keep you to true principles of piety, virtue, and honour; you shall never want a kingdom.

A principal point of your honour will consist in your deferring all respect, love, and protection to your mother, my wife, who hath many ways deserved well of me, and chiefly in this, that having been a means to bless me with so many hopeful children (all which, with their mother, I recommend to your love and care), she hath been content with incomparable magnanimity and patience to suffer both for and with me and you.

My prayer to God Almighty is (whatever becomes of me, who am, I thank God, wrapt up and fortified in my own innocency, and His grace) that He would be pleased to make you an anchor, or harbour rather, to these tossed and weather-beaten kingdoms; a repairer, by your wisdom, justice, piety, valour, of what the folly and wickedness of some men have so far ruined, as to leave nothing entire in Church or State, to the Crown, the nobility, the clergy, and the Commons, either as to laws, liberties, estates, order, honour, conscience, or lives.

When they have destroyed me (for I know not how far God may permit the malice and cruelty of my enemies to proceed, and such apprehensions some men's words and actions have already given me) as I doubt not my blood will cry aloud for vengeance to Heaven; so I beseech God not to pour out His wrath upon the generality of the people who have either deserted me, or engaged me, through the artifice and hypocrisy of their leaders, whose inward horror will be their first tormentor, nor will they escape exemplary judgements.

For those that loved me, I pray God they may have no miss

of me when I am gone; so much I wish and hope that all good subjects may be satisfied with the blessings of your presence and virtues.

For those that repent of any defects in their duty toward me, as I freely forgive them in the word of a Christian King, so I believe you will find them truly zealous to repay, with interest, that loyalty and love to you which was due to me.

In sum, what good I intended do you perform, when God shall give you power: much good I have offered, more I proposed to Church and State, if times had been capable of it.

The deception will soon vanish, and the vizards will fall off apace; this mark of religion on the face of rebellion (for so it now plainly appears since my restraint and cruel usage, that they fought not for me, as was pretended) will not long serve to hide some men's deformities.

Happy times, I hope, attend you, wherein your subjects, by their miseries, will have learned that religion to their God, and loyalty to their King, cannot be parted without both their sin and infelicity.

I pray God bless you and establish your kingdoms in righteousness, your soul in true religion, and your honour in the love of God and your people.

And if God will have disloyalty perfected by my destruction, let my memory ever, with my name, live in you; as of your father, that loves you, and once a King of three flourishing kingdoms; whom God thought fit to honour, not only with the sceptre and government of them, but also with the suffering many indignities and an untimely death for them; while I studied to preserve the rights of the Church, the power of the laws, the honour of my crown, the privilege of Parliaments, the liberties of my people and my own conscience, which I thank God, is dearer to me than a thousand kingdoms.

I know God can—I hope He will—restore me to my rights. I cannot despair, either of His mercy, or my people's love and pity.

At worst, I trust I shall but go before you to a better kingdom, which God hath prepared for me, and me for it, through my Saviour Jesus Christ, to whose mercy I commend you, and all mine.

Farewell, till we meet, if not on earth, yet in Heaven.

On January 29th, 1649, Charles was executed, outside the Banqueting Hall in Whitehall. A few minutes before his death, he remarked to the Bishop of London, 'I go from a corruptible to an incorruptible crown, where there will be no more trouble.'

APPENDICES

APPENDIX I

CHAPTER I

I. Maitland Collection.
II. Maitland Collection.
III. Harl. MSS. 6986, f. 83.
IV. Bishop Goodman's *History of His Own Times*, vol. ii, pp. 209-10.
V. Harl. MSS. 6987, art. 96.
VI. Rawlinson MSS.
VII. Harl. MSS. 6987, art. 6.
VIII. Harl. MSS. 6987, art. 10.
IX. Harl. MSS. 6987, art. 11.
X. Harl. MSS. 6987, art. 16.
XI. Harl. MSS. 6011, p. 11.
XII. Harl. MSS. 6011, p. 11.
XIII. Harl. MSS. 6987, art. 22.
XIV. Lansdowne MSS. 1236, art. 1.
XV. Harl. MSS. 6987, art. 34.
XVI. Harl. MSS. 6987, art. 39.
XVII. Harl. MSS. 6987, art. 42.
XVIII. Harl. MSS. 6987, art. 43.
XIX. Harl. MSS. 6987, art. 46.
XX. Harl. MSS. 6987, art. 52.
XXI. Harl. MSS. 6987, art. 73.
XXII. Harl. MSS. 6987, art. 55.
XXIII. Harl. MSS. 6987, art. 56.
XXIV. Harl. MSS. 6987, art. 61.
XXV. Harl. MSS. 6987, art. 71.
XXVI. Harl. MSS. 6987, art. 76.
XXVII. H.M.C. MSS. of G. W. Digby, Esq.
XXVIII. H.M.C. MSS. of G. W. Digby, Esq.
XXIX. H.M.C. MSS. of G. W. Digby, Esq.
XXX. H.M.C. MSS. of G. W. Digby, Esq.
XXXI. Harl. MSS. 6987, art. 113.
XXXII. H.M.C. MSS. of G. W. Digby, Esq.

CHAPTER II

I. H.M.C. Traquair MSS.
II. Harl. MSS. 6988, art. 96.
III. Harl. MSS. 6988, art. 1
IV. Harl. MSS. 6988, art. 3.
V. Rawlinson MSS.

277

VI. Harl. MSS. 6988, art. 6.
VII. H.M.C. Kenyon MSS.
VIII. H.M.C. Rye MSS.
IX. Harl. MSS. 6988, art. 20.
X. Harl. MSS. 6988, art. 22.
XI. Harl. MSS. 6988, art. 23.
XII. Harl. MSS. 6988, art. 24.
XIII. Harl. MSS. 6988, art. 25.
XIV. Harl. MSS. 6988, art. 26.
XV. Harl. MSS. 6988, art. 31.
XVI. House of Lords' Journals, vol. iv, pp. 789-90.
XVII. Rushworth's *Historical Collections*, vol. i, appendix i.

CHAPTER III

I. Add. MSS. 2293, art. 3.
II. H.M.C. Add. MSS. of Sir Hervey Bruce.
III. Clarendon State Papers, vol. i, p. 547.
IV. H.M.C. Rye MSS.
V. H.M.C. Report 13, appendix vi.
VI. Harl. MSS. 2173, art. 29.
VII. H.M.C. Wells MSS.
VIII. H.M.C. Wells MSS.
IX. H.M.C. Wells MSS.
X. H.M.C. Wells MSS.
XI. H.M.C. Wells MSS.
XII. H.M.C. Buccleugh MSS.
XIII. Rushworth's *Historical Collections*, vol. ii, p. 257.
XIV. *Select Collection of Original Letters*, vol. i, p. 118. (London, 1755.)
XV. *Letters and Dispatches of the Earl of Strafford*, vol. i, p. 331.
XVI. *Letters and Dispatches of the Earl of Strafford*, vol. i, p. 365.
XVII. *Letters and Dispatches of the Earl of Strafford*, vol. ii, p. 32.
XVIII. *Letters and Dispatches of the Earl of Strafford*, vol. ii, p. 78.
XIX. *Letters and Dispatches of the Earl of Strafford*, vol. ii, p. 211.
XX. *Letters and Dispatches of the Earl of Strafford*, vol. ii, p. 228.
XXI. *Letters and Dispatches of the Earl of Strafford*, vol. ii, p. 244.
XXII. *Letters and Dispatches of the Earl of Strafford*, vol. ii, p. 275.

XXIII. *Letters and Dispatches of the Earl of Strafford*, vol. ii, p. 292.

XXIV. *Letters and Dispatches of the Earl of Strafford*, vol. ii, p. 361.

XXV. *Letters and Dispatches of the Earl of Strafford*, vol. ii, p. 362.

XXVI. *Letters and Dispatches of the Earl of Strafford*, vol. ii, p. 372.

XXVII. *Letters and Dispatches of the Earl of Strafford*, vol. ii, p. 409.

XXVIII. H.M.C. Report 11, appendix.

XXIX. H.M.C. Report 11, appendix.

XXX. H.M.C. Report 11, appendix.

XXXI. H.M.C. Report 11, appendix.

XXXII. H.M.C. Report 11, appendix.

XXXIII. H.M.C. Report 11, appendix.

XXXIV. H.M.C. Dovaston MSS.

CHAPTER IV

I. *Letters and Dispatches of the Earl of Strafford*, vol. ii, p. 416.

II. Journals of the House of Lords, vol. iv, p. 245.

III. Sloane MSS. 1467, art. 37.

IV. Journals of the House of Lords, vol. v, p. 12 *et seq.*

V. Journals of the House of Lords, vol. v, p. 111-12.

VI. Journals of the House of Lords, vol. v, p. 127.

VII. Journals of the House of Lords, vol. v, p. 178.

VIII. Journals of the House of Lords, vol. v, p. 224.

IX. Journals of the House of Lords, vol. v, p. 231.

X. Journals of the House of Lords, vol. v, p. 327.

XI. Harl. MSS. 6988, art. 69.

XII. H.M.C. Traquair MSS.

XIII. Harl. MSS. 6988, art. 71.

XIV. Harl. MSS. 6988, art. 74.

XV. Harl. MSS. 6988, art. 75.

XVI. Carte's *History of the Life of James, Duke of Ormonde*, vol. v, pp. 1-3.

XVII. Carte's *History of the Life of James, Duke of Ormonde*, vol. v, p. 3.

XVIII. Carte's *History of the Life of James, Duke of Ormonde*, vol. v, p. 6.

XIX. Carte's *History of the Life of James, Duke of Ormonde*, vol. v, p. 445.

XX. Carte's *History of the Life of James, Duke of Ormonde*, vol. v, pp. 445-6.

XXI. Sanderson's *Compleat History of the Life and Raigne of King Charles*, p. 648.
XXII. H.M.C. Somerset MSS.
XXIII. Harl. MSS. 6988, art. 88.
XXIV. H.M.C. Mar MSS.

CHAPTER V

I. Harl. MSS. 6988, art. 104.
II. Harl. MSS. 6988, art. 106.
III. MSS. in the Heralds' College.
IV. Nalson's MS. Collections, British Museum.
V. Nalson's MS. Collections, British Museum.
VI. Nalson's MS. Collections, British Museum.
VII. Harl. MSS. 6988, art. 107.
VIII. Rushworth's *Historical Collections*, vol. v, p. 858.
IX. Carte's *History of the Life of James, Duke of Ormonde*, vol. vi. pp. 8-9.
X. Carte's *History of the Life of James, Duke of Ormonde*, vol. vi, pp. 9-10.
XI. Carte's *History of the Life of James, Duke of Ormonde*, vol. vi, p. 13.
XII. Carte's *History of the Life of James, Duke of Ormonde*, vol. vi, p. 14.
XIII. Harl. MSS. 6988, art. 12.
XIV. H.M.C. Traquair MSS.
XV. Evelyn MSS.
XVI. Harl. MSS. 6988, art. 116.
XVII. Carte's *History of the Life of James, Duke of Ormonde*, vol. vi, pp. 15-16.
XVIII. Original in the Vatican Library.
XIX. Carte's *History of the Life of James, Duke of Ormonde*, vol. vi, p. 16.
XX. Journals of the House of Lords, vol. viii, p. 46.
XXI. Journals of the House of Lords, vol. viii, p. 72.
XXII. *Letters of Charles I to Queen Henrietta Maria*, pp. 1-3.
XXIII. *Letters of Charles I to Queen Henrietta Maria*, pp. 6-7.
XXIV. Journals of the House of Lords, vol. viii, pp. 108-9.
XXV. Journals of the House of Lords, vol. viii, pp. 125-6.
XXVI. Journals of the House of Lords, vol. viii, pp. 132-3.
XXVII. *Letters of Charles I to Queen Henrietta Maria*, pp. 18-20.
XXVIII. Clarendon MSS. in the Bodleian Library.
XXIX. Ormonde Papers, appendix.

CHAPTER VI

I. Evelyn MSS.
II. Journals of the House of Lords, vol. viii. p. 329.
III. Add. MSS. 11252, f. 1.
IV. Clarendon MSS. in the Bodleian Library.
V. Journals of the House of Lords, vol. viii, p. 334.
VI. *Letters of Charles I to Queen Henrietta Maria*, pp. 48-9.
VII. Clarendon MSS. in the Bodleian Library.
VIII. *Letters of Charles I to Queen Henrietta Maria*, p. 55.
IX. Journals of the House of Lords, vol. viii, p. 460.
X. Clarendon MSS. in the Bodleian Library.
XI. Clarendon MSS. in the Bodleian Library.
XII. Clarendon MSS. in the Bodleian Library.
XIII. Lambeth Palace MSS. 679, f. 183.
XIV. Clarendon MSS. in the Bodleian Library.
XV. Journals of the House of Lords, vol. viii, p. 627.
XVI. Journals of the House of Lords, vol. ix, p. 26.
XVII. Journals of the House of Lords, vol. ix, p. 69.
XVIII. Journals of the House of Lords, vol. ix, p. 193.
XIX. Rushworth's *Historical Collection*, vol. vii, p. 810.
XX. Sanderson's *Compleat History of the Life and Raigne of King Charles*, p. 995.
XXI. Sloane MSS. 3299.
XXII. Clarendon MSS. in the Bodleian Library.
XXIII. Lauderdale Papers, Camden Soc., vol. i, p. 2.
XXIV. Sloane MSS. 3299, art. 85.
XXV. Holmes's MSS. *Historical Collections*.
XXVI. *State Trials*, vol. iv.
XXVII. Rushworth's *Historical Collections*, vol. vii, p. 1403.
XXVIII. Sanderson's *Compleat History of the Life and Raigne of King Charles*, pp. 1140-9.

APPENDIX II

THE GRAND REMONSTRANCE, AND ACCOMPANYING PETITION

Most Gracious Sovereign,

Your Majesty's most humble and faithful subjects the Commons in this present Parliament assembled, do with much thankfulness and joy acknowledge the great mercy and favour of God, in giving your Majesty a safe and peaceable return out of Scotland into your kingdom of England, where the pressing dangers and distempers of the State have caused us with much earnestness to desire the comfort of your gracious presence, and likewise the unity and justice of your royal authority, to give more life and power to the dutiful and loyal counsels and endeavours of your Parliament, for the prevention of that eminent ruin and destruction wherein your kingdoms of England and Scotland are threatened. The duty which we owe to your Majesty and our country cannot but make us very sensible · and apprehensive, that the multiplicity, sharpness and malignity of those evils under which we have now many years suffered, are fomented and cherished by a corrupt and ill-affected party, who amongst other their mischievous devices for the alteration of religion and government, have sought by many false scandals and imputations, cunningly insinuated and dispersed amongst the people, to blemish and disgrace our proceedings in this Parliament, and to get themselves a party and faction amongst your subjects, for the better strengthening themselves in their wicked courses, and hindering those provisions and remedies which might, by the wisdom of your Majesty and counsel of your Parliament, be opposed against them.

For preventing whereof, and the better information of your Majesty, your Peers and all other your loyal subjects, we have been necessitated to make a declaration of the state of the kingdom, both before and since the assembly of this Parliament, unto this time, which we do humbly present to your Majesty, without the least intention to lay any blemish upon your royal person, but only to represent how your royal authority and trust have been abused, to the great prejudice and danger of your Majesty, and of all your good subjects.

And because we have reason to believe that those malignant parties, whose proceedings evidently appear to be mainly for the advantage and increase of Popery, is composed, set up, and acted by the subtle practice of the Jesuits and other engineers and factors for Rome, and to the great danger of this kingdom, and most grievous affliction of your loyal subjects, have so far prevailed as to corrupt divers of your Bishops and others in prime places of the Church, and also to bring divers of these instruments to be of your Privy Council, and other employments of trust and nearness about your Majesty, the Prince, and the rest of your royal children.

And by this means have had such an operation in your council and the most important affairs and proceedings of your government, that a most dangerous division and chargeable preparation for war betwixt your kingdoms of England and Scotland, the increase of jealousies betwixt your Majesty and your most obedient subjects, the violent distraction and interruption of this Parliament, the insurrection of the Papists in your kingdom of Ireland, and bloody massacre of your people, have been not only endeavoured and attempted, but in a great measure compassed and effected.

For preventing the final accomplishment whereof, your poor subjects are enforced to engage their persons and estates to the maintaining of a very expensive and dangerous war, notwithstanding they have already since the beginning of this Parliament undergone the charge of £150,000 sterling, or thereabouts, for the necessary support and supply of your Majesty in these present and perilous designs. And because all our most faithful endeavours and engagements will be ineffectual for the peace, safety and preservation of your Majesty and your people, if some present, real and effectual course be not taken for suppressing this wicked and malignant party:

We, your most humble and obedient subjects, do with all faithfulness and humility beseech your Majesty:

1. That you will be graciously pleased to concur with the humble desires of your people in a parliamentary way, for the preserving the peace and safety of the kingdom from the malicious designs of the Popish party:

For depriving the Bishops of their votes in Parliament, and abridging their immoderate power usurped over the Clergy, and other your good subjects, which they have perniciously abused to the hazard of religion, and great prejudice and oppression to the laws of the kingdom, and just liberty of your people:

For the taking away such oppressions in religion, Church government and discipline, as have been brought in and fomented by them:

For uniting all such your loyal subjects together as join in the same fundamental truths against the Papists, by removing some oppressive and unnecessary ceremonies by which divers weak consciences have been scrupled, and seem to be divided from the rest, and for the due execution of those good laws which have been made for securing the liberty of your subjects.

2. That your Majesty will likewise be pleased to remove from your council all such as persist to favour and promote any of those pressures and corruptions wherewith your people have been grieved; and that for the future your Majesty will vouchsafe to employ such persons in your great and public affairs, and to take such to be near you in places of trust, as your Parliament may have cause to confide in; that in your princely goodness to your people you will reject and refuse all mediation and solicitation to the contrary, how powerful and near soever.

3. That you will be pleased to forbear to alienate any of the

forfeited and escheated lands in Ireland which shall accrue to your Crown by reason of this rebellion, that out of them the Crown may be the better supported, and some satisfaction made to your subjects of this kingdom for the great expenses they are like to undergo in this war.

Which humble desires of ours being graciously fulfilled by your Majesty, we will, by the blessing and favour of God, most cheerfully undergo the hazard and expenses of this war, and apply ourselves to such other courses and counsels as may support your real estate with honour and plenty at home, with power and reputation abroad, and by our loyal affections, obedience and service, lay a sure and lasting foundation of the greatness and prosperity of your Majesty, and your royal posterity in future times.

The Grand Remonstrance

The Commons in this present Parliament assembled, having with much earnestness and faithfulness of affection and zeal to the public good of this kingdom, and His Majesty's honour and service, for the space of twelve months wrestled with great dangers and fears, the pressing miseries and calamities, the various distempers and disorders which had not only assaulted, but even overwhelmed and extinguished the liberty, peace and prosperity of this kingdom, the comfort and hopes of all His Majesty's good subjects, and exceedingly weakened and undermined the foundation and strength of his own royal throne, do yet find an abounding malignity and opposition in those parties and factions who have been the cause of those evils, and do still labour to cast aspersions upon that which hath been done, and to raise many difficulties for the hindrance of that which remains yet undone, and to foment jealousies between the King and Parliament, that so they may deprive him and his people of the fruit of his own gracious intentions, and their humble desires of procuring the public peace, safety and happiness of this realm.

For the preventing of those miserable effects which such malicious endeavours may produce, we have thought good to declare the root and the growth of these mischievous designs: the maturity and ripeness to which they have attained before the beginning of the Parliament: the effectual means which have been used for the extirpation of those dangerous evils, and the progress which hath therein been made by His Majesty's goodness and the wisdom of the Parliament: the ways of obstruction and opposition by which that progress hath been interrupted: the courses to be taken for the removing those obstacles, and for the accomplishing of our most dutiful and faithful intentions and endeavours for restoring and establishing the ancient honour, greatness and security of this Crown and nation.

The root of all this mischief we find to be a malignant and pernicious design of subverting the fundamental laws and principles of government, upon which the religion and justice of this kingdom are firmly established. The actors and promoters hereof have been:

1. The Jesuited Papists, who hate the laws, as the obstacles of that change and subversion of religion which they so much long for.

2. The Bishops, and the corrupt part of the Clergy, who cherish formality and superstition as the natural effects and more probable supports of their own ecclesiastical tyranny and usurpation.

3. Such Councillors and Courtiers as for private ends have engaged themselves to further the interests of some foreign princes or states to the prejudice of His Majesty and the state at home.

The common principles by which they moulded and governed all their particular counsels and actions were these:

First, to maintain continual differences and discontents between the King and the people upon questions of prerogative and liberty, that so they might have the advantage of siding with him, and under the notions of men addicted to his service, gain to themselves and their parties the places of greatest trust and power in the kingdom.

A second, to suppress the purity and power of religion and such persons as were best affected to it, as being contrary to their own ends, and the greatest impediment to that change which they thought to introduce.

A third, to conjoin those parties of the kingdom which were most propitious to their own ends, and to divide those who were most opposite, which consisted in many particular observations.

To cherish the Arminian part in those points wherein they agree with the Papists, to multiply and enlarge the difference between the common Protestants and those whom they call Puritans, to introduce and countenance such opinions and ceremonies as are fittest for accommodation with Popery, to increase and maintain ignorance, looseness, and profaneness in the people; that of those three parties, Papists, Arminians and Libertines, they might compose a body fit to act such counsels and resolutions as were most conducible to their own ends.

A fourth, to disaffect the King to Parliaments by slander and false imputations, and by putting him upon other ways of supply, which in show and appearance were fuller of advantage than the ordinary course of subsidies, though in truth they brought more loss than gain both to the King and people, and have caused the great distractions under which we both suffer.

As in all compounded bodies the operations are qualified according to the predominant element, so in this mixed party, the Jesuited counsels, being most active and prevailing, may easily be discovered to have had the greatest sway in all their determinations, and if they be not prevented, are likely to devour the rest, and to turn them into their own nature.

In the beginning of His Majesty's reign the party began to revive and flourish again, having been somewhat damped by the breach with

Spain in the last year of King James, and by His Majesty's marriage with France; the interests and counsels of that State being not so contrary to the good of religion and the prosperity of this kingdom as those of Spain; and the Papists of England, having been ever more addicted to Spain than France, yet they still retained a purpose and resolution to weaken the Protestant parties in all parts, and even in France, whereby to make way for the change of religion which they intended at home.

1. The first effect and evidence of their recovery and strength was the dissolution of the Parliament at Oxford, after there had been given two subsidies to His Majesty, and before they received relief in any one grievance many other more miserable effects followed.

2. The loss of the Rochel fleet, by the help of our shipping, set forth and delivered over to the French in opposition to the advice of Parliament, which left that town without defence by sea, but likewise to the loss of all the strength and security of the Protestant religion in France.

3. The diverting of His Majesty's course of wars from the West Indies, which was the most facile and hopeful way for this kingdom to prevail against the Spaniard, to an expenseful and successless attempt upon Cadiz, which was so ordered as if it had rather been intended to make us weary of war than to prosper in it.

4. The precipitate breach with France, by taking their ships to a great value without making recompense to the English, whose goods were thereupon imbarred and confiscated in that kingdom.

5. The peace with Spain without consent of Parliament, contrary to the promise of King James to both Houses, whereby the Palatine's cause was deserted and left to chargeable and hopeless treaties, which for the most part were managed by those who might justly be suspected to be no friends to that cause.

6. The charging of the kingdom with billeted soldiers in all parts of it, and the concomitant design of German horse, that the land might either submit with fear or be enforced with rigour to such arbitrary contributions as should be required of them.

7. The dissolving of the Parliament in the second year of His Majesty's reign, after a declaration of their intent to grant five subsidies.

8. The exacting of the like proportion of five subsidies, after the Parliament dissolved, by commission of loan, and divers gentlemen and others imprisoned for not yielding to pay that loan, whereby many of them contracted such sicknesses as cost them their lives.

9. Great sums of money required and raised by privy seals.

10. An unjust and pernicious attempt to extort great payments from the subject by way of excise, and a commission issued under the seal to that purpose.

11. The Petition of Right, which was granted in full Parliament, blasted, with an illegal declaration to make it destructive to itself, to the power of Parliament, to the liberty of the subject, and to that

purpose printed with it, and the Petition made of no use but to show the bold and presumptuous injustice of such ministers as durst break the laws and suppress the liberties of the kingdom, after they had been so solemnly and evidently declared.

12. Another Parliament dissolved 4 Car., the privilege of Parliament broken, by imprisoning divers members of the House, detaining them close prisoners for many months together, without the liberty of using books, pen, ink or paper; denying them all the comforts of life, all means of preservation of health, not permitting their wives to come unto them even in the time of their sickness.

13. And for the completing of that cruelty, after years spent in such miserable durance, depriving them of the necessary means of spiritual consolation, not suffering them to go abroad to enjoy God's ordinances in God's house, or God's ministers to come to them to minister comfort to them in their private chambers.

14. And to keep them still in this oppressed condition, not admitting them to be bailed according to law, yet vexing them with informations in inferior courts, sentencing and fining some of them for matters done in Parliament; and extorting the payments of those fines from them, enforcing others to put in security of good behaviour before they could be released.

15. The imprisonment of the rest, which refused to be bound, still continued, which might have been perpetual if necessity had not the last year brought another Parliament to relieve them, of whom one died by the cruelty and harshness of his imprisonment, which would admit of no relaxation, notwithstanding the imminent danger of his life did sufficiently appear by the declaration of his physician, and his release, or at least his refreshment, was sought by many humble petitions, and his blood still cries either for vengeance or repentance of those Ministers of State, who have at once obstructed the course both of His Majesty's justice and mercy.

16. Upon the dissolution of both these Parliaments, untrue and scandalous declarations were published to asperse their proceedings, and some of their members unjustly; to make them odious, and colour the violence which was used against them; proclamations set out to the same purpose; and to the great dejecting of the hearts of the people, forbidding them even to speak of Parliaments.

17. After the breach of the Parliament in the fourth of His Majesty, injustice, oppression and violence broke in upon us without any restraint or moderation, and yet the first project was the great sums exacted through the whole kingdom for default of knighthood, which seemed to have some colour and shadow of a law, yet if it be rightly examined by that obsolete law which was pretended for it, it will be found to be against all the rules of justice, both in respect of the persons charged, the proportion of the fines demanded, and the absurd and unreasonable manner of their proceedings.

18. Tonnage and Poundage hath been received without colour or pretence of law; many other heavy impositions continued against law,

and some so unreasonable that the sum of the charge exceeds the value of the goods.

19. The Book of Rates lately enhanced to a high proportion, and such merchants that would not submit to their illegal and unreasonable payments, were vexed and oppressed above measure; and the ordinary course of justice, the common birthright of the subject of England, wholly obstructed unto them.

20. And although all this was taken upon pretence of guarding the seas, yet a new unheard-of tax of ship-money was devised, and upon the same pretence, by both which there was charged upon the subject near £700,000 some years, and yet the merchants have been left so naked to the violence of the Turkish pirates, that many great ships of value and thousands of His Majesty's subjects have been taken by them, and do still remain in miserable slavery.

21. The enlargements of forests, contrary to *Carta de Foresta*, and the composition thereupon.

22. The exactions of coat and conduct money and divers other military charges.

23. The taking away the arms of trained bands of divers counties.

24. The desperate design of engrossing all the gunpowder into one hand, keeping it in the Tower of London, and setting so high a rate upon it that the poorer sort were not able to buy it, nor could any have it without licence, thereby to leave the several parts of the kingdom destitute of their necessary defence, and by selling so dear that which was sold to make an unlawful advantage of it, to the great charge and detriment of the subject.

25. The general destruction of the King's timber, especially that in the Forest of Deane, sold to Papists, which was the best storehouse of this kingdom for the maintenance of our shipping.

26. The taking away of men's right, under the colour of the King's title to land, between high and low water marks.

27. The monopolies of soap, salt, wine, leather, sea-coal, and in a manner of all things of most common and necessary use.

28. The restraint of the liberties of the subjects in their habitation, trades and other interests.

29. Their vexation and oppression by purveyors, clerks of the market and saltpetre men.

30. The sale of pretended nuisances, as building in and about London.

31. Conversion of arable into pasture, continuance of pasture, under the name of depopulation, have driven many millions out of the subjects' purses, without any considerable profit to His Majesty.

32. Large quantities of common and several grounds have been taken from the subject by colour of the Statute of Improvement, and by abuse of the Commission of Sewers, without their consent, and against it.

33. And not only private interest, but also public faith, have been broken in seizing of the money and bullion in the mint, and the whole

kingdom like to be robbed at once in that abominable project of brass money.

34. Great numbers of His Majesty's subjects, for refusing those unlawful charges, have been vexed with long and expensive suits, some fined and censured, others committed to long and hard imprisonments and confinements, to the loss of health in many, of life in some, and others have had their houses broken up, their goods seized, some have been restrained from their lawful callings.

35. Ships have been interrupted in their voyages, surprised at sea in a hostile manner by projectors, as by a common enemy.

36. Merchants prohibited to unlade their goods in such ports as were for their own advantage, and forced to bring them to those places which were much for the advantage of the monopolizers and projectors.

37. The Court of Star Chamber hath abounded in extravagant censures, not only for the maintenance and improvement of monopolies and their unlawful taxes, but for divers other causes where there has been no offence, or very small; whereby His Majesty's subjects have been oppressed by grievous fines, imprisonments, stigmatizings, mutilations, whippings, pillories, gags, confinements, banishments; after so rigid a manner as hath not only deprived men of the society of their friends, exercise of their professions, comfort of books, use of paper or ink, but even violated that near union which God hath established between men and their wives, by forced and constrained separation, whereby they have been bereaved of the comfort and conversation one of another for many years together, without hope of relief, if God had not by His overruling providence given some interruption to the prevailing power, and counsel of those who were the authors and promoters of such peremptory and heady courses.

38. Judges have been put out of their places for refusing to go against their oaths and consciences; others have been so awed that they dared not do their duties, and the better to hold a rod over them, the clause *Quam diu se bene gesserit* was left out of their patents, and a new clause *Durante bene placito* inserted.

39. Lawyers have been checked for being faithful to their clients; solicitors and attorneys have been threatened, and some punished, for following lawful suits. And by this means all the approaches to justice were interrupted and forecluded.

40. New oaths have been forced upon the subject against law.

41. New judicatories erected without law. The Council Table have by their orders offered to bind the subjects in their freeholds, estates, suits and actions.

42. The pretended Court of the Earl Marshal was arbitrary and illegal in its being and proceedings.

43. The Chancery, Exchequer Chamber, Court of Wards, and other English Courts, have been grievous in exceeding their jurisdiction.

V

THE LETTERS OF KING CHARLES I

44. The estate of many families weakened, and some ruined by excessive fines, exacted from them for composition of wardships.

45. All leases of above a hundred years made to draw on wardship contrary to law.

46. Undue proceedings used in the finding of offices to make the jury find for the King.

47. The Common Law Courts, feeling all men more inclined to seek justice there, where it may be fitted to their own desire, are known frequently to forsake the rules of the Common Law, and straying beyond their bounds, under pretence of equity, to do injustice.

48. Titles of honour, judicial places, serjeantships at law, and other offices have been sold for great sums of money, whereby the common justice of the kingdom hath been much endangered, not only by opening a way of employment in places of great trust, and advantage to men of weak parts, but also by giving occasion to bribery, extortion, partiality, it seldom happening that places ill-gotten are well used.

49. Commissions have been granted for examining the excess of fees, and when great exactions have been discovered, compositions have been made with delinquents, not only for the time past, but likewise for immunity and security in offending for the time to come, which under colour of remedy has but confirmed and increased the grievance to the subject.

50. The usual course of pricking Sheriffs not observed, but many times Sheriffs made in an extraordinary way, sometimes as a punishment and charge unto them; sometimes such were pricked out as would be instruments to execute whatsoever they would have to be done.

51. The Bishops and the rest of the Clergy did triumph in the suspensions, excommunications, deprivations, and degradations of divers painful, learned and pious ministers, in the vexation and grievous oppression of great numbers of His Majesty's good subjects.

52. The High Commission grew to such excess of sharpness and severity as was not much less than the Romish Inquisition, and yet in many cases by the Archbishop's power was made much more heavy, being assisted and strengthened by authority of the Council Table.

53. The Bishops and their Courts were as eager in the country; although their jurisdiction could not reach so high in rigour and extremity of punishment, yet were they no less grievous in respect of the generality and multiplicity of vexations, which lighting upon the meaner sort of tradesmen and artificers, did impoverish many thousands.

54. And so afflict and trouble others, that great numbers to avoid their miseries departed out of the kingdom, some into New England and other parts of America, others into Holland.

55. Where they have transported their manufactures of cloth, which is not only a loss by diminishing the present stock of the

kingdom, but a great mischief by impairing and endangering the loss of that particular trade of clothing, which has been a plentiful fountain of wealth and honour to this nation.

56. Those were fittest for ecclesiastical preferment, and soonest obtained it, who were most officious in promoting superstition, most virulent in railing against godliness and honesty.

57. The most public and solemn sermons before His Majesty were either to advance prerogative above law, and decry the property of the subject, or full of such kind of invectives.

58. Whereby they might make those odious who sought to maintain the religion, laws and liberties of the kingdom, and such men were sure to be weeded out of the commission of the peace, and out of all other employments of power in the government of the country.

59. Many noble personages were councillors in name, but the power and authority remained in a few of such as were most addicted to this party, whose resolutions and determinations were brought to the table for countenance and execution, and not for debate and deliberation, and no man could offer to oppose them without disgrace and hazard to himself.

60. Nay, all those that did not wholly concur and actively contribute to the furtherance of their designs, though otherwise persons of never so great honour and abilities, were so far from being employed in any place of trust and power, that they were neglected, discountenanced, and upon all occasions injured and oppressed.

61. This faction was grown to that height and entireness of power, that now they began to think of finishing their work, which consisted of these three parts.

62. I.—The Government must be set free from all restraint of laws concerning our persons and estates.

63. II.—There must be a conjunction between Papists and Protestants in doctrine, discipline and ceremonies; only it must not yet be called Popery.

64. III.—The Puritans, under which name they include all those that desire to preserve the laws and liberties of the kingdom, and to maintain religion in the power of it, must be either rooted out of the kingdom with force, or driven out with fear.

65. For the effecting of this it was thought necessary to reduce Scotland to such Popish superstitions and innovations as might make them apt to join with England in that great change which was intended.

66. Whereupon new canons and a new liturgy were pressed upon them, and when they refused to admit of them, an army was raised to force them to it, towards which the Clergy and the Papists were very forward in their contribution.

67. The Scots likewise raised an army for their defence.

68. And when both armies were come together, and ready for a bloody encounter, His Majesty's own gracious disposition, and the counsel of the English nobility and dutiful submission of the Scots,

did so far prevail against the evil counsel of others, that a pacification was made, and His Majesty returned with peace and much honour to London.

69. The unexpected reconciliation was most acceptable to all the kingdom, except to the malignant party; whereof the Archbishop and the Earl of Strafford being heads, they and their faction began to inveigh against the peace, and to aggravate the proceedings of the states, which so incensed His Majesty, that he forthwith prepared again for war.

70. And such was their confidence, that having corrupted and distempered the whole frame and government of the kingdom, they did now hope to corrupt that which was the only means to restore all to a right frame and temper again.

71. To which end they persuaded His Majesty to call a Parliament, not to seek counsel and advice of them, but to draw countenance and supply from them, and to engage the whole kingdom in their quarrel.

72. And in the meantime continued all their unjust levies of money, resolving either to make the Parliament pliant to their will, and to establish mischief by a law, or else to break it, and with more colour to go on, by violence to take what they could not obtain by consent. The ground alleged for the justification of this war was this:

73. That the undutiful demands of the Parliaments in Scotland was a sufficient reason for His Majesty to take arms against them, without hearing the reason of those demands, and thereupon a new army was prepared against them, their ships were seized in all ports both of England and Ireland, and at sea, their petitions rejected, their commissioners refused audience.

74. This whole kingdom most miserably distempered with levies of men and money, and imprisonments of those who denied to submit to those levies.

75. The Earl of Strafford passed into Ireland, caused the Parliament there to. declare against the Scots, to give four subsidies towards that war, and to engage themselves, their lives and fortunes, for the prosecution of it, and gave directions for an army of eight thousand foot and one thousand horse to be levied there, which were for the most part Papists.

76. The Parliament met upon the 13th of April, 1640. The Earl of Strafford and Archbishop of Canterbury, with their party, so prevailed with His Majesty, that the House of Commons was pressed to yield a supply for maintenance of the war with Scotland, before they had provided any relief for the great and pressing grievances of the people, which being against the fundamental privilege and proceeding of Parliament, was yet in humble respect to His Majesty, so far admitted as that they agreed to take the matter of supply into consideration, and two several days it was debated.

77. Twelve subsidies were demanded for the release of ship-

money alone, a third day was appointed for conclusion, when the heads of that party began to fear the people might close with the King, in satisfying his desires for money; but that withal they were like to blast their malicious designs against Scotland, finding them very much indisposed to give any countenance to that war.

78. Thereupon they wickedly advised the King to break off the Parliament and to return to the ways of confusion, in which their own evil intentions were most likely to prosper and succeed.

79. After the Parliament ended the 5th of May, 1640, this party grew so bold as to counsel the King to supply himself out of his subjects' estates by his own power, at his own will, without their consent.

80. The very next day some members of both Houses had their studies and cabinets, yea, their pockets searched: another of them not long after was committed close prisoner for not delivering some petitions which he received by authority of that House.

81. And if harsher courses were intended (as was reported), it is very probable that the sickness of the Earl of Strafford, and the tumultuous rising in Southwark and about Lambeth were the causes that such violent intentions were not brought into execution.

82. A false and scandalous Declaration against the House of Commons was published in His Majesty's name, which yet wrought little effect with the people, but only to manifest the impudence of those who were authors of it.

83. A forced loan of money was attempted in the City of London.

84. The Lord Mayor and Aldermen in their several wards, enjoined to bring in a list of the names of such persons as they judged fit to lend, and of the sums they should lend. And such Aldermen as refused to do so were committed to prison.

85. The Archbishop and the other Bishops and Clergy continued the Convocation, and by a new commission turned it into a provincial Synod, in which, by an unheard-of presumption, they made canons that contain in them many matters contrary to the King's prerogative, to the fundamental laws and statutes of the realm, to the right of Parliaments, to the property and liberty of the subject, and matters tending to sedition and of dangerous consequence, thereby establishing their own usurpations, justifying their altar-worship, and those other superstitious innovations which they formerly introduced without warrant of law.

86. They imposed a new oath upon divers of His Majesty's subjects, both ecclesiastical and lay, for maintenance of their own tyranny, and laid a great tax on the Clergy, for supply of His Majesty, and generally showed themselves very affectionate to the war with Scotland, which was by some of them styled *Bellum Episcopale*, and a prayer composed and enjoined to be read in all churches, calling the Scots rebels, to put the two nations in blood and make them irreconcilable.

87. All those pretended canons and constitutions were armed

with the several censures of suspension, excommunication, deprivation, by which they would have thrust out all the good ministers, and most of the well-affected people of the kingdom, and left an easy passage to their own design of reconciliation with Rome.

88. The Popish party enjoyed such exemptions from penal laws as amounted to a toleration, besides many other encouragements and Court favours.

89. They had a Secretary of State, Sir Francis Windebanck, a powerful agent for speeding all their desires.

90. A Pope's Nuncio residing here, to act and govern them according to such influences as he received from Rome, and to intercede for them with the most powerful concurrence of the foreign princes of that religion.

91. By his authority the Papists of all sorts, nobility, gentry and clergy, were convocated after the manner of a Parliament.

92. New jurisdictions were erected of Romish Archbishops, taxes levied, another state moulded within this state, independent in government, contrary in interest and affection, secretly corrupting the ignorant or negligent professors of our religion, and closely uniting and combining themselves against such as were found in this posture, waiting for an opportunity by force to destroy those whom they could not hope to seduce.

93. For the effecting whereof they were strengthened with arms and munitions, encouraged by superstitious prayers, enjoined by the Nuncio to be weekly made for the prosperity of some great design.

94. And such power had they at Court, that secretly a commission was issued out, or intended to be issued to some great men of that profession, for the levying of soldiers, and to command and employ them according to private instructions, which we doubt were framed for the advantage of those who were the contrivers of them.

95. His Majesty's treasure was consumed, his revenue anticipated.

96. His servants and officers compelled to lend great sums of money.

97. Multitudes were called to the Council Table, who were tired with long attendances there for refusing illegal payments.

98. The prisons were filled with their commitments; many of the Sheriffs summoned into the Star Chamber, and some imprisoned for not being quick enough in levying the ship-money; the people languished under grief and fear, no visible hope being left but in desperation.

99. The nobility began to weary of their silence and patience, and sensible of the duty and trust which belong to them: and thereupon some of the most ancient of them did petition His Majesty at such a time, when evil counsels were so strong, that they had occasion to expect more hazard to themselves, than redress of those public evils for which they interceded.

100. Whilst the kingdom was in this agitation and distemper, the Scots, restrained in their trades, impoverished by the loss of many

of their ships, bereaved of all possibility of satisfying His Majesty by any naked supplication, entered with a powerful army into the kingdom, and without any hostile act or spoil in the country they passed, more than forcing a passage over the Tyne at Newburn, near Newcastle, possessed themselves of Newcastle, and had a fair opportunity to press on further upon the King's army.

101. But duty and reverence to His Majesty, and brotherly love to the English nation, made them stay there, whereby the King had leisure to entertain better counsels.

102. Wherein God so blessed and directed him that he summoned the Great Council of Peers to meet at York upon the 24th of September, and there declared a Parliament to begin the 3rd of November then following.

103. The Scots, the first day of the Great Council, presented an humble Petition to His Majesty, whereupon the Treaty was appointed at Ripon.

104. A present cessation of arms agreed upon, and the full conclusion of all differences referred to the wisdom and care of the Parliament.

105. As our first meeting, all oppositions seemed to vanish, the mischiefs were so evident which those evil counsellors produced, that no man durst stand up to defend them: yet the work itself afforded difficulty enough.

106. The multiplied evils and corruptions of fifteen years, strengthened by custom and authority, and the concurrent interest of many powerful delinquents, were now to be brought to judgement and reformation.

107. The King's household was to be provided for: they had brought him to that want, that he could not supply his ordinary and necessary expenses without the assistance of his people.

108. Two armies were to be paid, which amounted very near to eighty thousand pounds a month.

109. The people were to be tenderly charged, having been formerly exhausted with many burdensome projects.

110. The difficulties seemed to be insuperable, which by the Divine Providence we have overcome. The contrarieties incompatible, which yet in a great measure we have reconciled.

111. Six subsidies have been granted and a Bill of poll-money, which if it be duly levied, may equal six subsidies more, in all £600,000.

112. Besides, we have contracted a debt to the Scots of £220,000, yet God hath so blessed the endeavours of this Parliament, that the kingdom is a great gainer by all these charges.

113. The ship-money is abolished, which cost the kingdom about £200,000 a year.

114. The coat and conduct-money, and other military charges are taken away, which in many countries amounted to little less than the ship-money.

115. The monopolies are all suppressed, whereof some few did prejudice the subject, above £1,000,000 yearly.

116. The soap £100,000.

117. The wine £300,000.

118. The leather must needs exceed both, and salt could be no less than that.

119. Besides the inferior monopolies, which, if they could be exactly computed, would make up a great sum.

120. That which is more beneficial than all this is, that the root of these evils is taken away, which was the arbitrary power pretended to be in His Majesty of taxing the subject, or charging their estates without consent in Parliament, which is now declared to be against law by the judgement of both Houses, and likewise by an Act of Parliament.

121. Another step of great advantage is this, the living grievances, the evil counsellors and actors of these mischiefs have been so quelled.

122. By the justice done upon the Earl of Strafford, the flight of the Lord Finch and Secretary Windebanck,

123. The accusation and imprisonment of the Archbishop of Canterbury, of Judge Berkeley; and

124. The impeachment of divers other Bishops and Judges, that it is like not only to be an ease to the present times, but a preservation to the future.

125. The discontinuance of Parliaments is prevented by the Bill for a triennial Parliament, and the abrupt dissolution of this Parliament by another Bill, by which it is provided it shall not be dissolved or adjourned without the consent of both Houses.

126. Which two laws well considered may be thought more advantageous than all the former, because they secure a full operation of the present remedy, and afford a perpetual spring of remedies for the future.

127. The Star Chamber.

128. The High Commission.

129. The Courts of the President and Council in the North were so many forges of misery, oppression and violence, and are all taken away, whereby men are more secured in their persons, liberties and estates, 'than they could be by any law or example for the regulation of those Courts or terror of the Judges.

130. The immoderate power of the Council Table, and the excessive abuse of that power is so ordered and restrained, that we may well hope that no such things as were frequently done by them, to the prejudice of the public liberty, will appear in future times but only in stories, to give us and our posterity more occasion to praise God for His Majesty's goodness, and the faithful endeavours of this Parliament.

131. The canons and power of canon-making are blasted by the votes of both Houses.

132. The exorbitant power of Bishops and their courts are much abated, by some provisions in the Bill against the High Commission Court, the authors of the many innovations in doctrine and ceremonies.

133. The ministers that have been scandalous in their lives, have been so terrified in just complaints and accusations, that we may well hope they will be more modest for the time to come; either inwardly convicted by the sight of their own folly, or outwardly restrained by the fear of punishment.

134. The forests are by a good law reduced to their right bounds.

135. The encroachments and oppressions of the Stannary Courts, the extortions of the clerk of the market.

136. And the compulsion of the subject to receive the Order of Knighthood against his will, paying of fines for not receiving it, and the vexatious proceedings thereupon for levying of those fines, are by other beneficial laws reformed and prevented.

137. Many excellent laws and provisions are in preparation for removing the inordinate power, vexation and usurpation of Bishops, for reforming the pride and idleness of many of the clergy, for easing the people of unnecessary ceremonies in religion, for censuring and removing unworthy and unprofitable ministers, and for maintaining godly and diligent preachers through the kingdom.

138. Other things of main importance for the good of this kingdom are in proposition, though little could hitherto be done in regard of the many other more pressing businesses, which yet before the end of this Session we hope may receive some progress and perfection.

139. The establishing and ordering the King's revenue, that so the abuse of officers and superfluity of expenses may be cut off, and the necessary disbursements for His Majesty's honour, the defence and government of the kingdom, may be more certainly provided for.

140. The regulating of courts of justice, and abridging both the delays and charges of law-suits.

141. The settling of some good courses for preventing the exportation of gold and silver, and the inequality of exchanges between us and other nations, for the advancing of native commodities, increase of our manufactures, and well balancing of trade, whereby the stock of the kingdom may be increased, or at least kept from impairing, as through neglect hereof it hath done for many years last past.

142. Improving the herring-fishing upon our coasts, which will be of mighty use in the employment of the poor, and a plentiful nursery of mariners for enabling the kingdom in any great action.

143. The oppositions, obstructions and the difficulties wherewith we have been encountered, and which still lie in our way with some strength and much obstinacy, are these; the malignant party whom we have formerly described to be the actors and promoters of all our misery, they have taken heart again.

144. They have been able to prefer some of their own factors and agents to degrees of honour, to places of trust and employment, even during the Parliament.

145. They have endeavoured to work in His Majesty ill impressions and opinions of our proceedings, as if we had altogether done our own work, and not his; and had obtained from him many things very prejudicial to the Crown, both in respect of prerogative and profit.

146. To wipe out this slander we think good only to say thus much: that all that we have done is for His Majesty, his greatness, honour and support, when we yield to give £25,000 a month for the relief of the Northern Counties; this was given to the King, for he was bound to protect his subjects.

147. They were His Majesty's evil counsellors, and their ill instruments that were actors in those grievances which brought in the Scots.

148. And if His Majesty please to force those who were the authors of this war to make satisfaction, as he might justly and easily do, it seems very reasonable that the people might well be excused from taking upon them this burden, being altogether innocent and free from being any cause of it.

149. When we undertook the charge of the army, which cost above £50,000 a month, was not this given to the King? Was it not His Majesty's army? Were not all the commanders under contract with His Majesty, at higher rates and greater wages than ordinary?

150. And have we not taken upon us to discharge all the brotherly assistance of £300,000, which we gave the Scots? Was it not toward repair of those damages and losses which they received from the King's ships and from his ministers?

151. These three particulars amount to above £1,100,000.

152. Besides, His Majesty hath received by impositions upon merchandise at least £400,000.

153. So that His Majesty hath had out of the subjects' purse since the Parliament began, £1,500,000, and yet these men can be so impudent as to tell His Majesty that we have done nothing for him.

154. As to the second branch of this slander, we acknowledge with much thankfulness that His Majesty hath passed more good Bills to the advantage of the subjects than have been in many ages.

155. But withal we cannot forget that these venomous councils did manifest themselves in some endeavours to hinder these good acts.

156. And for both Houses of Parliament we may with truth and modesty say thus much: that we have ever been careful not to desire anything that should weaken the Crown either in just profit or useful power.

157. The triennial Parliament for the matter of it, doth not extend to so much as by law we ought to have required (there being two statutes still in force for a Parliament to be once a year), and for the

manner of it, it is in the King's power that it shall never take effect, if he by a timely summons shall prevent any other way of assembling.

158. In the Bill for continuance of this present Parliament, there seems to be some restraint of the royal power in dissolving of Parliaments, not to take it out of the Crown, but to suspend the execution of it for this time and occasion only: which was so necessary for the King's own security and the public peace, that without it we could not have undertaken any of these great charges, but must have left both the armies to disorder and confusion, and the whole kingdom to blood and rapine.

159. The Star Chamber was much more fruitful in oppression than in profit, the great fines being for the most part given away, and the rest stalled at long times.

160. The fines of the High Commission were in themselves unjust, and seldom or never came into the King's purse. These four Bills are particularly and more especially instanced.

161. In the rest there will not be found so much as a shadow of prejudice to the Crown.

162. They have sought to diminish our reputation with the people, and to bring them out of love with Parliaments.

163. The aspersions which they have attempted this way have been such as these:

164. That we have spent much time and done little, especially in those grievances which concern religion.

165. That the Parliament is a burden to the kingdom by the abundance of protections which hinder justice and trade; and by many subsidies granted much more heavy than any formerly endured.

166. To which there is a ready answer; if the time spent in this Parliament be considered in relation backward to the long growth and deep root of those grievances, which we have removed, to the powerful supports of those delinquents, which we have pursued, to the great necessities and other charges of the commonwealth for which we have provided.

167. Or if it be considered in relation forward to many advantages, which not only the present but future ages are like to reap by the good laws and other proceedings in this Parliament, we doubt not but it will be thought by all indifferent judgements, that our time hath been much better employed than in a far greater proportion of time in many former Parliaments put together; and the charges which have been laid upon the subject, and the other inconveniences which they have borne, will seem very light in respect of the benefit they have and may receive.

168. And for the matter of protections, the Parliament is so sensible of it that therein they intended to give them whatsoever ease may stand with honour and justice, and are in a way of passing a Bill to give them satisfaction.

169. They have sought by many subtle practices to cause jealousies and divisions betwixt us and our brethren of Scotland, by

slandering their proceedings and intentions towards us, and by secret endeavours to instigate and incense them and us one against another.

170. They have had such a party of Bishops and Popish lords in the House of Peers, as hath caused much opposition and delay in the prosecution of delinquents, hindered the proceedings of divers good Bills passed in the Commons' House, concerning the reformation of sundry great abuses and corruptions both in Church and State.

171. They have laboured to seduce and corrupt some of the Commons' House to draw them into conspiracies and combinations against the liberty of the Parliament.

172. And by their instruments and agents they have attempted to disaffect and discontent His Majesty's army, and to engage it for the maintenance of their wicked and traitorous designs; the keeping up of Bishops in votes and functions, and by force to compel the Parliament to order, limit, and dispose their proceedings in such manner as might best concur with the intentions of this dangerous and potent faction.

173. And when one mischievous design and attempt of theirs to bring on the army against the Parliament and the City of London hath been discovered and prevented;

174. They presently undertook another of the same damnable nature, with this addition to it, to endeavour to make the Scottish army neutral, whilst the English army, which they had laboured to corrupt and envenom against us by their false and slanderous suggestions, should execute their malice to the subversion of our religion and the dissolution of our government.

175. Thus they have been continually practising to disturb the peace, and plotting the destruction even of all the King's dominions; and have employed their emissaries and agents in them, all for the promoting their devilish designs, which the vigilancy of those who were well affected hath still discovered and defeated before they were ripe for execution in England and Scotland.

176. Only in Ireland, which was farther off, they have had time and opportunity to mould and prepare their work, and had brought it to that perfection that they had possessed themselves of that whole kingdom, totally subverted the government of it, routed out religion, and destroyed all the Protestants whom the conscience of their duty to God, their King and country, would not have permitted to join with them, if by God's wonderful providence their main enterprise upon the city and castle of Dublin had not been detected and prevented upon the very eve before it should have been executed.

177. Notwithstanding they have in other parts of that kingdom broken out into open rebellion, surprising towns and castles, committing murders, rapes and other villainies, and shaken off all bonds of obedience to His Majesty and the laws of the realm.

178. And in general have kindled such a fire, as nothing but God's infinite blessing upon the wisdom and endeavours of this State will be able to quench it.

179. And certainly had not God in His great mercy unto this land discovered and confounded their former designs, we had been the prologue to this tragedy in Ireland, and had by this been made the lamentable spectacle of misery and confusion.

180. And now what hope have we but in God, when as the only means of our subsistence and power of reformation is under Him in the Parliament?

181. But what can we the Commons, without the conjunction of the House of Lords, and what conjunction can we expect there, when the Bishops and recusant lords are so numerous and prevalent that they are able to cross and interrupt our best endeavours for reformation, and by that means give advantage to this malignant party to traduce our proceedings?

182. They infuse into the people that we mean to abolish all Church government, and leave every man to his own fancy, for the service and worship of God, absolving him of that obedience which he owes under God unto His Majesty, whom we know to be entrusted with the ecclesiastical law as well as with the temporal, to regulate all the members of the Church of England, by such rules of order and discipline as are established by Parliament, which is his great council, in all affairs both in Church and State.

183. We confess our intention is, and our endeavours have been, to reduce within bounds that exorbitant power which the prelates have assumed unto themselves, so contrary both to the Word of God and to the laws of the land, to which end we passed the Bill for the removing them from their temporal power and employments, that so the better they might with meekness apply themselves to the discharge of their functions, which Bill themselves opposed, and were the principal instruments of crossing it.

184. And we do here declare that it is far from our purpose or desire to let loose the golden reins of discipline and government in the Church, to leave private persons or particular congregations to take up what form of Divine Service they please, for we hold it requisite that there should be throughout the whole realm a conformity to that order which the laws enjoin according to the Word of God.   And we desire to unburden the consciences of men of needless and superstitious ceremonies, suppress innovations, and take away the monuments of idolatry.

185. And the better to effect the intended reformation, we desire there may be a general synod of the most grave, pious, learned and judicious divines of this island; assisted with some from foreign parts, professing the same religion with us, who may consider of all things necessary for the peace and good government of the Church, and represent the results of their consultations unto the Parliament, to be there allowed of and confirmed, and receive the stamp of authority, thereby to find passage and obedience throughout the kingdom.

186. They have maliciously charged us that we intend to destroy and discourage learning, whereas it is our chiefest care and desire to

advance it, and to provide a competent maintenance for conscionable and preaching ministers throughout the kingdom, which will be a great encouragement to scholars, and a certain means whereby the want, meanness and ignorance, to which a great part of the clergy is now subject, will be prevented.

187. And we intended likewise to reform and purge the fountains of learning, the two Universities, that the streams flowing from thence may be clear and pure, and an honour and comfort to the whole land.

188. They have strained to blast our proceedings in Parliament, by wresting the interpretations of our orders from their genuine intention.

189. They tell the people that our meddling with the power of episcopacy hath caused sectaries and conventicles, when idolatrous and Popish ceremonies, introduced into the Church by the command of the Bishops, have not only debarred the people from thence, but expelled them from the kingdom.

190. Thus with Elijah, we are called by this malignant party the troublers of the State, and still, while we endeavour to reform their abuses, they make us the authors of those mischiefs we study to prevent.

191. For the perfecting of the work begun, and removing all future impediments, we conceive these courses will be very effectual, seeing the religion of the Papists hath such principles as do certainly tend to the destruction and extirpation of all Protestants, when they shall have opportunity to effect it.

192. It is necessary in the first place to keep them in such condition as that they may not be able to do us any hurt, and for avoiding of such connivance and favour as hath heretofore been shown unto them.

193. That His Majesty be pleased to grant a standing Commission to some choice men named in Parliament, who may take notice of their increase, their counsels and proceedings, and use all due means by execution of the laws to prevent all mischievous designs against the peace and safety of this kingdom.

194. Thus some good course be taken to discover the counterfeit and false conformity of Papists to the Church, by colour whereof persons very much disaffected to the true religion have been admitted into place of greatest authority and trust in the kingdom.

195. For the better preservation of the laws and liberties of the kingdom, that all illegal grievances and exactions be presented and punished at the sessions and assizes.

196. And that Judges and Justices be very careful to give this in charge to the grand jury, and both the Sheriff and Justices to be sworn to the due execution of the Petition of Right and other laws.

197. That His Majesty be humbly petitioned by both Houses to employ such councillors, ambassadors and other ministers, in managing his business at home and abroad as the Parliament may

have cause to confide in, without which we cannot give His Majesty such supplies for support of his own estate, nor such assistance to the Protestant party beyond the sea, as is desired.

198. It may often fall out that the Commons may have just cause to take exceptions at some men for being councillors, and yet not charge those men with crimes, for there be grounds of diffidence which lie not in proof.

199. There are others, which though they may be proved, yet are not legally criminal.

200. To be a known favourer of Papists, or to have been very forward in defending or countenancing some great offenders questioned in Parliament; or to speak contemptuously of either Houses of Parliament or Parliamentary proceedings.

201. Or such as are factors or agents for any foreign prince of another religion; such are justly suspected to get councillors' places, or any other of trust concerning public employment for money; for all these and divers others we may have great reason to be earnest with His Majesty, not to put his great affairs into such hands, though we may be unwilling to proceed against them in any legal way of charge or impeachment.

202. That all Councillors of State may be sworn to observe those laws which concern the subject in his liberty, that they may likewise take an oath not to receive or give reward or pension from any foreign prince, but such as they shall within some reasonable time discover to the Lords of His Majesty's Council.

203. And although they should wickedly forswear themselves, yet it may herein do good to make them known to be false and perjured to those who employ them, and thereby bring them into as little credit with them as with us.

204. That His Majesty may have cause to be in love with good counsel and good men, by showing him in a humble and dutiful manner how full of advantage it would be to himself, to see his own estate settled in a plentiful condition to support his honour; to see his people united in ways of duty to him, and endeavours of the public good; to see happiness, wealth, peace and safety derived to his own kingdom, and procured to his allies by the influence of his own power and government.

The Remonstrance was only carried by 159 votes to 148. ' Had it been rejected,' Cromwell said, ' I would have sold all I had the next morning and never have seen England any more; and I know there are many other honest men of this same resolution.' Upon which Clarendon observes, ' So near was the poor kingdom at that time to its deliverance.'

APPENDIX III

YOUR MAJESTY's most humble and faithful subjects, the Lords and Commons in Parliament, having nothing in their thoughts and desires more precious and of higher esteem (next to the honour and immediate service of God) than the just and faithful performance of their duty to your Majesty and this kingdom: and being very sensible of the great distractions and distempers, and of 'the imminent dangers and calamities which those distractions and distempers are like to bring upon your Majesty and your subjects; all which have proceeded from the subtle insinuations, mischievous practices and evil counsels of men disaffected to God's true religion, your Majesty's honour and safety, and the public peace and prosperity of your people, after a serious observation of the causes of those mischiefs, do in all humility and sincerity present to your Majesty their most dutiful petition and advice, that out of your princely wisdom for the establishing your own honour and safety, and gracious tenderness of the welfare and security of your subjects and dominions, you will be pleased to grant and accept these their humble desires and propositions, as the most necessary effectual means, through God's blessing, of removing those jealousies and differences which have unhappily fallen betwixt you and your people, and procuring both your Majesty and them a constant course of honour, peace, and happiness.

The Nineteen Propositions

1. That the Lords and others of your Majesty's Privy Council, and such great officers and Ministers of State, either at home or beyond the seas, may be put from your Privy Council, and from those offices and employments, excepting such as shall be approved of by both Houses of Parliament; and that the persons put into the places and employments of those that are removed may be approved of by both Houses of Parliament; and that the Privy Councillors shall take an oath for the due execution of their places, in such form as shall be agreed upon by both Houses of Parliament.

2. That the great affairs of the kingdom may not be concluded or transacted by the advice of private men, or by any unknown or unsworn councillors, but that such matters as concern the public, and are proper for the High Court of Parliament, which is your Majesty's great and supreme council, may be debated, resolved and transacted only in Parliament, and not elsewhere: and such as shall presume to do anything to the contrary shall be reserved to the censure and

judgement of Parliament: and such other matters of state as are proper for your Majesty's Privy Council shall be debated and concluded by such of the nobility and others as shall from time to time be chosen for that place, by approbation of both Houses of Parliament: and that no public act concerning the affairs of the kingdom, which are proper for your Privy Council, may be esteemed of any validity, as proceeding from the royal authority, unless it be done by the advice and consent of the major part of your Council, attested under their hands: and that your Council may be limited to a certain number, not exceeding five and twenty, nor under fifteen: and if any councillor's place happen to be void in the interval of Parliament, it shall not be supplied without the assent of the major part of the Council, which choice shall be confirmed at the next sitting of Parliament, or else to be void.

3. That the Lord High Steward of England, Lord High Constable, Lord Chancellor, or Lord Keeper of the Great Seal, Lord Treasurer, Lord Privy Seal, Earl Marshall, Lord Admiral, Warden of the Cinque Ports, Chief Governor of Ireland, Chancellor of the Exchequer, Master of the Wards, Secretaries of State, two Chief Justices and Chief Baron, may always be chosen with the approbation of both Houses of Parliament; and in the intervals of Parliament, by assent of the major part of the Council, in such manner as is before expressed in the choice of councillors.

4. That he, or they unto whom the government and education of the King's children shall be committed, shall be approved of by both Houses of Parliament; and in the intervals of Parliament, by the assent of the major part of the Council, in such manner as is before expressed in the choice of councillors; and that all such servants as are now about them, against whom both Houses shall have any just exceptions, shall be removed.

5. That no marriage shall be concluded or treated for any of the King's children, with any foreign prince, or other person whatsoever, abroad or at home, without the consent of Parliament, under the penalty of a premunire, upon such as shall conclude or treat of any marriage as aforesaid; and that the said penalty shall not be pardoned or dispensed with but by the consent of both Houses of Parliament.

6. That the laws in force against Jesuits, priests, and Popish recusants, be strictly put in execution, without any toleration or dispensation to the contrary; and that some more effectual course may be enacted, by authority of Parliament, to disable them from making any disturbance in the State, or eluding the law by trusts or otherwise.

7. That the votes of Popish lords in the House of Peers may be taken away, so long as they continue Papists: and that your Majesty will consent to such a Bill as shall be drawn for the education of the children of Papists by Protestants in the Protestant religion.

8. That your Majesty will be pleased to consent that such a

w   305

reformation be made of the Church government and liturgy, as both Houses of Parliament shall advise; wherein they intend to have consultations with divines, as is expressed in their declaration to that purpose; and that your Majesty will contribute your best assistance to them, for the raising of a sufficient maintenance for preaching ministers throughout the kingdom; and that your Majesty will be pleased to give your consent to laws for the taking away of innovations and superstition, and of pluralities, and against scandalous ministers.

9. That your Majesty will be pleased to rest satisfied with that course that the Lords and Commons have appointed for ordering of the militia, until the same shall be further settled by a Bill; and that your Majesty will recall your Declarations and Proclamations against the Ordinance made by the Lords and Commons concerning it.

10. That such members of either House of Parliament as have, during the present Parliament, been put out of any place and office, may either be restored to that place and office, or otherwise have satisfaction for the same, upon the petition of that House whereof he or they are members.

11. That all Privy Councillors and Judges may take an oath, the form whereof to be agreed on and settled by Act of Parliament, for the maintaining of the Petition of Right and of certain statutes made by the Parliament, which shall be mentioned by both Houses of Parliament: and that an inquiry of all the breaches and violations of those laws may be given in charge by the Justices of the King's Bench every Term, and by the Judges of Assize in their circuits, and Justices of the Peace at the sessions, to be presented and punished according to law.

12. That all the Judges, and all the officers placed by approbation of both Houses of Parliament, may hold their places *quam diu bene se gesserint.*

13. That the justice of Parliament may pass upon all delinquents, whether they be within the kingdom or fled out of it; and that all persons cited by either House of Parliament may appear and abide the censure of Parliament.

14. That the general pardon offered by your Majesty may be granted, with such exceptions as shall be advised by both Houses of Parliament.

15. That the forts and castles of this kingdom may be put under the command and custody of such persons as your Majesty shall appoint, with the approbation of your Parliament: and in the intervals of Parliament, with approbation of the major part of the Council, in such manner as is before expressed in the choice of councillors.

16. That the extraordinary guards and military forces now attending your Majesty, may be removed and discharged; and that for the future you will raise no such guards or extraordinary forces, but according to the law, in case of actual rebellion or invasion.

17. That your Majesty will be pleased to enter into a more strict alliance with the States of the United Provinces, and other neighbouring princes and states of the Protestant religion, for the defence and maintenance thereof, against all designs and attempts of the Pope and his adherents to subvert and suppress it; whereby your Majesty will obtain a great access of strength and reputation, and your subjects be much encouraged and enabled, in a Parliamentary way, for your aid and assistance, in restoring your royal sister and her princely issue to those dignities and dominions which belong unto them, and relieving the other Protestant princes who have suffered in the same cause.

18. That your Majesty will be pleased, by Act of Parliament, to clear the Lord Kimbolton and the five members of the House of Commons, in such manner that future Parliaments may be secured from the consequence of that evil precedent.

19. That your Majesty will be graciously pleased to pass a Bill for restraining peers made hereafter, from sitting or voting in Parliament, unless they be admitted thereunto with the consent of both Houses of Parliament.

And these our humble desires being granted by your Majesty, we shall forthwith apply ourselves to regulate your present revenue in such sort as may be for your best advantage; and likewise to settle such an ordinary and constant increase of it, as shall be sufficient to support your royal dignity in honour and plenty, beyond the proportion of any former grants of the subjects of this kingdom to your Majesty's royal predecessors. We shall likewise put the town of Hull into such hands as your Majesty shall appoint, with the consent and approbation of Parliament, and deliver up a just account of all the magazine, and cheerfully employ the uttermost of our power and endeavours in the real expression and performance of our most dutiful and loyal affections, to the preserving and maintaining the royal honour, greatness and safety of your Majesty and your posterity.

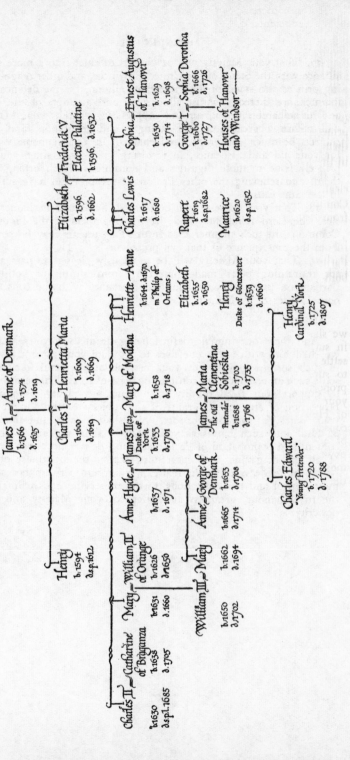

GENEALOGICAL TABLE OF THE STUART KINGS OF ENGLAND

SHORT BIBLIOGRAPHY

BELLOC, H.   *Charles the First.*

BROOKES, J.   *A Vindication of Charles I.*

BUCHAN, J.   *Montrose.*

CARTE, T.   *History of the Life of James, Duke of Ormonde.*

CLARENDON, EARL OF.   *History of the Rebellion and Civil Wars in England.*

COIT, C. W.   *The Royal Martyr.*

FEA, ALLAN.   *Memoirs of the Martyr King.*

GARDINER, S. R.   *History of England, 1603-1642.*

GARDINER, S. R.   *History of the Great Civil War.*

GIBBS, P.   *The Romance of George Villiers, First Duke of Buckingham.*

JOHN, E.   *King Charles I.*

MUDDIMAN, J. G.   *Trial of King Charles I.*

REID, R. R.   *The King's Council in the North.*

TRAILL, H. D.   *Lord Strafford.*

INDEX

ABBOTT, EDWARD, 87
Aboyne, Viscount of, 191
Acland, John, 192
Acton, Sir Thomas, 192
Airlie, Earl of, 191
America, emigration to, 290
Anabaptists, 233
Andrew, Michael, 13-14, 18
Anne of Austria, 8-9; Charles acknowledges obligation to, 40-1; dismissed retinue of, 45
Anne, Queen, mother of Charles, 3-4 letter to, 3
Antinomians, 233
Anti-Trinitarians, 233
Antrim, Marquess of (Earl of), recommended by Charles, 99, 102; negotiates with Irish, 134-5; commanded to lay down arms, 180
Appello Cæsarem, 68
Argyll, Earl of, 102, 182
Armin, Sir William, 190
Arminians, 233, 285
Army, waxing power of, 179, 214, 232; Parliament seeks control of, 186-9; commanded to disband, 219, 233; Charles in hands of, 219, 233, 241; Heads of Proposals of, 219-29; Declaration of, 227-9; payment of arrears to, 229; in possession of London, 234; victory of, 238
Articles of Religion, 68-9
Arundel, Earl of, 95
Arundel, Lord, of Wardour, 192
Ashburnham, Jack, 54-5, 164; and militia, 163; goes to France, 179-80; excepted from pardon, 191 letters to, 199, 203, 206, 210
Ashhurst, Mr., 190
Astley, Sir Jacob, 97, 101
Aston, Sir Walter, 33-4
Attainder, Bill of, 115-16
Audley, Lord, 192
Austria, and Palatinate, 99
Ayscough, Sir Edward, 190

BACON, Mr. Justice, 198
Balfour, Sir William, 51
Balmermoch, 182
Banks, Lord Chief Justice, 124
Barrois, Richard, 190
Barry, Colonel, 151
Bath and Wells, Bishop of, letter to, 88
Bayly, Dr., 213
Beale, Dr., 213

Bedingfield, Sir Henry, 192
Beecher, messenger, 50-2
Bellasis, Henry, 163
Bellievre, M. de, 211
Benion, Sir George, 192
Bennet, Humphrey, 192
Berkeley, Judge, imprisonment of, 296
Berwick, Charles determines to secure, 102, 108; settling of garrison of, 190; Scots army authorized to take, 236
Berwick, Treaty of, 112
Beverley, 241
Billingham, Mr., 190
Bishops' Wars, 112, 291-3
Blackiston, John, 190
Blaney, John, 192
Bodmin, 242
Bohemia, Elector accepts throne of, 5
Bolton, 144
Boston, letter to Mayor of, 126
Bradshaw, John, Lord President of trial, 243 *et seq.*
Bramhall, Dr., 191
Brentwood, 241-2
Brereton, Sir William, 190
Brett, Colonel, 54
Bristol, Charles sends for powder to, 144; Rupert surrenders, 156-8
Bristol, Earl of, sent to negotiate Spanish marriage, 7; and proxy of marriage, 28-9, 30, 32; disgrace of, 31-4; excepted from pardon, 191 letters to, 30, 31, 32, 34
Brooke, Sir Basil, 192
Brownists, 233
Bruce, Henry, 104
Bruce, Thomas, Lord, 190
Brudenell, Lord, 192
Buckingham, Duke of, his relations with Charles, 4, 39, 52; sets off for Madrid, 7; letters to James I, with Charles, 7, 9, 10, 12, 13, 14, 17, 18, 20, 21, 22, 24, 25, 27, 28, 29; in disguise in France, 7-9; arrives in Spain, 9; and dukedom, 19, 39; anxious to leave Madrid, 24; and disgrace of Bristol, 31, 33; real ruler of England, 39; sent to fetch Henrietta Maria, 39; in Holland, 42; besieges La Rochelle, 50-7; takes Rhé, 50; supplies and reinforcements for, 51, 54-5; attempted assassination of, 52-3; and powers to treat with France, 55-6; evacuates Rhé, 56; assassination of, 57; Parliament and, 76

311

Leeds, 130
Legge, Will, 156-7
Leicester, 242
Leith, 108
Leslie of Auchintoul, 191
Lesley, David, 165
Lesley, Sir James, 180
Lexington, Lord, 163
Libertines, 233, 285
Liddell, Sir Thomas, 192
Lincoln, Earl of, 190
Lincolnshire, drainage of Fens in, 85-6; protection for Royalists in, 130
Lindsay, 182
Lingen, Henry, 192
Liverpool, 144
Lloyd, Hugh, 192
Lloyd, Sir Richard, 191
London, sheriff of, committed to Tower, 74; levying of ship-money in, 92-4; prosecution of citizens of, 99; Charles refuses to return to, 121-2; plan of Royalist advance on, 143; Charles asks for safe-conduct to, 163, 202, 211; forces of City of, 189; militia of, 197; Act for granting and confirming liberties, etc., of, 197; engrossing of gunpowder in Tower of, 288; forced loan levied in, 293
letter to Lord Mayor of, 92, 181
London, Bishop of, 213; takes letter for Prince of Wales, 262; takes Charles's last words, 273
letter to, 208
Long Parliament, summoning of, 112, 295; results achieved by, 295-7; Bill for continuance of, 296, 299; money granted to Charles by, 298
Lords, House of, message to, on Petition of Right, 61; passes Bill of Attainder, 115; Bishops and Catholics in, 300-1, 305. See also Parliament
letters to, 116, 161, 162, 167, 168, 170, 202, 211, 212, 213, 214, 229
Lords of the Council, letter to, 49
Lostwithiel, 147
Lothian, Earl of, 182
Loudoun, Lord, 237
Louis XIII, King of France, 8; and dismissal of French retinue, 45
letter to, 39
Lucas, Lord, 163
Lucas, Sir John, 192
Ludovisio, Cardinal, 11
Lyttleton, Edward Lord, conveys Great Seal from Parliament, 189; confiscation of estates of, 195

MACDONALD, ALASTER, 191

Madrid, Charles and Buckingham in, 10-30; quarrels between English and Spanish in, 28
Magna Charta, 58-9, 62
Manchester, Earl of, 163, 190
Mandy, Sir John, 192
Mansfeld, fights for Palatinate, 42
Mar, Earl of, letter to, 138
March, Dr., 213
Marie de Medici, 8
Marley, Sir John, 191
Marshall, Mr., 213
Marston Moor, battle of, 145
Martin, Henry, 190
Mathews, Toby, 22
Maurice, Prince, excepted from pardon, 191
letters to, 137, 158
Maxwell, John, 191
Mazarin, Cardinal, 164
Militia, Justices ordered to muster, 48; attempt to increase efficiency of, 49-50, 83-4; Charles calls up, 112; Parliament seeks control of, 117, 122-124, 306; Charles's Proclamation concerning, 122; Charles on Crown's right to control of, 122, 200, 217; Charles forbids assembly of, 126; Charles's propositions concerning, 163, 172, 217; of London, 197; Army's propositions concerning, 222-223
Millington, Gilbert, 190
Minshull, Sir Richard, 192
Molynew, Caryl, 192
Monopolies, 227, 288, 296
Montagu, Lord, letter to, 91
Montague, Richard, *Appeal to Cæsar* of, 68
Montgomery, Lord, 4
Montreuil, 165, 176, 182
Montrose, Earl of, defeat of, 159; commanded to lay down arms, 180; faction of, 182; excepted from pardon, 191
Morton, Lord, 51
Murray, Mrs., 19
Murray, Will, 209-10
Musgrave, Sir Philip, 192
Muskerry, Lord, 151

NASEBY, battle of, 153, 242
National Covenant. See Covenant
Navy, use of supplies for, 70; ships of, held against Charles, 125-6; Army's propositions concerning, 223
letter to officers of, 125
Neale, Sir Paul, 192
New England, 290